D0968987

THE
WAR
YEARS
1939–1945

By I. F. Stone

A NONCONFORMIST HISTORY OF OUR TIMES

THE
WAR
YEARS

1939–1945

I. F. STONE

LITTLE, BROWN AND COMPANY

BOSTON   TORONTO

COPYRIGHT © 1988 BY I. F. STONE

ALL RIGHTS RESERVED. NO PART OF THIS BOOK MAY BE REPRODUCED IN ANY FORM OR BY
ANY ELECTRONIC OR MECHANICAL MEANS, INCLUDING INFORMATION STORAGE AND
RETRIEVAL SYSTEMS, WITHOUT PERMISSION IN WRITING FROM THE PUBLISHER, EXCEPT BY
A REVIEWER WHO MAY QUOTE BRIEF PASSAGES IN A REVIEW.

FIRST EDITION

10   9   8   7   6   5   4   3   2   1

All the articles that make up this book originally appeared in *The Nation*.

Library of Congress Cataloging-in-Publication Data

Stone, I. F. (Isidor F.), 1907–
    The war years / I. F. Stone: — 1st ed.
        p.   cm.
    Originally published in *The Nation* from 1939 to 1945.
    Includes index.
    ISBN 0-316-81771-6
    1. World War, 1939–1945 — United States — Sources.   2. World
War, 1939–1945 — Sources.   I. Title.
    D769.S76 1988
    940.53'73 — dc19   87-37228
                                                             CIP

MV

Designed by Robert G. Lowe

Published simultaneously in Canada
by Little, Brown & Company (Canada) Limited

PRINTED IN THE UNITED STATES OF AMERICA

To my brothers, Marc and Lou

With acknowledgment to Beth Rashbaum and Perdita Burlingame
for their assistance in the selection and organization
of this collection

Contents

❧   ❧

Cast of Characters

ⅇ ⁓

ARNOLD, THURMAN   Assistant Attorney General, anti-trust division, 1939–1942.

CROWLEY, LEO T.   Custodian of Alien Property, 1942. Head of Office of Economic Warfare (OEW), later Foreign Economic Administration (FEA), 1943–1945.

DIES, MARTIN   U.S. Congress, 1931–1945, 1953–1959. Established in 1938 and was chairman of House Un-American Activities Committee.

HENDERSON, LEON   Director for Price Administration, National Defense Advisory Commission (NDAC), 1940. Federal Price Administrator, Office of Price Administration (OPA), 1941–1942.

HILLMAN, SIDNEY   Director for Labor and Employment, National Defense Advisory Commission (NDAC), 1940. Codirector of Office of Production Management (OPM), later War Production Board (WPB) 1940–1942.

HULL, CORDELL   Secretary of State, 1933–1944.

JONES, JESSE   Head of Reconstruction Finance Corporation (RFC) 1932–1945. Federal Loan Administrator 1939–1945. Secretary of Commerce 1940–1944.

KNOX, WILLIAM F.   Secretary of the Navy, 1940–1944.

KNUDSON, WILLIAM S.   Director for Industrial Production, National Defense Advisory Commission (NDAC), 1940. Codirector of Office of Production Management (OPM), 1941.

MORGENTHAU, HENRY JR.   Secretary of the Treasury, 1934–1945.

NELSON, DONALD M.   Chairman War Production Board (WPB), 1942–1944.

STETTINIUS, EDWARD R., JR.   Chairman War Resources Board 1939–1940. Administered Lend-Lease 1941–1943. Under Secretary of State, 1943–1944. Secretary of State, 1944–1945. Chairman of delegation to San Francisco United Nations Conference, 1945.

STIMSON, HENRY L.   Secretary of War, 1940–1945.

WALLACE, HENRY A.   Secretary of Agriculture, 1933–1940. Vice-President, 1941–1945. Chairman Board of Economic Warfare (BEW), 1942–1943. Secretary of Commerce 1945–1946.

WELLES, SUMNER   Under Secretary of State 1937–1943.

PART I

1939

Chamberlain's Russo-German Pact

I

A GLANCE BACK over the newspaper reports and news of the past two years may help to clarify current discussion of the Russo-German non-aggression consultation pact.[1] One way to judge the pact is to recall the cries of "canard" that rose from the pro-Soviet press when the first hints began to appear that an agreement of this kind was a possibility. The Communists were not alone in rejecting these reports. All of us who felt that the Soviet Union was the core of the world front against fascism shared their indignation and contemptuous disbelief. If a non-aggression pact were indeed a way to "stiffen the democracies" and "prevent a Munich" — I quote some of the apologists-after-the-fact — it is odd that no anti-fascist met these early speculations by asking whether a Russo-German agreement might not be a feasible and clever maneuver. On the contrary the idea was dismissed as either the propaganda of reactionaries or the wishful thinking of oppositionists who felt — as we all did — that a pact of this kind would discredit the Soviet Union. All this may seem elementary. It is already being forgotten.

I have been able to find three stories by foreign correspondents during the year 1938 which speculated on the possibility of some kind of rapprochement between the U.S.S.R. and Nazi Germany. On May 28 William Bird cabled the New York *Sun* from Paris that too little attention had been paid to the resumption of normal diplomatic relations between the two countries. He said the return of von Schulenburg to the German embassy at Moscow and the nomination of A. T. Merekalov as

---

[1] The Hitler-Stalin pact signed in Moscow on August 23, 1939 allowed Germany to invade Poland without interference from Russia.

ambassador to Berlin "cannot be regarded as simple routine. There is no doubt that Russo-German relations have taken a new turning. . . ." Bird felt that "the important thing for Germany is to get access to the wheat fields of the Ukraine; the important thing for Stalin is to have the German machine-shop at his disposal when war comes in the East. It is no accident that a specialist in steel is the new Soviet ambassador to Berlin." This dispatch was discounted on the ground that the *Sun* is anti-Soviet. Similar reasons made it easy to brush aside a cable sent by H. R. Knickerbocker from Prague on June 18, 1938, to the Hearst-owned International News Service. Knickerbocker said there was a report that von Schulenburg was trying to negotiate a pact with Stalin. He wrote that "on the surface" this was to be a new pact of non-aggression, but a non-aggression pact of such a nature as to cancel the Franco-Soviet pact. The agreement since signed exactly fits that description. Knickerbocker went on to say that both countries denied this report and that the Czechs regarded it as an attempt to frighten England into giving Germany a free hand with Czechoslovakia. "One odd feature of the projected plan in its present version," Knickerbocker declared, "is that Hitler is said to have laid down two conditions. First, that Maxim Litvinov must resign as Soviet Foreign Commissar; second, that Gregori Dimitrov, of Reichstag-fire-trial fame, be removed from the chairmanship of the Communist International." Knickerbocker seemed skeptical of his own story. "Acceptance by Stalin of the plan itself, much less its conditions, is believed in authoritative circles to be absolutely excluded."

The next hint came not from a Hearst correspondent but from Walter Duranty, who had come to be regarded as an unofficial spokesman for the Kremlin. In a cable from Paris to the New York *Times* on October 10, 1938, he said, "There remains a possibility — I do not say probability — which makes the present leaders of France and England sleep uneasily at night, namely, a Russo-German rapprochement, cooperation instead of war." Duranty declared that when one got down to "brass tacks" the only obstacle to the policy of Russo-German collaboration Bismarck had always advocated was "Hitler's fanatic fury against what he calls 'Judeo-Bolshevism.' " There followed a sentence that was cynical and shocking: "But Hitler is not immortal and dictators can change their minds and Stalin has shot more Jews in two years of purge than were ever killed in Germany." Duranty said that should Hitler decline to imitate Napoleon and prefer the iron and coal of Alsace-Lorraine to the "distant riches" of the Donetz basin, "there is no reason to believe that Russia would refuse collaboration with Germany or shed tears over the ultimate fate of France and the British Empire." Was this a wink from Moscow to Berlin? Or was Duranty off on some queer tangent of his own? At the time the latter alone seemed a plausible explanation. Any unpleasant taste was removed a month later by Dimitrov's speech on the twenty-first anniversary of the revolution. Dimitrov did, indeed, warn against "the policy of warlike agreement between the fascist aggressors and England and France," but made no suggestion of rapprochement with Germany as a way out. "Nothing can be accomplished," he cried, "with more pacific declarations [non-aggression pacts?]. Active opposition against armed fascism is necessary to show the mailed fist of the people."

But the "canards" did not end. The first of the current year came on January 19. On that day the New York *Daily News* ran a copyright cable dated from London but declaring that "in Berlin tonight" economic and military collaboration between Soviet Russia and Nazi Germany "was envisaged." The *News* is a tabloid. Tabloids are sensational. The *News* is anti-Soviet. Union Square read and chuckled. The *News* said the first step would be taken the following week at a conference between German and Russian representatives either in Stockholm or Copenhagen. It declared the new move had been initiated by the Führer himself when he "astounded diplomats at his New Year's reception" by singling out the Soviet ambassador for a prolonged private conversation. Hitler had asked an exchange of views, given assurances on the Ukraine. Stalin had consented. "Maxim Litvinov's failure to attend the meeting of the Council of the League of Nations at Geneva, it was learned, was due to his opposition to the Hitler proposal. Stalin, it was said, ordered his chief foreign adviser of years past to remain, literally a prisoner, in Moscow." Germany, the *News* said, was ready to abandon its tie with Tokyo; Russia, "deserted during the September crisis by Great Britain and France," was ready "to cement new alliances." This cable, with its "it is learned's" and "it is said's" seemed a typical example of what is known on a newspaper as "a dope story."

Soon there came hints from Moscow itself. On January 31 *Pravda* quoted without comment the London *News-Chronicle*'s warning that it would be "extremely unwise to suppose that the existing disaccord between Moscow and Berlin will necessarily remain an unchangeable factor of international policy"; and the Associated Press correspondent in Moscow noted, "The fact that *Pravda* failed to reject indignantly the suggestion of a possible Soviet-German rapprochement increased its significance to foreign observers." On March 11 in his speech before the eighteenth All-Union Congress in Moscow, Stalin accused enemies of Russia of trying to foment war between the Soviet Union and Germany, and the Associated Press correspondent in Moscow voiced what many felt — that "in its emphasis upon a lack of any genuine basis for war between Germany and Russia, his speech sounded almost like a rapprochement between these two countries." To that correspondent the speech seemed "strikingly reminiscent" of Stalin's speech in 1934 before the seventeenth All-Union Congress, the year before the adoption of the Popular Front line. At that time Stalin said the real issue in so far as Russo-German relations were concerned was not the new fascist regime. "Naturally we are far from enthusiastic about that," he said, but Russia had enjoyed good relations with Italy despite fascism. The real issue, he declared, was the struggle within the Reich "between advocates of cooperation with Soviet Russia and opponents of that policy." Note that he said "cooperation" and not merely good relations. It is, in fact, "cooperation" with the U.S.S.R. that one wing of the Nazi Party, of the Reichswehr, and of German industry has always wanted.

II

Stalin's speech was made on March 11. German troops occupied Prague on March 15. March 15 was the Continental Divide of British policy. From that day on "appeasement" became overwhelmingly unpopular, and the demand in Britain for a Russian alliance rose in volume until it included even the London *Times,* the Cliveden set,[2] and the formerly pro-Nazi *Observer.* I think two conclusions are possible on the basis of what we now know, though we are far from knowing all that occurred. The first conclusion is that by March, 1938, the idea of a Russo-German agreement was not absolutely excluded by the Soviet Union, and by agreement I mean a non-aggression pact, even a non-aggression pact which would prevent the U.S.S.R. from entering the peace front against fascism that it had so long sought to erect. The second is that London needed no corps of spies in Berlin and Moscow to inform it that a Russo-German rapprochement of some kind was a possibility. On the contrary, if so much had appeared in the press, it is safe to assume that at least a little more was known to the British Intelligence Service and therefore to Chamberlain. If Chamberlain had shared the popular revulsion in Britain against Munichism, these scattered hints alone

[2] An influential group of prominent English men and women, including the editor of the London *Times,* who advocated a policy of appeasement toward Hitler. Cliveden was the country house where they gathered on weekends.

would have been sufficient to make him hasten negotiation of a pact with the Soviets.

But if one goes back day by day over the news reports, one finds strong reasons to suspect that Chamberlain, although he finally bowed before popular pressure, did not share the general reaction after Hitler took Bohemia and Moravia. Although the London *Times* called the invasion, "a crude, brutal act of oppression and suppression" and there were bitter questions in the Commons on March 15, Chamberlain's statement that day could hardly be described as fiery. "I have so often heard charges of a breach of faith bandied about," he said, "which do not seem to me to be founded on sufficient premises. I do not wish to associate myself today with any charges of that character, but I am bound to say that I cannot believe anything of the kind that has taken place was contemplated by any of the signatories of the Munich agreement. . . . But, finally, do not let us be deflected from our course." What did he mean by "our course"? "It was clear," Ferdinand Kuhn, Jr., wrote in his dispatch to the New York *Times,* "that he intended to pursue his policy of 'appeasement' whether Germany gave him any encouragement or not." On March 16 in the Commons Chamberlain was asked to tell the Führer that British indignation would be intensified if there were any attack "on the lives or liberties of leaders of the Czech people." He replied, "I think it would be wrong to assume that the German government has any such intention." When Lady Astor leaped to her feet and asked the Prime Minister to let the German government "know with what horror the whole of this country regards Germany's action," Chamberlain showed himself many degrees cooler than Cliveden. He made no reply. It was not until March 17 that the Prime Minister recalled Sir Neville Henderson from Berlin "to report" and made the famous speech in Birmingham in which he protested that Germany had extinguished the liberties of a "proud, brave people" and asked, "If it is so easy to discover good reasons for ignoring assurances so solidly and repeatedly given, what reliance can be placed upon other assurances which come from the same place?" Chamberlain was referring, of course, to Hitler's assurances, not to his own.

In itself this emotional lag on the part of Chamberlain might not be sufficient to support the conclusion that he still favored "appeasement." Mr. Chamberlain's nature shows little tendency toward the passionate. There are other indications that "appeasement" had not been abandoned. The day the German troops marched into Prague the Federation of British Industries announced that its delegates at Dusseldorf had concluded an agreement with its Nazi counterpart, the Reichsgruppe

Industrie, for joint exploitation of export markets. The news provoked protest, but not until four days later did Halifax announce that the government approval necessary to make the agreement binding "had to be and must be indefinitely postponed." Postponed, not abandoned. Two days afterward Chamberlain dropped a hint to the Reich that the postponement might not be too extended. He told the Commons, "There is no desire on the part of His Majesty's Government to stand in the way of any reasonable efforts on the part of Germany to expand her export trade. On the contrary, we were on the point of discussing in the most friendly way the possibility of trade agreements which would have benefited both countries when the events took place which, *for the time being at any rate,* put a stop to these discussions." The italics are mine. Nor were indications of a desire to "appease" absent in the hectic months which followed. In May, after Chamberlain had called the story a "mare's nest," the Commons learned that the Bank of England had indeed handed over five million pounds in Czech gold to the Reichsbank. In July the government first denied and then admitted that Robert S. Hudson, head of the Board of Trade, had tried to "appease" Germany with a billion-pound loan, and Hudson escaped with the mildest of rebukes. Chamberlain's long delay in making clear that Danzig was included in his pledge to Poland must be regarded as significant: the pledge to Poland was made on March 31; Danzig was not specifically mentioned until July 10. The long haggle over the five-million-pound cash loan the Poles needed to buy rifles was hardly calculated to stiffen Polish resistance; the loan never was granted. Sir John Simon was "standing firm" against the five-million-pound loan to Britain's ally, Poland, at the very time that Hudson was discussing a billion-pound loan to Britain's enemy, Germany.*

---

* It is an indication of how far we may trust a government headed by Chamberlain that the Federation of British Industries agreement would have hit American export trade; that the billion-pound loan to Germany would have required the cooperation of the American money market; but that one reason for denying Poland a cash loan was that "the British were afraid that it would go to the United States and have a weakening effect on the pound." (Robert P. Post dispatch from London, New York *Times,* July 27.)

Portrait of a Dollar-a-Year Man

⤳ ⤳

THE DOLLAR-A-YEAR-MEN are beginning to arrive in Washington. The first since 1917 were appointed by Secretary Morgenthau on September 5. W. R. Burgess, vice-chairman of the National City Bank, will advise on government financing. Tom K. Smith, president of the Boatmen's National Bank of St. Louis, and a past president of the American Banker's Association, will be "a sort of coordinator of all banking problems for the Treasury." Earle Bailie, chairman of the Tri-Continental Corporation and the leading partner in J. and W. Seligman and Company, will help the Secretary of the Treasury "on international monetary matters." These appointments are typical of the new men being brought into the government under cover of the war crisis. I wish to call attention at this time to only one of these appointees, Earle Bailie. For the case against the choice of Mr. Bailie as a Treasury adviser rests on more than surmise, and he may serve to illustrate the influences that will intrench themselves in the capital if the current *Anschluss* with Wall Street is completed.

Part of the story I have to tell has never been told before, but there are Senators who know the unpublished document on which it is based, a memorandum submitted by the late Senator Couzens to an executive session of the Senate Finance Committee on January 4, 1934. The day after that meeting the New York *Times* carried a story from Washington saying that "it was understood" that Senator Couzens has protested to the President against the appointment of Bailie as Morgenthau's special assistant in charge of fiscal affairs. It was also "understood," according to the *Times,* that the Senator had "sought to obtain from Mr. Morgenthau information as to the exact date when Mr. Bailie would relinquish his post." Morgenthau had been Acting Secretary since the death of Mr. Woodin. His nomination as Secretary was before the Senate Finance Committee. Senator Couzens took the position that he would oppose Morgenthau's appointment unless assured that Bailie would resign. On January 6, two days after the executive session, Mr. Bailie tendered his resignation, and Mr. Morgenthau's nomination was favorably reported to the Senate.

Senator Couzen's chief objection to Mr. Bailie will stir unpleasant recollections among many small-town American bankers and investors who were unwise enough to buy Peruvian bonds in 1927 and 1928. Mr. Bailie's banking firm and the National City Company headed the syndicate which floated an issue of about $90,000,000 in Peruvian bonds in this country. When Senator Couzens addressed the Senate Finance Committee, these bonds were selling at less than six cents on the dollar, and even today they can be bought for less than eight cents on the dollar. Their precipitous decline was explained when a Senate committee in 1932 investigated foreign bond flotations in this country. The committee found that the employee sent to Peru by J. and W. Seligman to make an investigation before the bonds were issued warned that they would be in default in five years. The National City received, and likewise ignored, three warnings from its representatives. A vice-president called Peru "an adverse moral and political risk." The company's overseas manager described the government of Peru as "a president surrounded by a group of rascals." National City's representative in Peru reported the Peruvian treasury was "flat on its back and gasping for breath." Yet the bankers were so anxious to get the bonds that the Seligman firm paid the son of President Leguia of Peru a commission of approximately $415,000 to arrange for this high-class engraved Peruvian wallpaper. "The bonds were sold to the public," Senator Couzens's memorandum says, "without any statement by the bankers of the warning which they had received."

Senator Couzens did not seem to think that Mr. Bailie was away fishing while this $90,000,000 bond issue was arranged and sold. Mr. Bailie had been a partner in the Seligman firm for ten years when Senator Couzens objected to his appearance in the Treasury, and the Senator told the Senate Finance Committee that Mr. Bailie was not only an important partner, "but in fact has been in command, and at most periods actually first in command" during those ten years. Senator Couzens explained that the most important member of the firm, Frederick Strauss, had been "inactive for large periods of time during the past ten years, and the main authority has therefore fallen to Mr. Bailie as second in line." Senator Couzens further declared that Mr. Bailie's importance could be judged by the fact "that the half-dozen investment trusts controlled by that banking firm are under the direction of Mr. Bailie, as chairman of the board or president of each investment-trust corporation, and in most cases as both chairman and president." Of these investment trusts Senator Couzens asserted that they "are arranged in the dangerous crazy-quilt fashion that marks such situations as the Insull utility holding companies and pyramids." He referred to the fact that one of the interlocking companies had made a contract with another for "investment service" — "the same sort of dangerous practice that public-utility holding companies engage in when they provide management service to public-utility operating companies controlled by the holding companies." Senator Couzens pointed out that on the board of directors of Tri-Continental, top holding company of the Seligman pyramid, Mr. Bailie had associated with him Wiggin of Chase National and Groesbeck of Electric Bond and Share. Senator Couzens did not feel that these associations recommended him for a post in the Treasury — particularly so soon after Mr. Roosevelt had driven the money changers from the temple.

Senator Couzens said he thought it essential "that a man with an important place in the United States Treasury shall have (1) ability, (2) disinterestedness and a sense of the obligations of trusteeship, and (3) the character, experience, and standing which will instil confidence in the public asked to buy United States government bonds." He felt that Mr. Bailie's record had to be considered "in accordance with these criteria," and he did not rest his case only on the Peruvian bonds and Mr. Bailie's other associations.

Senator Couzens said that Mr. Bailie "has also had many interesting affiliations in connection with the reorganization of corporations." He took as an example the bankrupt St. Louis–San Francisco Railway Company, of which Mr. Bailie was a director and later "one of its so-called readjustment managers, the men who are to reorganize the corporation." He added that the plan of reorganization prepared by Mr. Bailie and his associates in July, 1932, had been attacked before the ICC [Interstate Commerce Commission] "by leading life-insurance companies and banks." Senator Couzens said that the plan was attacked for favoritism to certain bank creditors at the expense of the bondholders, and as "financially inadvisable and impracticable"; and that Mr. Bailie and his associates had obtained control of more than $100,000,000 of principal amount of the railroad's bonds by an advertising campaign that seems less than candid. "The chairman of the railway company's board," Senator Couzens told the Finance Committee, "recently admitted under oath in a proceeding conducted by the Interstate Commerce Commission that they realized that the company would have to be put in receivership in order to carry through their reorganization plan, but Mr. Bailie and his associates entered upon a nation-wide advertising campaign to get control of the bondholders' bonds by telling them that if the bondholders sent in their bonds in sufficient numbers, receivership could be averted."

Senator Couzens pointed out that the legal work for the railroad managers in this reorganization, as in so many great railroad reorganizations, was done by Cravath, de Gersdorff, Swaine, and Wood. The Senator said Mr. Bailie started out as a lawyer in that firm, "one of the most powerful, if not the most powerful, in Wall Street," and "his brother-in-law is now a member of this law firm." Senator Couzens declared that this firm had been "the guiding spirit in many of the big deals which have been criticized in recent years." "In consequence," he continued, "the relation of Mr. Bailie to that firm is of importance. That first will now have a friend in the Administration and a pipe-line to the activities and resources of the United States government."

Finally Senator Couzens took up Mr. Bailie's attitude toward reform legislation. He pointed out that Mr. Bailie, as chairman of the Committee on Railroad Securities of the Investment Bankers' Association of America, had objected in 1933 to those parts of the truth-in-securities act which affected railroad securities, though these were milder than the provisions governing non-railroad securities. He said that Bailie "was also an opponent of such provisions of the railroad-reorganization act of March 3, 1933, as seek to curb the power of bankers and others who have had an unfortunate influence over such reorganizations." Senator Couzens found it "difficult to reconcile a man of Mr. Bailie's viewpoint with the New Deal." The measured warning with which the Couzens memorandum ends cannot be ignored by New Dealers as the dollar-a-year men mobilize to make Washington safe for Wall Street. This is what Couzens said:

> Some of the least satisfactory elements in Wall Street now have direct access to the operations of the government. It is hard to estimate how much this can mean. The government is spending billions of dollars through the Reconstruction Finance Corporation and other organizations for projects some of which may not come up to those standards Congress

had in mind when it authorized such expenditures. Furthermore, the Treasury is going to take action of one kind or another which will profoundly benefit speculators or others who may have advance information of what is coming. The question which arises in connection with Mr. Bailie's occupation of an important post in the Treasury is whether he has shown himself to be the type of man who will be a bulwark against special favors and special opportunities for Wall Street men, or whether his connections and affiliations are such as to make this prospect dangerous for the public.

Is it not the Senate's duty today to make Secretary Morgenthau answer that question?

PART II

1940

August 17, 1940

Aviation's Sitdown Strike

෴ ෴

THE AVIATION INDUSTRY is still engaged in a sitdown strike against the national defense program. The purpose of this strike is to squeeze every possible financial concession out of the federal government. "This is no time," Congressman Barden of North Carolina lectured shipyard workers in Kearny's quickly quashed strike last June, "for labor to try and grab off 10 cents an hour more." No such petty stakes are involved in the aviation companies' sitdown. Their strike has forced the Administration and Congress to lift the profit limitations imposed on airplane contracts only a few weeks ago by the revised Vinson-Trammell Act, and is obtaining amortization privileges that will give aviation greatly expanded cost-free plants when the emergency of the war is over. But these concessions do not satisfy the industry. It is also seeking to block or postpone the enactment of an excess-profits tax. A huge backlog of British orders obtained on the juiciest terms the companies could extract from England's desperate need has provided the funds necessary to feed the industry during its sitdown against our defense program.

"Treason" was the cry of Congressman Cox of Georgia when United States Steel's shipyard employees at Kearny asked a raise of 10 cents an hour. No such harsh accusation has been made against the aviation companies, though plane contracts to the value of $85,000,000 have been held up by their recalcitrance. Instead, the blame is being placed upon the Administration in a propaganda campaign that is mounting in intensity. The sitdown strike may yet play a part in the coming election, and aviation hopes that its resistance may help to bring in a new

President who can be depended upon to grant it everything instead of *almost* everything. It need hardly be added that in all these objectives the aviation strikers are being helped by sympathetic picketing from the other defense industries, notably steel, which is staging a sitdown of its own on armorplate.

Last May the financial editor of the New York *Sun,* appalled by the British excess-profits tax, thought it "difficult for many Americans to understand how Britain can expect anyone to make the tremendous extra productive effort required by war without some stimulus other than the vague one that it is necessary to save the country." Aviation has demonstrated that it agrees with him that a national emergency is too vague a stimulus to call forth its best efforts. The companies which the Nye committee found were helping to build up Hitler's air fleet in violation of the treaty of peace with Germany are in no hurry to build up our own. Pratt and Whitney, Curtiss-Wright, and Douglas Aircraft were the companies named in the Nye report of April 20, 1936. Pratt and Whitney, Curtiss-Wright, and Douglas Aircraft are among the leaders of aviation's sitdown strike.

The *Wall Street Journal,* which knows its big business men, smelled a scandal of this kind coming a month ago and sent out a staff man to do a series of articles on industry and its relation to defense. It reported "with pleasure" that "these extensive investigations reveal that the armament program is progressing without undue delay and without sound basis for criticism." Its investigator, surely a descendant of Voltaire's Candide, found that "American industry is operating with its typical efficiency. If, in the future, delays inherent in the very size and scope of the program come to light, they certainly cannot be laid at the door of a fully cooperating private industry." On the contrary, the *Wall Street Journal* placed the blame on the War and Navy departments, in spite of their readiness to speak for big business before Congressional committees. "The difficulty of getting action out of the government and particularly the Army and Navy departments," was cited as a principal cause for delay. But $85,000,000 worth of plane contracts cleared by army, navy, and Defense Commission are still waiting for the aviation industry to get into action. Since the President's call in May for 50,000 planes a year the industry has accepted contracts for only $900,378 worth of trainer planes. *Barron's Financial Weekly,* which cannot be accused of taking too implacable an attitude toward Wall Street, reported in its issue of July 29: "The attitude of some defense industries that they must be assured of a profit is souring many Washington dispositions, even in the pro-business War and Navy departments."

The phrase "assured of a profit" is something of an understatement. No one expects the aviation industry to serve for $21 a month. The Administration has been more than tender with it. When the National Defense tax bill was rushed through the House on June 11, a gag rule was imposed to prevent amendments that would tax war profits or excess profits. "The most inequitable tax bill enacted by Congress in the last decade" — the words are Senator La Follette's — lowered income-tax exemptions, imposed a 10 per cent supertax, enacted a long list of special sales and nuisance taxes, but added only 1 per cent to the corporation tax and imposed none on the mounting profits that industry will soon be drawing from defense. Trouble began when the Senate Naval Affairs Committee on June 18 discovered that the navy, without competitive bidding, had let a billion dollars' worth of shipbuilding contracts on the old World War basis of cost plus 10 per cent. The result was that Congress, just before the convention recess, revised the Vinson-Trammell Act of 1934 to lower profit limits on plane and ship contracts. The limit on the former had been 12 per cent; on the latter, 10 per cent. By the act of June 28 Congress reduced the profit limitation to 8 per cent on the cost of competitively bid contracts and 7 per cent on those negotiated privately. It was at that point that aviation's strike began.

These limitations governed, not the return on capital, but the margin of profit on the contract, and the profit allowed was clear profit. The government agreed to pay the cost not only of the work done but of any additional plant necessary to do the work. If by some chance the contractor failed to make his full 8 or 7 per cent he was to be allowed to make up the deficiency on other contracts during the succeeding four years. These conditions hardly seem confiscatory. The entire industry, nevertheless, lined up at the wailing wall. The *United States News,* edited by David Lawrence, accused the Treasury of harboring "a belief that patriotism rather than a desire for profits should motivate industry." The New Deal seems to have been innocent of any such subversive intention. The *Wall Street Journal* set out to show how ruinous the profit limitations could be: they might affect the raising of funds for expansion; research work would be cut. It applied the profit limits to the year 1939, admitting that the comparison was not quite fair because in that year production was not continuous or at capacity. Even on this basis the figures in the *Wall Street Journal* seemed less than disastrous. On the 7 per cent basis the return on capital for eight major aviation companies would have ranged from 4.3 per cent for Consolidated Aircraft to 28 per cent for Lockheed. Lockheed's high return was due to its high capital turnover in 1939, but all the companies will show a vastly increased capital turnover with the defense program under way. Here are the *Wall Street Journal*'s estimates:

Boeing	21.5 per cent
Consolidated	4.3 per cent
Curtiss-Wright	9.8 per cent
Douglas	18.3 per cent
Lockheed	28.0 per cent
G. I. Martin	9.4 per cent
North American	20.2 per cent
United Aircraft	11.2 per cent

These rates on profit seem adequate, particularly in a national emergency, to "preserve and strengthen" — we quote from the National City Bank's July bulletin — "the system of private enterprise." Men in the trenches manage to sustain morale on a lower profit margin.

The bill embodying the new profit limits was signed by the President on June 28. On July 10 he surrendered to the sitdowners. The Administration agreed to drop the profit limits. In addition it promised to enact legislation that would permit companies building a new plant or installing new equipment to amortize these additions in five years. This means that 20 per cent of the cost of this new plant or equipment may be deducted by the companies from their income before arriving at the net on which income taxes and excess-profits taxes must be paid. At the end of the five-year period the companies would have plants completely paid off out of the sums received from the government for planes. William S. Knudsen, head of the National Defense Advisory Commission, was jubilant. He emerged from the July 10 conference with the President to say that the tax-and-amortization agreement "would expedite many defense contracts with companies which have been reluctant to undertake such work." The commission announced "the placing of contracts totaling approximately $100,000,000 since July 1 in a program under which negotiations have been conducted looking to the supply of 25,000 airplanes for our national defense." Louis Johnson, at that time Assistant Secretary of War, sent out a letter asking all plane manufacturers to begin work immediately on the contracts ready for them. He pointed out that the entire program would be delayed at least sixty days if they waited for Congress to enact the Administration agreement into law. It was reported that the letter offered the protection of price revisions later if anything occurred to change the situation.

That the Administration had the power to make good on its promise cannot be doubted. Any Congressman who refused to back the agreement could be accused of sabotaging the defense program. The companies decided to wait. "Although contracts for some 4,000 planes have been drawn and are awaiting signature," the *Wall Street Journal* reported, "it is understood that the industry has declined to accept the business until definite regulations are forthcoming on amortizing new plants. It was generally felt by government officials — after an agreement between Administration officials and Congressional tax leaders that new plants would be amortized over a five-year period and the 8 per cent profit limitation removed in favor of a new excess-profits tax — that contracts could be entered into immediately. However, the industry is reported to feel that it would be unwise to accept new business until exact regulations under whatever new law is passed are made known." The President was still hopeful. On July 16 he announced that replies to Assistant Secretary Johnson's letter "indicated that arrangements are being made now by the companies for tooling their plants to fill the orders, and in some instances they are proceeding with plant-expansion plans." These indications seem to have been slightly exaggerated.

The Administration surrendered on July 10, but the strike was still on a month later. The excuse was that Congress has not yet written into law the promise made by the President and Congressional leaders to repeal the limitation on plane profits and grant five-year amortization. What really lay behind the continued strike was a struggle over the excess-profits tax. President Roosevelt coupled his announcement that he would back repeal of the profit-limit law with a pledge to impose excess-profits taxes on industry as a whole. The demand of the aviation companies for five-year amortization gave the Administration a bargaining weapon in pushing an excess-profits tax bill through Congress. Those who must pay the taxes naturally preferred a more leisurely pace — no action on excess profits at all, if that could be managed. The strategy of the aviation companies, acting in this respect as a spearhead for a drive by big business, was to sit tight, refuse to build planes, continue the cry for protection on amortization. If amortization could be rushed through Congress in a separate bill, it would be easier to delay or defeat an excess-profits tax.

Closely examined, the amortization issue itself is not a very real one.

Under the Vinson-Trammell profit-limitation law, the cost of any additional plant or equipment is included in the contract costs before the profit margin is figured. Without any change in the tax law a measure of protection exists for companies which, for defense purposes, build plants that will be of no use to them in peace time. The Treasury may allow for obsolescence, and a plant can become obsolete because there is no market for its products. Or an allowance can be obtained for the cost of turning it to peace-time uses. There will be a peace-time market for airplanes, perhaps a greater market than ever. If the companies are allowed five-year amortization, they will have cost-free plants with which to build planes when the war is over.

Unless they obtain five-year amortization the risk for the plane companies is that if at the end of the emergency they have no use for the plants, they may have no net income against which to take an obsolescence allowance. The allowance, of course, is an allowance against income or profits taxes. This risk is not very serious, particularly in view of the prices the companies are charging for planes. These should cover at least part of their capital expenditures. But even this slight measure of risk is more theoretical than real in the light of the way in which plant expansions will probably be financed. The case of Wright Aeronautical Corporation will illustrate the financial featherbed on which the companies may be wafted through this emergency.

Any plane company that needs a government loan to finance plant expansion for defense will get it. Wright Aeronautical is the first to be offered such a loan, and the same terms are available to other companies. Engines are one of the bottlenecks in the plane program. United Aircraft and Wright are the only producers of high-powered air-cooled engines in this country. The government began negotiations last May with the Wright company for the erection of a plant in Cincinnati to build these engines. Originally the Wright company was to be given a loan of $20,000,000 by the RFC. This was raised to $55,000,000 on June 20 and on July 26 to $92,000,000. The interest rate was reported to be 4 per cent. The Wright company was to have an eight-year lease with the right to renew for another eight years. The Treasury ruled that the Wright company could amortize the plant in eight years. The government was to pay the Wright company enough on the engine contracts to repay the loan in eight years. At the end of the eight years the Wright company could renew the lease for another eight years with a cost-free plant, or it could sell the plant back to the government, in which case the government would pay for the plant twice. It cannot be said that under this arrangement the Wright company would be embarking on a speculative venture. But just to eliminate any possible risk the loan was offered as a non-recourse loan, that is, the government would have no claim against the Wright company if it failed to pay the loan. All the government could do in that case would be to take the factory. Since the plant would be financed entirely by the government, the government would really be taking back its own property if the Wright company for some reason wanted to drop it. The amount of the loan also would provide a generous margin of safety for the Wright company. The *Wall Street Journal* reported on August 2 that while the loan was for $92,000,000, "the cost of the proposed plant and its equipment is understood to be only $37,000,000 or $38,000,000." When asked by the *Journal* correspondent about "this apparent discrepancy," Jesse Jones said, "We don't believe it would be in the public interest to break down that total at this time." As this is being written, the Wright contract has yet to be signed. The company is now asking for five-year amortization instead of eight. Incidentally, a vice-president of this finicky company, T. P. Wright, was assigned to the Defense Commission on June 8 to help speed up production. The home office doesn't seem too cooperative.

At the risk of tugging at the reader's heartstrings, I want to conclude with the *Wall Street Journal*'s analysis of what excess-profits taxes might do to the aviation companies. The joint Congressional committee has recommended a 40 per cent tax on earnings above the average for the years 1936–39. The Treasury wants a sliding scale ranging from 25 per cent of profits over a 15 per cent return on invested capital to 50 per cent on profits over a 30 per cent return. The *Wall Street Journal* applied the Canadian excess-profits tax to six major aviation companies on the basis of their 1940 business as shown by reports for the first six months of this year. Canada takes 75 per cent of earnings over average earnings from 1936 to 1939. The net profit for the six companies, after deducting a 75 per cent excess-profits tax, would range from a low of 14.37 per cent for Curtiss-Wright to a high of 53.35 per cent for North American. These are the *Wall Street Journal*'s figures, not mine, and the *Wall Street Journal* is not one to underestimate the plight to which a national emergency has reduced the 100 per cent (if they can get it) patriots of the aviation industry.

Mr. Hull and the Pact

NOWHERE IN WASHINGTON was the news of the Berlin-Rome-Tokyo pact[1] greeted with so elaborate a lack of surprise as in the State Department. "We knew it all the time," was the refrain of the statement the Secretary of State gave the press, a statement which managed to achieve prolixity though but three sentences long. Mr. Hull began by saying that the alliance did not "substantially alter a situation which has existed for several years." He went on to declare that it "merely makes clear a situation which has long existed in effect and to which this government has repeatedly called attention." That such an agreement "has been in process of conclusion," Mr. Hull assured the correspondents, "has been well known for some time, and that fact has been fully taken into account by the government of the United States in the determining of this country's policies." It is impossible to take these words at their face value without passing a harsh verdict on our diplomats. For if the announcement of the pact does not alter a situation which has existed for several years and if that situation was "fully taken into account" by our government, why did the State Department so long refuse to embargo war materials which armed one of the principal participants in the most dangerous alliance that has ever confronted this country?

It is more charitable to assume that Secretary Hull's statement was a bold front on a diplomatic defeat. For the dominant faction in the State Department has hoped to appease Japan and keep it from joining the

[1] The Axis nations, Germany, Italy, and Japan, had agreed in September to form a military and economic alliance.

Axis, and this group continued to act on the basis of that hope long after it had been abandoned everywhere but in the British Foreign Office. Secretary Hull, like Secretary Stimson before him, provided an accompaniment of lofty moral discourses for the Japanese advance down the China coast. The discourses made veiled use of that most foolhardy of weapons, threats which the other side knew were hollow. Within the department, over the objections of a more farsighted minority, the experts made a joke of the discourses by protecting the profits accruing to American business from the aggressions we were so nobly denouncing. It was not until July of 1939, after almost eight years of Sino-Japanese warfare, that the State Department finally gave notice of intention to abrogate our commercial treaty with Japan, a necessary step if an embargo was to be imposed with a full legal decorum.

The six months' notice that was stipulated in the treaty expired in January of this year, but it was not until July that an "embargo" on oil and scrap was announced. I have been told that the White House originally intended this embargo to be an actual embargo on oil and scrap, but that the details were left to the State Department experts. When the regulations were promulgated it was found that the only scrap "embargoed" was No. 1 heavy melting, that the only petroleum "embargoed" was aviation gas, and that the "embargo" itself was only a system of licensing. It is now revealed that few if any licenses were denied under these regulations. Now, when an embargo is finally to be placed on all the seventy-five varieties of iron and steel scrap instead of on just one, the Japanese are given almost three weeks' notice, and will therefore be able to add another 100,000 to 200,000 tons of scrap to the 9,000,000 tons we have so generously supplied to them in the last six years.

When Mr. Hull appeared before a Congressional committee on trade agreements a year ago, a Republican member, exasperated by the Secretary's ability to say little at great length, asked him whether he ever answered a question with a yes or no. The State Department, despite the events of the past week, has yet to give a final yes or no to Japan. The momentum of events may itself supply the answer. The $25,000,000 loan to China, the help now vaguely promised French Indo-China, and the embargo on iron and scrap are the result of a number of factors: a new confidence that Britain will be able to hold out, Anglo-Australian desire for our protection in the Far East, advance knowledge that the Berlin-Rome-Tokyo pact would be signed in a few days, and the belated "discovery" that national-defense needs require an embargo on scrap.

This discovery itself has a rather interesting background. The Japanese, with about a year's supply on hand, do not need our scrap as much as they did, and the scrap industry, with a defense boom in the offing, does not need Japanese orders. The big steel companies cannot oppose an embargo on scrap by claiming that we have an over-supply of steel and at the same time ask for a higher price for steel on the ground of a shortage. The embargo implies and advertises a shortage, and the shortage may provide a basis for asking higher prices. Both big steel and the scrap industry have accepted the embargo with a curious equanimity. This may be the result of a new sense of patriotism or it may be something else. The test of steel will come on proposals to embargo pig iron and semi-finished steel; Japan took 126,000 tons of pig and semi-finished during the first seven months of this year. The test of the State Department will come on proposals to embargo oil, copper, and other raw materials that are as necessary to the Japanese war machine as steel; particularly oil, a commodity for which the department has shown a tender concern in the past.

Other questions are raised by the crucial development of the past few days. Will we end our pinch-penny policy on loans for China? Will we insist that Canada stop selling scrap to Japan and that British Malaya stop supplying it with pig iron? Have we obtained assurances that the Burma road will be reopened on October 8? What commitments are we making and what concessions are we getting in the Far East? Are we going to use Singapore for a naval base? What steps are we taking toward a rapprochement with Russia, our natural counterpoise to Japan? Are we going to make the same mistakes with respect to Russia that the British made in 1939?

At the moment the chances that Moscow will do anything to displease Berlin seem slimmer than ever. The possibility that our State Department could or would move swiftly enough to outmaneuver the Nazi Foreign Office is even more remote.

October 12, 1940

Hitler Profits from Our Defense

〜 〜

HARD-METAL COMPOSITION is an alloy of basic importance to national defense. It is used to cut tools needed for the manufacture of munitions, aircraft tanks, and ships. According to a report by the Senate Committee on Interstate Commerce, it costs about $25 a pound to produce "hard-metal composition." In August it was selling at $205 a pound and 10 per cent of the price was being paid to a German trust. In 1929 this trust entered into an international cartel agreement with American interests making the alloy. Restriction of production was part of the agreement. "Hard-metal composition," which had sold as low as $48 a pound before the agreement, has sold as high as $453 a pound since. Agreements of this kind enable the Nazis (1) to make a profit on our defense program, (2) to restrict production of materials essential to that program, and (3) to keep themselves well informed on American military plans and preparedness.

The case of "hard-metal composition" is but one of many examples of international business tie-ups dangerous to defense. A resolution introduced by Senator Wheeler calling for an investigation of the subject has just been adopted after a hard struggle. The Department of Justice, which is itself prosecuting participants in a number of these agreements, approved the proposed investigation. The Senate Committee on Interstate Commerce submitted a unanimous report recommending adoption of the resolution. But Senator Warren R. Austin, Republican, of Vermont, succeeded in blocking passage on the unanimous consent calendar, and the Senate committee was so fearful of reactionary opposition to the Wheeler resolution that it struck out its original request for $50,000 to finance the inquiry. The resolution now carries no request for funds, and because of that fact the investigation authorized by it will be terribly handicapped. The request for funds was struck out so that the resolution would not have to run the gauntlet of the Senate Audit and Control Committee. The chairman of this committee is Senator Byrnes. Senator Byrnes believes in "economy."

American experience in the last war showed the importance of knowing the extent of German influence and investment in our industrial machine. The decision of United States Circuit Judge Woolley in the Chemical Foundation case after the war revealed the extent of this influence. Through the Bosch Magneto Company the German government had been able "by a policy of deception and delays" to postpone delivery for fifteen months on special apparatus needed for airplanes. German-owned fire-insurance companies had forwarded plans of American industrial plants to Berlin. The Florida Lumber Company, controlled by German interests, "had acquired every advantageous place on the finest harbor on the Gulf of Mexico, the nearest harbor on American soil to the Panama Canal. Its files, instead of containing matters pertaining to the lumber business, were filled with pan-German literature." German-dominated concerns had cornered the market in coal tar to hamper the manufacture of munitions. "Their achievements," according to Judge Woolley, "in acquiring essential chemicals were regarded by the German government authorities as equivalent to the destruction of a train of 400 cars loaded with explosives." Indisputably German interests in those years not only managed to impede preparedness but to make a profit in the process. There are indications that this is true today, perhaps to an even greater extent than last time. Senator Wheeler proposes to find out. It is hard to believe that anyone sincerely concerned with the defense of this country would object to a full disclosure of the facts.

Until July, 1940, when the Department of Justice was successful in breaking up the practice, an American corporation manufacturing bomb sights declined to sell or quote prices on its products without the permission of a German corporation which was its cartel partner. A German group controls patents in this country on the manufacture of beryllium, a light metal used in making planes. Magnesium is widely used in German aviation, but the supply of it here has been restricted by patents in which a German chemical trust has a half-interest. Long-term contracts made some years ago by a number of American concerns with German and Japanese companies require them to disclose any newly developed secret military devices to these foreign companies. How many of these agreements are still in force? American companies have $2,000,000,000 invested in Germany. To what extent has this been made a basis for blackmail? "To the extent that reports, secret processes, formulas, and personnel are exchanged between German and American plants," the Senate Committee on Interstate Commerce believes, "there may arise the danger of disclosing to a foreign power matters which defense considerations make it unwise to reveal." Isn't it unsafe to embark on a great defense program without full knowledge of these international connections?

October 19, 1940

Defense and the Wagner Act

M R. ROOSEVELT is a master of the art of changing the subject, and his skill in this important branch of politics is being applied to the explosive question of whether companies violating the Wagner Act[1] shall continue to be given defense contracts. On this issue there is silence at the White House and pained embarrassment at the Defense Commission. Mr. Hoover's favorite device as a statesman was to appoint a commission of inquiry and pray the subject would be forgotten before a report could be made. The Administration is trying similar tactics. One is told (off the record) that nothing can be said (off the record) because a subcommittee of Defense Commission lawyers has been assigned to study the question. No effort will be made to hasten their deliberation; it is hoped that the lawyers will continue splitting hairs until after the election. Whether this is possible depends on Mr. Roosevelt's ability to placate Mr. Knudsen without too far antagonizing Mr. Lewis,[2] and vice versa — no easy feat. The crawl that Attorney General Jackson and Defense Commissioner Hillman were forced to execute before the sadistic Smith committee last week can only be understood in the light of this precarious necessity. It is feared that if an attempt is made to enforce the Wagner Act on defense contracts Mr. Knudsen will pick up his marbles and come out for Willkie.[3] It is likewise feared that if an attempt is *not* made to enforce the Wagner Act on defense contracts

---

[1] The National Labor Relations Act of 1935, which affirmed labor's right to organize and bargain collectively.
[2] John L. Lewis. President of the United Mine Workers of America, founder of the C.I.O. He supported Wendell Willkie in the 1940 election.
[3] Wendell Willkie. Republican presidential candidate, 1940.

Mr. Lewis may stage a walkout of his followers from Mr. Hillman's labor advisory committee or call a general strike in Bethlehem Steel. All this might have been avoided if the New Deal had shown more courage in the past. The Labor Relations Board since 1936 and the C.I.O. since its organization have sought to bar Wagner Act violators from government contracts. A bill to that effect was introduced by Senator Wagner early in 1938, and although William Green — who has since changed his mind — helped to block its passage, similar measures have twice passed the Senate and once the House. Clever parliamentary footwork and the House Rules Committee always managed to prevent enactment. The Administration would neither put up a fight for these bills nor agree to Mr. Lewis's repeated request for an Executive Order requiring observance of the Wagner Act on government contracts. The demand was renewed when Mr. Hillman was named to the Defense Commission, and some concession on this basic labor issue became necessary. The first step was the statement of labor policy unanimously adopted by the commission on August 31. "All work carried on as part of the defense program," it said, "should comply with federal statutory provisions affecting labor . . . the Walsh-Healey Act, the Fair Labor Standards Act, the National Labor Relations Act, etc." The second was the adoption on September 6 of general principles to govern the letting of new defense contracts. "Adequate consideration," these instructions said, "must be given to labor. This means compliance with the principles on this subject stated by the commission in its release of August 31." If plain words mean what they seem to, this was a guaranty of justice to labor in the defense program.

Mr. Lewis expressed his satisfaction on September 16 and inquired what procedure should be followed "in advising the commission of the corporations which are violating the labor laws in order that these corporations be precluded from receiving government contracts until they comply with the mandate of the law." Mr. Hillman took up the question. On October 1 he released letters from Secretary of the Navy Knox and Assistant Secretary of the Navy Patterson saying they were working out the procedure "whereby the substance . . . of the aforesaid principles and the statement of labor policy . . . is properly made a condition of all contracts to be awarded."

Mr. Hillman's demeanor when he gave these statements to the press was that of a man who had won a great victory; and so it seemed. It is now clear in retrospect that he would have been better advised to wait for the procedural regulations promised. Instead, accepting these pledges at their face value, and in good faith, he went on to the other question raised: Would a company asking for a defense contract be held in violation of the Wagner Act as soon as the Labor Board so ruled, or would it be able to go on getting government work until a final decision was handed down on appeal? Mr. Knudsen, at best no Wagner Act enthusiast, thought the commission, if it acted at all, should wait for the courts. That might, with good fortune, take several years, and in the meantime Bethlehem, Ford, and du Pont could enjoy the benefit of the doubt, and defense contracts.

When Attorney General Jackson ruled to the contrary, big business sprang to arms with a celerity it has yet to show in the manufacture of planes or the production of armorplate. The press — with honorable exceptions — has rarely staged a more effective campaign of misrepresentations. The Jackson ruling was made public on Thursday, October 3. By the following Tuesday Mr. Jackson was explaining to the Smith committee that he had merely been answering a theoretical problem in elementary administrative law; and Mr. Hillman, that he hadn't said nothin'. The War and Navy departments revealed that they had never taken the declaration of labor policy seriously. To Assistant Secretary of War Patterson it was only "one of a dozen factors or so that are to be taken into consideration by the contracting officers to work out." Secretary of the Navy Knox agreed. The War and Navy departments did not intend to let the Labor Board or the Attorney General decide for them. "We would have to take into account in any case going before the Labor Board," Judge Patterson said, "how serious the thing was, the stage of the proceeding — whether it had been concluded or whether it was on appeal — and so forth." The Attorney General was forced to say that it was no concern of his "if the defense-contracting authorities decide to deal with men who are in violation of the [Wagner] act." Mr. Hillman's bitterest moment came when he was asked whether he agreed with Patterson and Knox that nothing in the statement of labor policy, the decision of the Attorney General, "or any implications that could be drawn from it" prohibits the War or Navy Department from giving defense contracts to firms which are not obeying the Wagner Act. "I have to agree with whatever they think is their opinion," Mr. Hillman answered, "because they have the power to award contracts."

New Dealers understand the importance of the common man's morale in defense, and there is anguish over this humiliating acquiescence in industrial arrogance. They solace themselves with the belief that all will be different after the election, and this vision of pie in the

November sky is held with Messianic fervor. It may be justified. But one test of whether appeasement of big business will end after November will be what Mr. Roosevelt does about that vacancy on the Labor Board. I am reliably informed that Mr. Madden will not be reappointed. This does not sound to me as if the cooperative commonwealth were just around the corner.

The Rat and Res Judicata

THOSE WHO READ "Native Son" may want to supplement it with the decision of the Supreme Court last week in Hansberry *vs.* Lee. I can promise them no scene so unforgettable as that in which the rat attacks Bigger. Justice Stone's opinion may appear to be no more than a formidably technical discussion of the doctrine of *res judicata*. But "Native Son" and Hansberry *vs.* Lee both grew out of Chicago's black belt, where Negroes, Chicago's most poorly paid workers, living 70,000 to the square mile, pay the highest rent.

This may seem an odd moment in the world's history to discuss the housing troubles of Chicago's Negroes, but I am not sure that their difficulties are entirely irrelevant to the great struggle before us. The weak points in our democratic armor are those in which we are untrue to ourselves, and this is certainly one of them. Rents in the black belt, higher per cubic foot than along the exclusive Michigan lake front, are high because space for black men is limited. Space is limited because so-called restrictive covenants covering 80 per cent of the property in Chicago bind the owners not to rent or sell to Negroes. These covenants are the walls of Chicago's black ghetto, and they have their counterparts in almost every city in our country. Hansberry *vs.* Lee indicates the lengths to which the courts of a great Northern state were prepared to go to uphold these covenants; it also demonstrates how far the United States Supreme Court must still go before it overturns them.

For the layman the questions raised by the case are simple enough. Does one American have the same right as another to live where he pleases? Is every American equal in the eyes of the law? Will the courts enforce covenants that place some Americans in the status of an inferior race? These questions deserve the same unequivocal answer in the courts that we are accustomed to give them in patriotic oratory. Unfortunately, these are not the answers supplied by our constitutional law. We have yet to establish the rule that contracts involving racial discrimination are contrary to public policy. The Illinois courts decline to recognize the principle despite the presence on their statute books of a Civil Rights Act which forbids discrimination against Negroes in public places. In the Hansberry case the Illinois courts showed themselves equally agile in evading evidence that favored a Negro. Hansberry, who is colored, bought a home in Woodlawn, a white island in the black belt of Chicago. Other property owners brought suit to take the property away from him on the ground that it had been sold to him in violation of a restrictive covenant. Hansberry pointed out that the covenant, by its own terms, was not to become effective unless owners of 95 per cent of the frontage in Woodlawn signed it. He proved that only 54 per cent had signed, and that the covenant was therefore invalid, but the court ingeniously managed to avoid a ruling in favor of the Negro.

Several years earlier a friendly suit had been arranged between two white property owners to test the validity of the covenant. Both sides agreed in advance — stipulated is the legal term for it — that the agreement did have the required 95 per cent. The court which later tried the Hansberry case in Illinois admitted that the stipulation in this earlier suit was "false and fraudulent." It nevertheless held that this earlier decision made the case *res judicata,* that is, a closed question no longer open to litigation in the courts. Hansberry appealed to the United States Supreme Court on the ground that this ruling denied him the fair trial guaranteed by the Fourteenth Amendment. He also argued that the covenant, even if it had had the required number of signatures, would be unenforceable under the Fourteenth Amendment because it was discriminatory. The court, by deciding the case on the first point in Hansberry's favor, did not have to decide the second. The decision thus invalidates one particular restrictive covenant in Chicago but leaves restrictive agreements as valid as they were before.

This result may seem strikingly inadequate in view of the composition of the present court. Justice Stone is a great and good man, and a true friend of the Negro. The Chief Justice, in his present as in his previous term on the bench, has distinguished himself as a champion of the black man's rights. The attitude of Justice Frankfurter, as of the other New Deal appointees, toward the Negro requires no testimonial. It need only be noted that no member of the court has shown himself more eager to fight for the rights of the colored man than Justice Black. From this court one would normally have expected not a sterile disquisition on *res judicata* but a factual study, in the Brandeis tradition, of the effects of racial discrimination in bad housing, bad health, bad morals, and bad feeling. It is explained that the court did not write that kind of decision because the way in which this case came before it did not permit consideration of these broader questions. The significant point, perhaps, is that while this decision will seem a meager victory to the Negro, it appears to the court as a daring and novel interference with the authority of state tribunals. The United States Supreme Court, as it was constituted in the '20s, would probably have affirmed the action of the Illinois courts. That the decision in Hansberry *vs.* Lee should present progress in the recognition of Negro rights is the best evidence of how poorly established those rights still are.

The court in this case was as much the prisoner of its past as Chicago's black folk are of their white neighbors' prejudices. The Fourteenth Amendment has been held a bar against discrimination by the state but not by private persons. The court has forbidden any Southern state to keep a Negro out of the Democratic primaries. But it permits a Democratic state committee to enforce the same barrier on the theory that a political party, like the Racquet Club, is a private association that can exclude whom it pleases. Similarly the court has ruled in the past that the Fourteenth Amendment forbids a state or city government to establish a Negro ghetto. But it also held in a famous District of Columbia case that property owners may reach the same result by covenant among themselves.

The loophole by which the Supreme Court could have escaped its past in that case is that these restrictive covenants can only be enforced in the courts. The courts are an agency of the state and therefore subject to the Fourteenth Amendment. This is a loophole which the present court may yet utilize, for it cannot permit our basic law to remain in the state in which Hansberry *vs.* Lee leaves it without inviting painful comparisons. These restrictive covenants are our Nürnberg laws, used as often against the Jew as against the Negro. To the latter they are more than a social annoyance.

PART III

1941

January 11, 1941

Munichman from Montana

SENATOR WHEELER was dressed in the costume favored by statesmen — cutaway and gray striped trousers. When I went in he was sitting behind the small desk at which he works. As the conversation warmed up he rose and walked round and round the room, twirling his silver-rimmed spectacles in one hand with the solemnity of a college dean. He spoke of the huge volume of mail he received after his "peace" speech. He said that the network over which he broadcast had only a tenth as many stations as that over which the President spoke Sunday night. He thought the President probably had not received more than twice as much mail as he did. These comparative figures gave him great satisfaction. I began by saying that *The Nation* wanted me to ask him just how he envisaged a negotiated peace at this time.

The Senator replied by remarking that he thought the President ought to try to bring about peace. He did not agree with colleagues like Senator Clark who believed that Mr. Roosevelt's strongly anti-Axis speeches made it impossible for him to act as a mediator. Senator Wheeler also thought that before giving more aid to Great Britain we ought to know what its war aims were. Last time these had been Versailles, and Versailles had created Hitler. Could one, after the events of the past few years, expect a Hitler peace to be anything more than a breathing spell for new aggression? "Let us assume," Senator Wheeler said, "that we can't believe Nazi promises." Nevertheless, peace now was better than continued slaughter.

He did not think the English could win. "I am one of those who don't want to see England annihilated," he said, "but those who are encouraging the British to resist by intimating that we are going to enter the war are doing them a disservice." He was convinced the President would take us into the war if he could. He thought it doubtful that a resolution declaring war could be put through Congress. "I think Congress has gone just about as far as it will go along that line." Unless we enter the war the British, in his opinion, could not win, and there was a question in his mind as to whether we could. In order to defeat Germany we should have to land troops on the Continent. Every military and naval expert he had talked to — and he had talked to many — agreed on that point. "If Germany can't land troops twenty-two miles across the Channel," the Senator said, "it isn't likely that we can land troops on the Continent." Only an alliance of Russia, the United States, and England, he added, could defeat Germany.

"Consequently," he said, "Russia and the United States could do a great deal to bring about peace in Europe, perhaps not a just peace from the standpoint of England, or of Germany or Italy for that matter, but surely the effort should be made." Some day there was going to be a negotiated peace. Almost every peace had been a negotiated peace. Why not try for one now? I suggested that Hitler had been underestimated here and abroad from the beginning. Wasn't it about time to begin to take him at face value? Hitler said he wanted to rule the world. "This talk about Hitler wanting to dominate the world, as he expounded it in 'Mein Kampf,'" the Senator answered, "doesn't impress me any more than did the boasts of Lenin and Trotsky a few years ago that they were going to make a world revolution. These are fantastic boasts by unpractical egotists. Japan boasts that she's going to rule the world. There are people in the United States who think that we, or at least the English-speaking peoples, should dominate the world."

"I appreciate the fact," the Senator continued, "that some fanatics who want to get us into war right away will brand me a Laval or something worse for what I have said. In some high circles there seem to be people who have the idea that those who are talking peace should be intimidated." We were not a totalitarian power, and some people talking blithely of tolerance and democracy were at the same time using "the very methods that Hitler, Stalin, and Mussolini used to maintain themselves in power." Those howling down the advocates of peace were "intolerant to the *nth* degree." They were breeding intolerance and racial and religious hatreds, which were always the forerunner of the destruction of democratic ideals. He had been attacked for his anti-war views by a Polish-American paper. He wasn't worried about what was going to happen to the Poles. He was concerned with what might happen to Americans. He had told some of his friends — he named some close Jewish advisers who share his isolationist views — that the backwash of the current hysteria was a rising tide of anti-Semitism. He feared a really virulent anti-Semitism if we became involved in the war. He wished some of the Jews in New York would have sense enough to keep their mouths shut. He felt they were being used by politicians for their own ends.

What kind of peace did the Senator think we could get? Would he take peace at any price? What would he consider terms impossible to accept? Well, he had been in Europe, and he felt then as he did now that a United States of Europe was the only way out. Did he think we could get a United States of Europe from Hitler? "I don't know," the Senator replied, "I'm not in his confidence. But there can be nothing lost in trying to bring about peace. Every American citizen from the President down ought to be working toward that end." Wouldn't a negotiated peace merely be an armed truce? "That," said the Senator, "is just a guess." Didn't he think the guess had some pretty good grounds after the events of the past few years? I didn't get an answer.

England, said the Senator, was opposed to a United States of Europe. "I don't think Hitler today would accept one either," he added. "Any peace in Europe," Senator Wheeler said, "has got to be based on letting the ordinary man live. That wasn't done when the Versailles treaty was written. I don't know that it can be done under Hitler." The Senator felt that peace could have been obtained in September, 1939, if Poland had given up Danzig, the Polish Corridor, and Silesia. He felt that the United States would be in a stronger moral position today if it had brought about peace then on those terms, and I kept coming back to, and the Senator kept getting away from, the issue of whether Hitler's signature on a peace treaty would be worth anything. The Senator said he thought we had to trust someone, that we had got along with tyrants in the past and would have to do so again in the future. If Britain was our first line of defense, he said, then we ought to go into the war immediately. But we weren't ready for war. High army and navy officers afraid to speak publicly had told him we weren't prepared. "The President," they said, "won't listen to us." The British, the Senator declared, were in a bad way. British labor's morale wouldn't hold up much longer. Wages were too low. "Talk about freedom," the Senator asked, "what of India, what of Hongkong?" By this time his secretary was at his elbow.

From NDAC to OPM

THE COURSE of human affairs may not proceed with Euclidean neatness, but the bitter fight being waged here for control of the defense machinery will be better understood if we start with a few simple axioms. War increases the demand for labor and for capital. Capital in war time invariably seeks to use its increased bargaining power with government as a means of reducing labor's newly enhanced power to bargain with capital. Capital tries to prevent labor from "taking advantage of the crisis" while itself fully exploiting the improved bargaining position conferred on capital by the war-time market. The organized cry to outlaw strikes on defense contracts is proof of the one. The ease with which capital last year obtained repeal of profit limitations on defense contracts is proof of the other. For both purposes capital needs control of the defense machinery. Basically it is this which lies behind the alphabet soup reshuffle from NDAC [National Defense Advisory Commission] to OPM [Office of Production Management], and it is this which accounts for the disappointment felt in business circles over the President's refusal to make William S. Knudsen the one-man boss of the new Office for Production Management. The executive order naming Sidney Hillman as Knudsen's associate was the greatest setback the dollar-a-year men have suffered since the election.

In a very real sense the behind-the-scenes fight over the executive order was an extension of the election campaign. The masters of enterprise are not content to cast a ballot once every four years. Their failure to install a Willkie in the White House only made them the more eager to install a Willkie in the defense machinery. They complain that the new OPM order divides authority between Knudsen and Hillman. They wanted to divide authority between Knudsen and Roosevelt. The division of authority between Knudsen and Hillman makes Mr. Roosevelt the final arbiter on defense matters. That is what they resent, and that is what they sought to avoid by a palace cabal. The President's intentions, despite claims to the contrary, were made quite clear in the December 20 press conference, at which he first announced the establishment of the OPM. At that time he decried talk of a one-man boss for production for defense, explaining that there were three elements in the productive picture, management, labor, and the buyer, and that he wanted all three equally represented in the OPM. Knudsen was to represent management, Hillman to represent labor, Stimson and Knox the army and navy as purchasers. Obviously this was quite different from the one-man setup proposed by the conservative press and from the three-man board made up of Knudsen, Stimson, and Knox which was suggested by the army and navy. The drafting of the executive order to carry out the President's instructions was left with Budget Director Harold Smith, White House Administrative Assistant William McReynolds, and Louis Brownlow, coauthor of the President's government-reorganization plan. To attribute what they did to the "extreme vagueness" of the President's instructions, as two conservative newspaper columnists have since done, is feeble apologetics.

What these three gentlemen did was to confer with Knudsen's counsel, Frederick Eaton, and Stettinius's counsel, Blackwell Smith, both Wall Streeters, and emerge with a draft that would have made Knudsen the "director general" of the new Office of Production Management and left Hillman a mere "adviser." Characteristic of the way the dollar-a-year men tend to operate was their failure to consult with Sidney Hillman, who was laid up with the grippe, or with Hillman's devoted counsel, Maxwell Brandwen. Neither side in this fight will do much talking, but so far as I can determine, Brandwen first learned of this order from a story about it in the *Wall Street Journal.* Stimson and Knox, the story said, were to retain their administrative functions under Knudsen, and these three would comprise the administrative board of the OPM; Hillman would be "relegated to a position of 'adviser' to Knudsen with no administrative authority." Brandwen read this and went to battle.

Harry Hopkins and Attorney General Jackson helped to defeat the dollar-a-year men. I hope revelation of the part he played will not cause trouble for the Attorney General. The day before I learned of the help he had given, I was informed by two persons, both in the government, that the FBI in checking on the household-help and landladies of government employees, was asking whether these employees had entertained or consorted with any persons of "communistic" or "pro-labor" views. My informants, neither of whom had any sympathy with the Communist Party, insisted that the phrase "pro-labor" had been used by FBI agents.

The bitter attacks made on Hillman in Congress last week were not accidental. "Let Congress act," the New York *Herald Tribune* demanded on January 9. "It has the power to direct the organization of the defense program upon a sound and efficient basis — with a single head in supreme control." The dollar-a-year men will seek to do through Congress what they have failed to do in the White House. Their defeat is essential if the United States is to be adequately prepared and to give increased aid to Britain. Knudsen, a man of winning sincerity and simplicity, did not lack authority before and does not lack it now. Legally, the shift from NDAC to OPM has given him more power. Actually he lacked not power but imagination, daring, and will. Spiritually he is still a General Motors employee and cannot be expected effectively to boss men who were his employers before and may be so again. He is neither a Baruch[1] nor a Beaverbrook,[2] and if he is given supreme power it will be exercised not by him but by shrewder and less honorable men in less conspicuous posts. The effect of giving Knudsen supreme power would be not to speed production but to push labor out of the picture.

The events of the past few weeks have vividly demonstrated the need for labor representation at the top of the defense picture, and not merely as an aid in winning justice for the worker and preserving his morale. Labor through the Reuther plan first brought home the existence of unused man-power and machines in the automotive industry. Labor through the S.W.O.C.[3] was the first to reveal the existence of unused capacity in steel. Experience in the last war showed that there is a tendency on the part of the big companies to monopolize war orders at the expense of productive efficiency. Only labor has an interest in maximum employment and maximum productivity. In the last war it did not matter that many American concerns failed miserably to provide

[1] Bernard M. Baruch. Successful financier, Chairman of War Industries Board, World War I.
[2] William M. Aitken, first Baron Beaverbrook. Newspaper proprietor, British Minister of Aircraft Production (1940–1941), Minister of Supply (1941–1942).
[3] The Socialist Workers Organizing Committee, predecessor of the Socialist Workers Party, a Trotskyist organization.

planes and ordnance in sizable quantities, for the factories of the Allies could supply our troops. This time the situation is different, and it is only on labor that we can rely for the discovery of the productive short cuts that may eat into profits but can speed output. Philip Murray is now preparing "Reuther plans" for other industries. Hillman in the past has had a kind of stepchild role. He was not consulted on production. He wasn't shown production contracts and could not see whether army and navy were keeping their pledges to labor, which they were not. Now, if he has the courage and energy, he can have a voice in the productive process. The public is waking up to the fact that labor can provide production leadership.

January 25, 1941

A Time for Candor

THIS IS WRITTEN at the close of the first week of hearings on
the lease-lend bill[1] before the House Foreign Affairs Committee.
By the time this letter appears the fireworks will have begun. Kennedy,
Norman Thomas, and Hanford MacNider will have been heard in
opposition to the bill. Lindberg and Hugh Johnson will be before the
committee. Perhaps the sharpest impression left by the hearings so far is
their undramatic character. The occasion itself is, in a word worn shabby
on lesser events, historic. We may be on the eve of the greatest armed
struggle of all time. The Navy Department is certainly thinking in terms
of protecting Singapore; the War Department may well be thinking of
the landing at Dakar. The State Department, in its own devious way, is
dickering with Franco and Stalin, Chiang and Weygand[2]. In Belgrade
and in Ankara, the newspapers postpone their press time three hours so
that they can present the full text of the American President's message
to Congress. We are reaching out for imperial responsibilities and have
become the focus of world-wide hopes and fears.

If 1776 stands as the symbol of our emergence from colonial status to
independence, H.R. 1776 is the symbol of our determination a century
and a half later to decide the destiny of the world. It seems foolish for
isolationists to believe, after the extraordinary events of the past few
years, that we can afford to make the same mistake about the British that
the British made about the Czechs and the Spanish Republic. But it also

[1] The Lend-Lease Act was signed by President Roosevelt on March 11, 1941. It provided for sale,
transfer, exchange, or lease of arms to U.S. allies.
[2] General Maxime Weygand. Governor General of Algeria under the Vichy regime, the puppet
government of unoccupied France.

seems unwise for interventionists to shut their eyes to the logic of the steps they propose and the commitments entailed. The lend-lease bill circumvents the Johnson Act and the Neutrality Act, perhaps also the national debt limitation.

It unquestionably places war-time powers in the hands of the President. The urgent necessities of the moment justify so sweeping a grant of authority, but they do not justify pretense in a situation that requires as much cool thinking as we can muster. The issues raised are momentous and deserve momentous presentation, but none of the Administration spokesmen during the first week of hearings was equal to the occasion.

First came Hull, as evasive as he always is with Congressional committees. He seems to find it hard ever to give a straight answer to a straight question. Morgenthau, flanked by five experts, whom he consulted on almost every question, was disarmingly meek, with the humility of a man who recognizes his own limitations. Stimson was franker and commanded more respect than either, but like Hull seemed appallingly the elderly gentleman caught up in a world of lightning war. Knox showed a vigor that they conspicuously lack and Knudsen seemed consciously the bashful Great Dane exploiting his natural charm. All five put together added very little to our knowledge of the lease-lend bill, and the aggregate impression left by their testimony was not one of candor.

The House Foreign Affairs Committee is no repository of genius, but after watching it for a few days one gets to like its members. They are as American as apple pie. The absence of brilliance makes them seem all the more representative of the decent democratic average, and with few exceptions they seem sincerely trying to do their best. The questions they ask tend to fumble, but so do the questions that most people ask about the bill, and in most cases they deserved plainer answers than they got. The committee has its oddities, chief among them its chairman. Sol Bloom perches his black ribboned pince nez on his nose at the angle of George Arliss playing Disraeli, but there the resemblance ends. Johnson of Texas, the ranking majority member, seems to be the brains of the Democratic side. To the majority members the hearings so far have seemed a formality. They already have the votes needed for passage in both Senate and House.

The House Foreign Affairs Committee is split along straight party lines on this bill; the handsome gray-haired Eaton of New Jersey seems to be the only Republican for it. The Republican members on the whole give an impression of genuine concern and sincerity, and I think no greater mistake could be made than to call their honesty and patriotism into question. Mrs. Rogers and Vorys of Ohio stand out in this respect.

I must confess that I took a dislike to Mundt of South Dakota, and some of his pettifogging questions. Fish, the ranking minority member, could not suppress a smirk of satisfaction as the camera flashlights boomed at the opening of the hearings and Tinkham gave the appearance of a ham actor playing prosecutor. Some of his questions deserved a better source and he made what was perhaps the most incisive remark of the first week of hearings. He asked Morgenthau whether the President could give away the Navy under the lend-lease bill and the Secretary replied that he thought that a violent assumption. "We are living in days," Tinkham retorted, "when the most violent assumption is apt to be the most correct assumption." No one recalled to him that he and his fellows regard it as a "violent assumption" that the United States will be in danger from the Third Reich if Great Britain is defeated.

A certain air of unreality has hung over the hearings so far, as of persons going through the motions before reaching a foregone conclusion. The Administration spokesmen said what was expected of them, and evaded most of the crucial questions. The Republicans for the most part fell back into the old rut of suspecting Roosevelt of intending to make himself a dictator; they have cried "wolf" so often that they can hardly take themselves too seriously. Much of the time the Republican members, as their party colleague Eaton complained, were chasing up "rabbit tracks" rather than keeping to the main issues. The feeblest theorizing of the hearings was Hull's excuse that we were substituting the "law of self-preservation" for international law; the one novel idea put forward was Knox's proposal for a customs union of all the nations in the Western hemisphere. Both Stimson and Knox will no doubt blush in the near future over their assurances to the committee that there is no intention under the bill to convoy merchant ships to Great Britain. It is hard to see what else we can do to lend additional aid to Britain within the next few months. For behind the question of lending or leasing materials to Britain is the more basic question of manufacturing these materials in sufficient time and quantity to be of help.

To the solution of this question the bill makes no contribution. The hearings themselves do, but in an unintended form. One came away from them impressed by the need for younger and abler leadership if the giant bureaucracies of army, navy, and business are to be shaken out of their customary ways of doing things. Until they are, the inadequacy of our present production effort and its business-as-usual pace will continue to endanger not only our British outpost but our own security.

Oil Is Still Neutral

ONE NEED POSSESS no inside information to see that war with Japan is a possibility. Gossip in circles on the Hill which are close to the army and navy say "within sixty days." Yet the same patriotic oil companies whose dollar-a-year men dominate the Defense Commission continue to send Japan the oil it needs. During the week ended February 15 we sent Japan 147,044 barrels of crude oil and 137,657 barrels of lubricating oils. We sent Britain 60,000 barrels of crude and 168,986 barrels of fuel oil the same week. Oil is still neutral.

When foreign countries, like domestic consumers, become annoyed with Standard Oil, the marines are called for. Otherwise business is business and a yen is as good as a dollar. For all the headlines about oil embargoes, American oil companies are enjoying a boom in exports to Japan. Here is the total value of our petroleum exports to Japan during the past four years:

1937	$43,733,000
1938	51,191,000
1939	45,285,000
1940	53,133,000

Lest the reader think these exports have been slowing down I give the figures for 1940 by quarters:

1st quarter	$ 8,584,000
2nd quarter	7,717,000
3rd quarter	14,160,000
4th quarter	22,675,000

Oil exports to Japan are running at a rate almost double any year since the "China incident" began.

The figures for gasoline alone show that we sent Japan three times as much gasoline in 1940 as in any of the three preceding years. Aviation gas is a story in itself. The Commerce Department, at the request of the State Department, changed the name of aviation gas last September to "high-grade motor fuel in bulk or containers." This was done, I was told, "so the State Department wouldn't be embarrassed by writers and newspapermen." In 1939 Japan took 628,560 barrels of aviation gas. In 1940 it took 556,703 barrels of "high-grade motor fuel in bulk or containers." The Export Control division says no aviation gas of higher than 87.5 octane content is going to Japan and that this other gas is inferior gas, not suitable for modern planes. Some authorities say flatly that it is good enough to be used in planes combatting an inferior air force like China's.

It is unfortunate that public attention has been centered on aviation gas, for war with Japan would be a naval war, and fuel oil runs battleships. Japan is being kept well supplied with fuel oil by American companies. Japan and Kwantung together (the State Department insists on separating them, although Japan's possession of Kwantung — the old Port Arthur region in South Manchuria — goes back to 1905) obtained almost 7,500,000 barrels of fuel oil from this country last year. Of basic importance, too, are Japan's heavy imports of crude oil, which amounted to more than 12,000,000 barrels in 1940. In December we exported 2,000,000 barrels of crude, of which half went to Canada, a fourth to Japan. Fuel oil and aviation gas are, of course, manufactured from crude oil. Japan has considerable facilities for refining and cracking, despite oil-company apologetics to the contrary. Latest published figures, which are several years behind, show Japan's refining capacity to be 52,600 barrels a day, as compared with Greater Germany's 68,770. Her cracking capacity is 16,250 barrels a day, as compared with Greater Germany's 7,920 barrels a day.

Exports to Japan are not the only contributions of American oil companies to the Axis. There are two sources through which Germany and Italy might obtain American oil — Soviet Russia and Spain. The attention paid to these two loopholes is in inverse ratio to the amount of oil going to them. The dollar value of all petroleum products shipped from this country to the U.S.S.R. last year was $1,850,000, as compared with the total of $53,135,000 sent to Japan.

Joseph Curran, of the National Maritime Union, testifying before the Senate Foreign Relations committee on February 10 against the Lease-Lend bill, provided a glimpse of Spanish possibilities. He told of the recent trip of a Standard Oil tanker, the W. H. Libby. "Not long ago," he said, "she went to Cartagena, Colombia, and loaded up with oil she took to Freetown, West Africa, for British use. Then she hurried back to Carapito, Venezuela, for another load of oil which she took, this time, to Teneriffe in the Canary Islands, where the cargo was transferred to a German and Italian tanker. . . ." The crew [of the W. H. Libby] found Teneriffe a busy port, with a steady stream of Standard Oil tankers pulling in and out. In the harbor when the W. H. Libby left, were three German and five Italian tankers, the crew reported.

This part of Curran's testimony was given scant attention in the press, whether it was for or against the Lease-Lend bill. It would have been easy to refute it from Standard Oil and official records. I am told in the Commerce Department that oil exports from this country to Spain are now running about 300,000 barrels a month. But no one knows how much oil is going to the Spanish islands for transhipment to the Axis from American oil companies and refineries in Venezuela and the Dutch West Indies. Japan is obtaining large quantities from American and British oil companies in the Dutch East Indies. The press has played up every story of Mexican oil going to Japan or the Axis powers but pays little attention to American oil bound for Japan and makes no attempt to investigate how much oil may be reaching Germany and Italy through Spain, although that would be a great story. Mexico has some excuse for her shipments. Standard, Dutch Shell, and the State Department have been doing their best to enforce an unofficial embargo on Mexican oil, as I disclosed in *The Nation* last fall. The navy on instructions from the State Department chose to pay Standard Oil ten cents a barrel more for fuel oil manufactured by Harry Sinclair from crude given him by the Mexican government in settlement of his claim under expropriation.

Behind the scenes Mexico is now being blackjacked into an agreement whereby Standard and Shell will get back operating control of their properties. The American taxpayer will be asked to foot the bill in the shape of a loan or an appropriation paying off the exaggerated estimates the American oil companies place on the value of their Mexican properties. The excuse will be that we must keep Mexican oil out of Japanese hands. Why not start by keeping American oil out of Japanese hands?

Wheeler's Cliveden Set

THE LEASE-LEND BILL, a measure no more extraordinary than the times in which we live, finally passed the Senate tonight. The future is in the hands of Mr. Roosevelt. Within a few weeks, it is probable that there will be a declaration of emergency, a move likewise without precedent. It will be imposed for its psychological effect. The hope is to obtain war-time powers at home, as abroad, without actual participation in war, a step which no responsible spokesman for the Administration regards as other than a last step, to be avoided as long as possible. The chances are that before the issuance of a declaration of this kind, a triple-barreled attack by the Axis powers, against England, in the Mediterranean, and in the Pacific, will amply provide the sense of urgency so necessary to an effective effort. The President, in his address tonight to diners commemorating the eighth anniversary of the New Deal's agricultural program, used the phrase which is the key to the period we are entering, "Total Defense."

Though it will interfere with business-as-usual, the adjective is total, not totalitarian. An opposition crystalized and united by the fight against the lease-lend bill will do its best to represent the defense effort in a sinister light, although this opposition is itself infected with the totalitarian virus. Senator Wheeler, with his excursion into Coughlinite demagogy, seems tempted to complement his record for tolerance in the last war with a little sly dabbling in anti-Semitism in this one. Last January 11 in the columns of the Washington *Daily News,* Senator Wheeler debated the lease-lend bill with Senator Wagner. The Senator from Montana was generous. "There are those," he admitted, "who are honest, sincere, patriotic, Christian gentlemen who oppose a negotiated peace at this time — certainly among them is my good friend, Senator Wagner." In a radio address delivered March 3, the Montanan said, "Now we find these same international bankers with their friends the royal refugees and with the Sassoons of the Orient and with the Rothschilds and Warburgs of Europe in another theme song ... 'Our investments in India, Africa and Europe must be preserved. Save democracy!' "

It is becoming increasingly difficult to believe that the resemblance of such remarks to the ranting of Father Coughlin is wholly coincidental. A prominent New Dealer recently told me that when he was at the Senator's home a year ago a telephone call came in from the Detroit priest and that the conversation was long and friendly, though the Senator, after it was over, seemed somewhat embarrassed. Even more disturbing to one who wishes to believe that the Senator's recent tone is due to a temporary hysteria and not a considered position was the conversation I had with Mrs. Wheeler, who is said to exert a strong influence over her husband. The Senator, she said, was in her opinion much too tolerant of the Jews, often defending them unjustifiably in conversations in the Wheeler home. She also told me that she thought the Jews were 100 per cent for the lease-lend bill and agreed to except only one Jew — an aide of her husband's — from her sweeping allegation.

Voltaire said if there were no God, we should have to invent one. If there were no Jews, Hitler would have to invent some. In the past Senator Reynolds of North Carolina — whose "courage and ability" are praised by Senator Wheeler on page A 887 of the *Congressional Record* for February 25 — was the only member of the upper House to show the benefits of the Third Reich's higher learning. Senator Holman of Oregon seems to have joined the happy little band. He was Reynolds's stooge on the Senate Immigration Committee in the fight against the Wagner-Rogers Child Refugee bill and he would like to save American labor from the Wagner Act. He expressed himself in opposition to Nazism but thought Hitler ought to be given credit for breaking "the control of the international bankers and traders over the rewards for the labor of the common people of Germany." Not in the same class with Wheeler, Reynolds, and Holman but in strange company lately is Senator Nye. The Senator seems to have been too busy doing research into the misdeeds of the British to catch up with those of the Third Reich. He is strongly opposed to aiding the "despotic" British Empire, but spoke at a

Gerald L. K. Smith mass meeting in Detroit recently — rather odd
auspices for so fervent a democrat.

We have our own Cliveden set, and its outlines became clearer during
the lease-lend debate. Most of those who opposed the bill did so from
considerations whose weight cannot be denied, however much one may
disagree with them, and their patriotism cannot be questioned. But there
was also a minority of appeasers, pro-Hitlerites, and a few native fascists
who have begun to develop a vested interest in defeat, for it is only in the
event of the British or Anglo-American reverse that they can hope to
take power. Their anxiety is to "make the record clear"; their strategy is
to inherit power in a debacle. A little anti-Semitism fits in with their
plans. Their chief campaigning grounds will be in the isolationist farm
belt; all Senators from Kansas, Wisconsin, North Dakota, Idaho, and
Colorado voted against the lease-lend bill and one each from South
Dakota, Missouri, Iowa, Nebraska, Illinois, Indiana, Minnesota, Michigan, and Ohio. The states of the Far West and all the states of New
England but Maine cast one vote against lease-lend. Only Senator
Reynolds from the South and "Pudler Jim" Davis from the industrial
East voted against the bill. These sectional differences are likely to grow
less as new victories bring the Nazis closer.

The appeasers, and their allies, have lost the battle against the
lease-lend bill but intend to fight the President every step of the way as
he puts it into effect. The bill itself authorizes the expenditure of but
$1,300,000,000, and it will soon be necessary to ask for more. The
Administration's first concern under the bill will be how to get war
materials to the British, and there will probably be a fight in Congress
over that as well. Convoys of American sub-chasers — the Canadians
have found these small fast boats effective for the purpose — may be
used to escort shipping part way across the Atlantic, not into the war
zone itself but perhaps to the Azores. Long-range bombers may also be
used for this purpose. More shipping may be transferred to the British,
for they will need it badly, and we may soon see a heavier burden thrown
upon our railroads, with freight priorities and probably government
operation as in the last war. All this will coincide with a speaking tour
by Wheeler, and there are reports that John L. Lewis will go back into
action with a series of speeches, starting with the "shrunken bellies" and
winding up with an attack on aid to Britain.

These sour reflections aside, there is more hope now for energetic
action on all-out aid than ever before. Harry Hopkins has been working
for the past two weeks on plans to put the lease-lend bill into effect. The

Bureau of the Budget is drawing up suggestions for a new organization of defense which will largely supersede the present set-up. The real problem, of course, is personnel, but a change in organization provides an excuse for a shake-up. Other plans are being presented to the President. The chances grow stronger that Justice Douglas will step down from the Supreme Court to become top executive of defense. It looks as though Tom Corcoran, whose energy, devotion, and enthusiasm have too long been left idle, will share direction of aircraft production with Robert Lovett. The pair of them can be trusted to see the possible uses of idle automotive equipment a good deal more clearly than Mr. Knudsen.

April 26, 1941

Pipe Lines and Profits

〜〜　〜〜

THE HOPE that the Russo-Japanese pact does not mean Soviet abandonment of China is growing dimmer here, and this would be the psychological moment for the Administration to make Morgenthau and Jesse Jones[1] stop piddling and fiddling over that $100,000,000 they promised the Chinese last fall. It would also be the psychological moment for an embargo on all oil shipments to Japan. The Chinese need a shot in the arm badly, and their continued resistance is as important to us in the East as Britain's is in the West. *Pravda*'s belly-crawling assurances yesterday to Hitler and its scarcely veiled invitation to the Japanese to help themselves to "vulnerable spots" in the East signal serious trouble ahead. I am informed in the Department of Commerce that our oil exports to Japan are still averaging about 400,000 barrels a week, and have been as high as 600,000 barrels. This includes crude oil for Japan's refineries, fuel oil for its navy, low-grade aviation gas, motor fuel for mechanized vehicles, and lubricating oils of all kinds. Since the oil companies are always asking for our intervention in their behalf in Latin America, since we helped them muscle in on the Near East fields after the last war, and since we may have to defend the Dutch East Indies, an embargo ought to apply to shipments from American oil-company properties anywhere — in the Dutch West Indies as well as the Dutch East Indies, on the Persian Gulf as well as the Gulf of Mexico.

[1] Jesse H. Jones. Simultaneously Secretary of Commerce and Federal Loan Administrator by a joint resolution of Congress, he also ran the Reconstruction Finance Corporation, although he had officially resigned as chairman. The RFC made loans to foreign governments and financed the construction and operation of war plants, among other activities.

A government too flabby to keep its oil companies from fueling our enemies is too flabby to fight a successful war.

Rancid is the word for the contrast between the unwillingness of the oil companies to make this contribution to the security of their country and the many favors they continue to ask and receive here in the name of national defense. The State Department is making a fatted calf of Camacho[2] in preparation for the return of our prodigal oil companies to Mexico. We have placed a Rockefeller[3] in charge of promoting our Good Neighbor policy, and he has the help of a Chase National Bank executive in passing on Export-Import Bank loans to Latin America. Chase National, based on Standard Oil millions, is well known for neighborliness in Latin America, particularly in Cuba, where it financed a man named Machado.[4] It and the oil dollar-a-year men could easily prove criticism unjust by exerting their influence to stop oil shipments to Japan. Some of them have been using their influence to obtain some extraordinary letters in behalf of their companies from Mr. Roosevelt, Mr. Stimson, and Mr. Knox. There is no good reason why this influence shouldn't work both ways.

So far the only embargo for which the oil trust's dollar-a-year men have been plugging is an embargo on Thurman Arnold. Thurman Arnold, like Senator O'Mahoney, derives ultimately from the oil state of Wyoming, and the oil companies aren't accustomed to back talk from that area. The Senator is so well house-broken that he didn't even mention the oil monopoly in the final report of his monopoly inquiry, a spectacle to make history gape. Arnold, though unpredictable, has backbone, and he started out last fall to use both the Sherman Act and the Elkins Act against the pipe lines. Control of transportation is as much the heart of the oil monopoly today as it was when Henry Demarest Lloyd wrote "Wealth Versus Commonwealth." The pipe lines are supposed to be common carriers; the oil monopoly has kept them private thoroughfares. The first move made by the oil companies was to obtain a report from the National Defense Commission, prepared by Leon Henderson, hinting that defense would be impaired if Arnold were permitted to demand divorcement of the pipe lines. The report said the companies would not build certain pipe lines badly needed for defense if he went ahead with this part of his anti-trust suit. When I asked where

[2] Manuel Avila Camacho, president of Mexico.
[3] Nelson A. Rockefeller, then coordinator of the Office of Inter-American affairs.
[4] Gerado Machado, president of Cuba 1925–1933. Originally a reformer, he degenerated into a dictator whose reign of terror grew so oppressive that the U.S. intervened and Machado was overthrown.

these pipe lines were to be built I was told that was a military secret. I then obtained possession of this military secret for 15 cents by buying a copy of the annual pipe-line number of the *Oil and Gas Journal,* which contained a map showing all existing pipe lines and the two proposed new ones referred to in the report.

One was to be built from Port St. Joe, Florida, to Chattanooga by Pure Oil (Dawes interests) and Gulf (Mellon). The other, from Baton Rouge to Portsmouth, was the competitive answer of Standard of New Jersey and Shell interests, which didn't propose to be put at a disadvantage in the Southeastern marketing area. The promoters of the first line ran into a snag to acquire property by condemnation. The companies obtained a letter from the President saying this was needed for national defense, but on March 19 the legislature, though intensely pro-Roosevelt, refused the request, and the companies are now about to ask Congress for a law giving them the right to eminent domain in Georgia. The Cole committee, which since 1933 has spent about $500,000 investigating oil without ever doing much about it, was chosen as the oil-company forum. On January 24 Rear Admiral H. A. Stuart, director of naval petroleum reserves, had written Congressman John M. Coffee of Washington that the proposed pipe line was "a purely private enterprise" for the importation into the Southeast of "imported refined petroleum products, probably from Mexico, Venezuela, Colombia, etc . . . and so far as I am aware would not be of any service to the navy." Admiral Stuart was forced to eat his words. On the witness stand before the Cole committee he was confronted with a letter from Secretary of the Navy Knox declaring that this pipe line was required for defense. Major Clifford V. Morgan, oil expert in the office of the Under Secretary of War, who also failed to see any connection between this pipe line and defense, was similarly confronted with a letter to the contrary from Secretary of War Stimson. The railroads and the brotherhoods claim that with 9,000 tank cars a day idle and a shortage of steel the defense argument really runs the other way. Congressman Lea elicited the information at the Cole committee's hearing that the Baton Rouge–Portsmouth line alone would require enough steel to build three 35,000-ton battleships.

Curiously enough, this is the amount at which the liberals on the ICC [Interstate Commerce Commission] have finally prevailed upon their colleagues to exercise, for the first time, the power given them by Congress thirty-seven years ago to regulate pipe lines. An order has been issued reducing crude-oil pipe line rates to an 8 per cent return (they have been averaging 25 per cent), and another order reduces the rates of two Midwestern gasoline pipe lines to a miserly 20 per cent (they have been averaging 30 per cent). No doubt the companies will use this as an additional argument for softening up the consent decree they are now negotiating behind the scenes with Thurman Arnold. Thus the ICC, like Providence, moves in mysterious ways. The joker is that very few independents can get to the pipe lines anyway. So long as we permit integrated companies to control the flow of oil from the well to the service-station pump, a reduction in the rates they charge themselves for the use of their own pipe lines merely forces them to put less in one pocket and more in another.

Why Knudsen Should Go

WALTER LIPPMANN suggests that we ought to take over the Azores. I think we ought to take over Detroit. Our confidence in our ability to wage a successful war stems in large part from the knowledge that we possess the world's greatest mass-production industries. The automotive industry is the outstanding example. But it is not enough to have these industries. It is necessary to use them. We cannot fight a war with convertible coupes or overawe a Panzer division with a brigade of statistics on automobile sales. The problem is to turn existing mass-production facilities as rapidly as possible to the production of armament. We are fumbling that problem, and we have no time to fumble. Let us look at the record of the automobile industry, the industry with which the director of the OPM [Office of Production Management], William S. Knudsen, is most familiar, the industry he should find it easiest to mobilize for defense.

On April 17 Mr. Knudsen called in the press and announced, with great satisfaction, that his industry had "willingly accepted an initial 20 per cent reduction" in the production of automobiles "to make available more man-power, materials, facilities, and management" for defense. The next day the newspapers carried the story of another sacrifice by the industry. This came in the form of a letter from Knudsen's former employer, Alfred P. Sloan, chairman of the board of General Motors. Mr. Sloan wrote that in the interest of national defense General Motors would give up its 1943 models — not its 1942 models but its 1943 models. "In this crisis," said a full-page advertisement placed by General Motors in our leading newspapers that day, "every hour counts. Every hour moves us closer to the day when defense materials will flow to our embattled friends in Europe in volume enough to swing the scale." So passionate is our devotion to their cause that we will do without new car models — year after next.

It is hard for a newspaper to look a full-page ad in the mouth, and these statements of sacrifice were not examined too closely. One notes first that the 20 per cent reduction in the output of cars applies not to the current production season but to next year's. One notes next that this year's production, which will probably end in June, will be one of the greatest in the history of the industry. Only two previous years, 1929 and 1937, topped the 5,000,000-car output which will be achieved this year. While we are promised a 20 per cent reduction next year in the interest of defense, this year's production will be 20 per cent above last year's. In the midst of the greatest defense emergency in our history, the automobile industry increased the production of cars by 20 per cent. Its facilities were mobilized, not for the production of armament, but to take advantage of the market created for automobiles by defense spending. Now, as a "sacrifice" for defense, it is reducing its production schedule for 1942 from the 1941 boom level to the more normal 1940 level. *C'est la guerre.*

These announcements of sacrifice are confessions of shortsightedness and greed. We are told, to impress us with the magnitude of the contribution the automobile industry will be making by its 20 per cent cut in next year's production, that this will save many metals in which shortages are developing: 5,000 tons of aluminum, 54,700 tons of lead, 18,200 tons of zinc, 4,796,000 pounds of nickel, 26,400 tons of copper, 1,437,000 tons of steel, much of it the high-grade alloys so important to defense. Aluminum represents our most serious shortage, and airplane production lines are already slowing down for lack of it. If a 20 per cent cut under this year's automobile production will save 5,000 tons of aluminum next year, the automobile industry this year must be using five times 5,000 tons of this precious metal. Multiply each of the other figures by five and you get some idea of the extent to which this year's boom production of cars is hobbling defense.

Informed circles in both the steel and automobile industries were surprised only that the 20 per cent reduction announced was so small and had been so long delayed. I quote two sources not conspicuously critical of either industry. "It has been known for some time," said a dispatch to the New York *Times* from Pittsburgh on April 21, "that automotive centers were producing at as good as full capacity in order to build up a backlog of finished cars against the day when production actually is curtailed because of the press of national-defense activity. *It has been this accelerated tempo of production by the automotive industry that taxed to the utmost the steel industry's facilities for the production of bars and sheets and strips."* The italics are mine. The same day David J. Wilkie, automotive editor of the Associated Press, reported from Detroit, "Some of the producers admit they have been thinking in terms of a curtailment of 33⅓ per cent or more." Knudsen had actually asked his old associates of the automobile business for a smaller "sacrifice" than some of them were prepared to make.

Mr. Sloan's first-quarter report this morning reveals the leisurely tempo of General Motors' work for defense. I can find no figures on total sales last year in this or in the last annual report, but some elementary arithmetic shows that the total defense sales of General Motors last year was less than $60,000,000. Its net earnings before deduction of income and excess-profits taxes last year — the greatest in its history — were over $320,000,000. In the first quarter of this year defense sales were almost $50,000,000 — out of total sales of $65,000,000. Not until "well into the third quarter" would General Motors begin to produce in quantity for defense. Mr. Sloan explained that this was because "by far the greatest number of projects" on which the company is engaged for defense involve the erection and equipment of new plants. Had the automobile industry been required to turn existing equipment to defense purposes it would have been unable to turn out 5,000,000 cars in the space of about seven months, as it is now doing. The automobile industry has been careful to keep defense from interfering not only with business as usual but with better-than-usual business. "The bulk of defense work assigned to the motor-car industry," the Associated Press explained from Detroit on April 12, "has so far been done in its engineering laboratories and in new plant construction.... *This explains to some extent how the industry has been able to roll out so great a volume of new cars and trucks during the last six months* (my italics). It may also explain why the industry has never been willing to give the Reuther plan a fair hearing.

The industry has ignored not only the Reuther plan but its modified version, the Knudsen plan, because the latter would also have interfered with capacity production of automobiles. It was announced in October that after a plea from Knudsen — who had heard of the Reuther plan the month before — all the major automobile manufacturers had formed an Automotive Committee for Air Defense to pool their machine-tool and stamping equipment for the production of the wing and body parts of 12,000 bombers. This program has since been quietly abandoned. Instead, the government is financing the construction of new plants for Ford, General Motors, Chrysler, and Hudson Goodyear. The bomber parts are to be built in these new plants instead of with existing automotive equipment. Under the bomber program General Motors was to supply parts for the new North American Aviation assembly plant at Kansas City. It was to, and eventually will, supply from 50 to 60 per cent of the parts needed. I notice that North American's annual report says, "Actually, however, North American will have to do much of the manufacturing itself, until the automotive industry can carry its share." If Knudsen had forced the automobile companies to carry out the program to which they were pledged, General Motors would have begun the task of making these parts seven months ago. "In this crisis," said the General Motors adverstisement, "every hour counts." It is a good thing that advertisements can't blush.

Knudsen can look a blueprint in the eye without flinching, but he gets bashful when he talks to Alfred P. Sloan. New models require machine tools. "Machine tools," as Secretary of the Navy Knox said last week, "are the critical item in nearly all cases of plant expansion, and the speed with which quantity production can be started is governed very largely by their availability." Machine tools require design and manufacture. Sloan's letter giving up any new models for year after next says this will release "a very considerable amount of managerial and technical talent that could be diverted to production and engineering problems in national defense." He also said, "We spend on an average model change from $35,000,000 to $40,000,000. This involves tooling, almost entirely. Probably 90 percent of this capacity could be diverted to defense purposes. In terms of production, there would be involved approximately 15,000,000 man-hours." He was talking here not of the entire industry but of General Motors alone. This means that the entire industry would probably have saved about three times that much labor — the most highly skilled kind of labor — had it decided last year to abandon 1942 models. It is interesting to compare this figure with the 52,000,000 man-hours — most of it unskilled — which were lost in all industry last year through strikes. The automobile industry's insistence on 1942 models cost the defense program almost as much in man-hours and more in terms of skill than all last year's strikes put together.

One of the points made by Reuther when he outlined his plan to Hillman last August was that the machine-tool bottleneck could be eased if the automobile industry were forced to make its private machine-tool facilities available for defense. Half the machine-tool capacity of Detroit is in the captive automotive tool-and-die shops. It was Knudsen's duty last fall to force his colleagues to abandon new models and turn these facilities over for armament production. The newspapers thought that was what was meant when he said to the automobile manufacturers last October, "If you gentlemen figure you are going to need a lot of machine tools in order to carry out your American way of life, you had better take another look." I think we had all better take another look at Knudsen. I expect to go farther into this problem of machine tools next week, but I want to suggest now that on the basis of this record Knudsen ought either to turn in his resignation and go back to Detroit or take a subordinate job where his real abilities as a production man could be utilized without requiring him to exercise the policy-making decision of which he has shown himself incapable. He is a very nice man, but this is no time for sentiment; as the General Motors ad says, "every hour counts." The clock of the defense program is ticking off not only minutes but lives.

May 24, 1941

Their Monopoly, Right or Wrong

～～ ～～

THE EXTRAORDINARY STORY on aluminum unfolded here this week before the Truman committee investigating national defense has been meagerly reported in the press, but it is one that the people of this country and their President dare not ignore. On Wednesday morning Richard S. Reynolds, president of the Reynolds Metals Company, testified that early in the summer of 1939 Philippe Levelle, one of the officials of the French Aluminum Company, visited him at his home in Richmond, Virginia. "I had become quite concerned," Reynolds told the Senate committee, "over the knowledge that Germany was buying more bauxite from France than the French were reducing to aluminum metal, and I asked Mr. Levelle in regard to this, and he said that Germany was short of brass and was using the excess aluminum for making things like window frames and door knobs." Reynolds wondered whether this was the real reason Germany was buying so much bauxite. "I stated to him at that time I thought they were using it for airplanes and that France would later hear about it." But Levelle was as complacent about bauxite sales to the Reich as our steel and oil men — and some of our admirals and State Department officials — are about our continued steel and oil exports to Japan.

Men like Levelle control production of most of the basic war materials in this country, and we risk the fate of France so long as we leave them in control. In May of last year, after the *Blitzkrieg* began, Reynolds came up to Washington to see Senator Lister Hill of Alabama, a member of the Senate Military Affairs Committee. "I had become convinced in my own mind," Reynolds testified, "that this would be a light-metal war, and I had figured from my inadequate source of information that Germany, her allies and conquered territories, including France if conquered, could produce one billion pounds of aluminum, while the total production in the United States at that time was less than one-third of that amount." Senator Hill asked what could be done, and Reynolds said he would see Arthur Davis, chairman of the board of the Aluminum Company of America. Reynolds went to Davis and told him that "he should inform our government of the true situation and not permit us to be caught in the same position as France." Reynolds, whose company at that time merely fabricated aluminum, suggested that Davis ask the government for funds to enable the Aluminum Company of America to raise its output to one billion pounds of aluminum a year. Since so vast an expansion of aluminum capacity would lessen its scarcity and lower its price, thus interfering with the Aluminum Company of America's monopoly policies, Reynolds thought Davis could ask the government for "full protection to his company . . . these emergency plants should be closed at the end of the emergency so as not to embarrass the Aluminum Company." Even on this basis, however, Davis did not care to cooperate. "Mr. Davis felt that I was unnecessarily alarmed," Reynolds said, ". . . stating that in his opinion there was ample aluminum and that there would be no shortage." Davis's optimism turns out to have been as fatuous as Levelle's.

The most favorable picture of our aluminum picture was presented to the committee by W. L. Batt, who came to the OPM's [Office of Production Management] production division from the SKF roller-bearing company. Batt said that, if all present plans for expansion work out perfectly and "100 per cent on schedule," we shall have only 1,209,000,000 pounds of aluminum next year, although our "direct" military needs on the basis of present plans will be 1,400,000,000. This does not include "indirect" military needs. A more pessimistic picture was presented by Leland Olds, chairman of the Federal Power Commission, who indicated that he felt the OPM estimates of productive possibility were much too high. The production of aluminum is closely tied in with production of power, and that in turn is affected by rainfall. Olds said that if weather conditions adversely affected the hydroelectric plants supplying the Aluminum Company of America, it would be able to produce only 500,000,000 pounds of aluminum. Even under average water conditions, Olds said the Aluminum Company would be able to generate only enough power for the production of 642,000,000 pounds of aluminum in 1942.

This is a terribly serious situation, but it will be less so if we shake loose from the grip of the business-as-usual crowd. With RFC [Reconstruction Finance Corporation] help, the comparatively tiny Reynolds Metals Company was able to build an aluminum plant and two metal-reduction plants in six months' time. Reynolds felt that the Aluminum Company of America could beat that record if it wanted to. "It is evident, in my mind," Reynolds testified, "that the production of aluminum ingots should not be allowed to embarrass or interfere with any possible requirement of defense. Aluminum ingots can be increased and multiplied as fast as aviation, automobile, and other defense contractors can expand their facilities." The way to get aluminum is to begin construction of a chain of government aluminum plants that will give us planes now and cheaper pots later.

The dollar-a-year men who make a great to-do about coming here to serve their country should be criticized even more severely than Mr. Davis and his Aluminum Company. Of these men, the one who bears the heaviest share of the responsibility for hiding the true facts on aluminum from the American people is Edward R. Stettinius, Jr. The testimony before the Truman committee provides a damning bill of particulars. Admissions wrung from the Aluminum Company's arrogant vice-president by Hugh Fulton, chief counsel for the committee, disclosed that at the time Stettinius was assuring the country that we had plenty of aluminum, the Aluminum Company of America was already unable to fill orders on its books. Moreover, according to the testimony of Grenville M. Holden of the Eastman Kodak Company, a dollar-a-year consultant on light metals, Stettinius and the men around him tried to discourage Reynolds Metals from entering the aluminum manufacturing field. They pigeon-holed an offer from a Swiss company to build an aluminum plant here at its own expense. They ignored offers of other companies to build aluminum-manufacturing plants, and they offered to help the Aluminum Company get around the Federal Power Commission's licensing regulations for the construction of a $37,000,000 power project at Fontana, North Carolina. The OPM in October announced that the Aluminum Company as its contribution to national defense was going to construct this power project to expand manufacture of aluminum. But the company abandoned the project rather than submit to the uniform accounting and unearned increment provisions of the Federal Power Act.

The subordination of public need and the country's safety to considerations of profit and monopoly was likewise disclosed in testimony on the priorities set up on aluminum. Priorities can be used by big business in war time to put smaller and less favored concerns out of business. One of the two civilian representatives on the Priorities Committee comes from General Motors, the other from a small aluminum-fabricating company completely at the mercy of Alcoa for its supplies. Senator Mead of New York expressed surprise that officials of companies using aluminum were allowed to determine priorities. "I can't imagine a Senator who was an officer in an aluminum company," he said, "participating in the tariff discussions of the Finance Committee and voting on that particular schedule in the Senate." In New York, he went on, the director of a private corporation was forbidden by law to vote on questions in which he had a private ax to grind. There has never been a bigger grinder of private axes than the OPM as now constituted.

June 14, 1941

Snub-and-Sell Diplomacy

꿍   꿍

VICHY[1] need not think it can collaborate with Hitler unscathed. I hope I am revealing no military secrets when I predict that after the Nazis have occupied Dakar, Mr. Hull will take note in the strongest terms of the grave allegations arising and, should a new situation on full inquiry be disclosed, resume freedom to act accordingly. "Accept, sir, the renewed assurances of my highest consideration. . . ." Beneath the imperturbable mask of protocol beat the hearts of tigers, and I consider it a duty to report a growing suspicion here that American diplomacy has already delivered a crushing blow to Vichy. On Friday M. Henry-Haye, the French Ambassador, asked Mr. Hull for an interview. M. Henry-Haye was kept waiting. M. Henry-Haye, after a wait, was informed that unfortunately the Secretary of State was very busy. The suspicion spread that M. Henry-Haye, as evidence of this government's displeasure, had been snubbed. The clever part of this, if I remember my Grotius, is that a snub, even the snub intentional, is not a casus belli. The sly old foxes of the State Department had again taken measures short of war.

The clumsy amateurs in Congress do not understand that a war of blitzsnub as waged by the State Department requires the utmost secrecy, lest the element of surprise be eliminated. The complex questions of national policy which led our State Department to seize the western end of M. Henry-Haye before the breathless Nazis have had time to consolidate their hold on the eastern end of the Mediterranean cannot be debated on the Hill.

[1] Authoritarian regime of Marshal Henri Pétain, which ruled unoccupied France as a puppet government under the Germans.

Mr. Hull sent an emissary to the House Rules Committee on Wednesday to block passage of the Gillette-Coffee resolution to investigate the leak — a mild word for it — of American supplies to the Axis. The State Department seems to be cleverer at office politics than at international, and I am sorry to report that its spokesman on this occasion was Dean Acheson, whom the President put into the department recently to leaven the sodden mass of Breckinridge Longs.[2] Though Mr. Acheson is no appeaser and is not in favor of providing the Axis with oil or other war supplies, he turned up neatly garroted in the old school tie. The department's point of view, as he presents it, seems somewhat lacking in clarity. It appears to be that disclosure of the facts would be unwise; that the facts are already disclosed in Department of Commerce reports on imports and exports; that exports to countries friendly to the Axis are being carefully watched; that of course, although they are being carefully watched, there is no way of being sure supplies are not being forwarded to the Axis; that one must be careful in shutting off supplies to countries friendly to the Axis because that would make them friendly to the Axis. If this still leaves you a trifle confused, remember that in diplomacy there are no blacks and whites — just fog.

In civil life a progressive and intelligent specimen of the corporation lawyer, Mr. Acheson seems something of a radical in the State Department. Unfortunately in this case he has let the old crowd in the department maneuver him into a position where he will take the rap for them. In a search for motives, proponents of the resolution point to the fact that last year Mr. Acheson appeared before the Supreme Court as counsel for the Ethyl Corporation. Ethyl is jointly owned by the du Ponts and Standard Oil of New Jersey. Neither can afford to have this resolution approved. Nor can those in the State Department who act as their international errand boys. I am prepared to vouch for Mr. Acheson's innocence and high state of subjective purity, but I still think it was improper for him to appear before the Rules Committee in opposition to a measure that would hurt important clients he had served in private life. The result will be to make him the lightning rod for less honorable elements in the department. I wish they handled our national affairs as skilfully as their own.

The Rules Committee held an executive session, but some of the facts presented there leaked to the press, as they should have. The figures on shipments to Japan are an old story; Brigadier General Russell L.

[2] Breckinridge Long. Assistant Secretary of State and former ambassador to Rome. An admirer of Mussolini.

Maxwell, administrator of export control, testified recently that we sent Japan 157,534,350 gallons of petroleum from July 1, 1940, to March 15, 1941, although oil was "embargoed" on July 31, 1940. The Rules Committee learned that Japan is not the only possible channel through which supplies are going to the Axis and that oil is not the only war material being sent them. Toluene is one of the constituents of TNT. We sent no toluene to Spain in 1939. We shipped 1,574,000 pounds to that country in 1940. Tinplate and taggers' tin have many military uses. Shipments to Spain rose from 6,105,000 pounds in 1939 to 20,436,000 pounds in 1940. Shipments to Portugal rose from 1,911,000 pounds in 1938 to 34,976,000 pounds in 1940. The State Department thinks this is for tinning sardines. I think we ought to make sure it isn't for tinning tools and plane parts for the Germans.

Cotton linters and pulp can be used for stuffing mattresses. They can also be used for explosives. Spanish imports of American cotton linters and pulp last year amounted to 2,337,000 pounds; there were none the year before. Spanish imports of lubricating greases rose from 577,000 pounds in 1938 to 3,931,000 pounds in 1940. Both the State Department and the British Ministry of Economic Warfare have explained that Spanish imports of petroleum have been sharply restricted to Spanish domestic needs. But Spain's imports of petroleum from this country rose from 2,571,000 forty-two-gallon barrels in 1938 to 4,456,000 barrels in 1940. The committee's attention was also called to the sensational rise in the shipments of American lard to Finland. We sent Finland 122,000 pounds in 1938, 732,000 pounds in 1939, 17,602,000 pounds in 1940. Finland today is in the German economic orbit.

For all its eulogies of democracy the State Department has always had an aristocratic professional dislike of democratic processes. This inquiry is feared (1) because it might interfere with the possibility of appeasing the Japanese, (2) because it would reveal the powerful influence of oil and other interests in the department, and (3) because it would thereby hurt the department's behind-the-scenes fight to control the long-postponed establishment of a Ministry of Economic Warfare. The only safe place for that ministry is in the Treasury. The State Department would sabotage economic warfare as it has the "oil embargo."

July 26, 1941

The G-String Conspiracy

I DO NOT THINK I am expounding a novel proposition when I suggest that you cannot kill an idea by putting its spokesmen in jail. The indictment obtained by the Department of Justice against the leaders of the Trotskyist Socialist Workers' Party and Local 544 in Minneapolis indicate that this is one of those platitudes better understood in the writing than in the making of history. The indictments say that the leaders of the Socialist Workers' Party, unless placed in jail, may overthrow the government of the United States, a task which would seem to call for more than a handful of men. The party claims that it has but 3,000 members. The department promises at the proper time to bring forward evidence to prove that the Socialist Workers' Party has all of 5,000.

Against this political gnat the government is about to let go with both barrels. One count of the indictments is based on the Smith Alien and Sedition Act,[1] which Congress passed last year over the objections of such radicals as Paul Scharrenberg of the American Federation of Labor. The other count is based on Section 6, Chapter 18 of the United States Code, which makes seditious conspiracy a felony. "Off the record" at least one official engaged in the prosecution is prepared to admit that the Supreme Court may find the sedition provisions of the Smith act unconstitutional. For the first time in peace since the Alien and Sedition Laws of John Adams a mere expression of opinion is made a federal crime. Under these provisions a man might be sent to jail for ten years because he circulated

[1] The so-called Smith Act refers to the sedition provisions of the Alien Registration Act of 1940; it is named for its principal sponsor, Senator Allison Smith of South Carolina.

such un-American documents as the Declaration of Independence and Lincoln's Second Inaugural, for both "advocate, abet, advise, or teach the duty, necessity, desirability, or propriety of overthrowing or destroying any government" by force. It is felt in the department that though this may be too much for the court, the convictions will stand under Section 6. There can be no doubt that Section 6 is constitutional. It was written to cope not with mere opinion but with an actual uprising. It was enacted in 1861 to deal with the Rebellion. The question is whether the courts will find it possible to equate the faint cannonading of Trotskyist popguns with the firing on Fort Sumter.

The rebellion of which the Trotskyist leaders of Local 544 are guilty was leaving the A.F. of L. for the C.I.O. Since the Trotskyists have been for revolution for a good many years and the Dunne brothers have been in control of Local 544 for a decade, one is entitled to wonder why no action was ever taken against them so long as they were content to carry on their subversive activities within Dan Tobin's International Brotherhood of Teamsters. Wendell Berge, assistant attorney general in charge of the Criminal Division in the Department of Justice, told me that while the actual decision to prosecute came after the union decided to leave Tobin's union for the C.I.O. the timing was a "fortuitous occurrence." The New York and Minneapolis offices of the FBI have been collecting material on the Trotskyists and on Local 544 for some time, and it may have been a happy coincidence which enabled the case to be filed in time to do a political favor for Mr. Tobin. The liberals in the department are either unhappy or confused about the case. Shrewder and more determined influences see in this prosecution of an easily isolated and unpopular minority a chance to establish precedents which can be applied more broadly. If the leaders of Local 544 can be convicted for their opinions, so can others and the National Maritime Union and the American Communications Association are next on the list.

No one questions the right of a government to protect itself, not only against overt acts but even against the expression of ideas, when there is really, in the formula of Justices Holmes and Brandeis, "a clear and present danger" that they will precipitate disorder or revolutionary action. Though the indictments allege that the Socialist Workers' Party is preparing to take over the government, officials of the department looked pained when one asks them about this charge. On the department's estimates $\frac{1}{260}$ of 1 per cent of the people of this country belong to the Socialist Workers' Party. In the Twin Cities, the party's stronghold, the ratio is much higher. There the party membership is $\frac{1}{18}$ of 1 per cent of the population. No minority is too small to cause some trouble, but the burden of proof is on the Justice Department.

To Acting Attorney General Biddle, to Mr. Berge and finally to Henry Schweinhaut, who is in charge of the prosecutions, I put the same questions: "What did these people *do?* What were they *about* to do? In what way did they menace Minneapolis?" All three were kind enough to discuss the case at length with me, but Mr. Biddle said he was not familiar enough with it to answer these questions and suggested that I ask Mr. Berge. Mr. Berge was also unable to provide particulars and suggested that I ask Mr. Schweinhaut when the latter returned from Minneapolis. Mr. Biddle, as Acting Attorney General, had to approve the prosecution before it could be begun. Mr. Berg heads the division in charge of the case. Without allegations as to overt acts or some clear and present danger these prosecutions are prosecutions of opinion. Yet Mr. Biddle and Mr. Berge were willing to take responsibility for them without the full inquiry warranted by a step so out of accord with our free traditions. If I understood Mr. Biddle rightly, he thinks a government need not wait for an overt act but can punish men for the probable consequences which would result if they tried to put their ideas into action. This reasoning is no different from that on which Trotskyists are jailed in the Third Reich or the Soviet Union. On this basis Thoreau could have been kept in jail for life.

From Mr. Schweinhaut I obtained a bill of particulars. They were not impressive. He is a well-meaning young man who headed the moribund Civil Liberties Division of the department until recently. He is now in charge of Commercial Frauds. He brought out pamphlets and quotations from speeches to prove that the Trotskyists do not believe in democratic processes and are opposed to participation in the war. He charged that party members were favored in the distribution of jobs through Local 544 and that every effort was made to place party members in key positions in other unions. He said the union had organized a defense guard of from 200 to 500 members — estimates vary. He said the defense guard had from ten to fifty guns to practice with and that its members did calisthenics regularly. The government has evidence that on one particular evening there was a test mobilization which brought all members of the guard to union headquarters within an hour. "What did they do when they got there?" I asked him. Mr. Schweinhaut said they went to the Gaiety, a local burlesque house. He said that each admission cost 75 cents and the government wants to know who paid for the tickets. This was told me in all seriousness. I have heard of the Gunpowder Plot. Maybe this will go down in history as the G-String Conspiracy.

F.D.R.'s First Task

IT IS AGAINST THE BACKGROUND of two sets of figures that the 203 to 202 vote in the House on extension of army service must be assessed. The first figures are naval; the second, military.

The day of the House vote Vichy fully joined the Axis. In doing so it brought the total naval tonnage of the Axis powers — Germany, Italy, Japan, and France — to 2,145,000 tons. Our total combatant tonnage is 1,277,000 tons. That two-ocean navy of ours will not be ready until 1945 at the earliest. With the British fleet to aid us, we can defend ourselves in both the Atlantic and the Pacific. In the event of a British defeat, the naval odds would be heavily against us. If the Axis obtained the fleet of a defeated Britain as it has that of a defeated France, it would be able to marshal 3,500,000 tons, a naval force more than twice as large as the one we have now and a half-million tons larger than the one we shall have in 1945 even if the present tempo of naval construction is speeded up considerably; that assumes, too, that the Axis itself builds no new ships in the intervening years. This is the measure of Britain's aid to us, and the basic necessity which dictates our aid to Britain.

The military situation is also grim. Representative Thomason of Texas, a member of the Military Affairs Committee, put the bald facts before the House in the debate on selective service. Germany has 260 army divisions. Germany, Italy, and Japan combined have 449 divisions. We have 33 divisions, most of them only partly trained and yet to be fully equipped. Germany has 40 new divisions in training which will be ready for combat service this year. The Axis has 37,000 fighting planes and 32,000 big tanks; it has a plane production of 3,160 per month and a tank production of 900 per month. We shall not begin to match those production figures until the end of 1942, and at the present rate not until then shall we have a fully equipped and trained army of 2,000,000 men against the 10,000,000 the Axis has under arms.

Hitler will not be defeated by bombing Berlin or scrawling V's on outhouses. To land an army in occupied Europe would require a huge force, and the best the British could provide might be 100 divisions. The problem of landing one division and of maintaining one bridgehead under German bombardment would be terrific enough. Fortunately for Britain and America, the Führer by his attack on the Soviet Union has "landed" a huge anti-Nazi army on the Continent, the only army in the world other than the German which is trained and prepared for modern mechanized war. He has presented Britain and America with an enormous bridgehead on the Eurasian continent, from which flank attacks can be launched on both the Nazis and the Japanese. If the Russians can hold the Nazis on the Dnieper or the Volga, we may not have to worry about Nazis on the Amazon; and if they can hold the Japanese at the Amur, we may not have to worry about the tin and rubber we need from Malaya and the Indies. This is the measure of Soviet aid to us, and the basic facts which dictate aid to Moscow. If either Britain or Russia is defeated, the defeat of the other will become easier; the defeat of both would leave us outnumbered and encircled and blockaded in a hostile world.

Hitler had hoped that dislike for Stalin's ideological table manners — and, conversely, Soviet dislike for ours — would keep the leadership of the Western free countries from effective united action, and it may. The Roosevelt-Churchill proposal for a conference with Stalin shows that our top leadership is robust enough to see the obvious. But the debate in the House on the Selective Service Act indicates that Mr. Roosevelt has yet to make America conscious of the realities confronting us. The British people see it; there is nothing like an incendiary bomb to illuminate an issue. But that hair-breadth victory in the House and the unanimous action of the Senate Appropriations Committee on the same day in voting down an army request for $1,347,000,000 for mechanized equipment show that too many Americans are still asleep. When a nation's leadership moves closer to war while its representative assembly moves farther away from it, danger is ahead.

To attribute Congressional action to Republican partisanship is to meet a crisis with a cliche. That a majority of the Republicans in Congress can play politics at a time like this indicates in itself that the issues have not been brought home to the people. Partisanship does not explain the vote of the Senate Appropriations Committee, which is controlled by Democrats, or the sixty-five Democratic votes against extension of army service. Nor does it account for the hostile votes of such all-outers as young Tom Eliot of Massachusetts or Voorhis of California. The Communist issue played a double role. There was a feeling that the Russians would "take care" of the Germans, and there was talk of "bloody Joe Stalin." But those who would lose a war rather than cooperate with the Soviets are distinctly a minority.

More fundamental than any of these factors was the feeling expressed over and over again in the debate by men whose devotion to country is beyond question that the Administration and the army chiefs have not taken the people into their confidence, have made promises only to break them, have not had the courage to be candid. Deepest of all was the rumble from the army training camps. Lack of material and failure to build morale have made extension of service unpopular, and this unpopularity was reflected in the vote. A contented people hates to fight until attacked, but recent history has shown over and over again that a people which waits until it is attacked waits until the enemy has chosen the best possible moment to attack it. Mr. Roosevelt, with the future of the world on his shoulders, has no task more important than to bring this home to the American people.

September 27, 1941

Making Defense Safe for Alcoa, I

LAST MONDAY the Truman committee, a Senate committee investigating the defense program, heard two witnesses. One was Jesse Jones. The other was Arthur H. Bunker, executive vice-president of the Lehman Corporation, now chief of the aluminum and magnesium section in the materials division of the OPM [Office of Production Management]. Both were unwilling witnesses. The story drawn from them, painfully and piecemeal, was a sensational story and an important story, for it dealt with aluminum. Without enough aluminum we cannot make enough planes, and without enough planes we can neither help the British and the Russians to survive nor defend ourselves in the event of their defeat.

Some important stories are dull stories — full of statistics and complicated facts. "Pig iron" we used to call them. The story developed by the Truman committee hearing was hardly dull. The testimony showed that (1) Bunker, the dollar-a-year man in charge of aluminum and magnesium, is still drawing his $60,000-a-year salary from Lehman Corporation, which owns stock in the Aluminum Company of America and its sister corporation, Aluminum Ltd., of Canada; (2) after four months not a shovelful of dirt has been turned on the 600,000,000 pound aluminum expansion program announced by the OPM last May; (3) the first contract to be signed under that program obligates the government to spend $52,000,000 to finance new alumina and aluminum plants but leaves the Aluminum Company of America to build these plants when it chooses and to operate them as it pleases; (4) this one-sided contract was negotiated by Jesse Jones, who can be the country's most hard-boiled horse-trader in dealing with some small business man or municipality; (5) Jones signed the contract two days after the receipt of a letter from Secretary of the Interior Ickes protesting that the contract was unfair to the government and contrary to the public interest, and ought not to be signed; (6) Jones testified that the contract was written "in the first instance" by "Mr. Cliff Durr, our general counsel," but a moment later Durr was forced to admit that the first draft was written by Oscar Ewing, counsel for the Aluminum Company of America. I can add, as my own contribution to this story, that there was very little difference between the first draft of that contract and the last, and that Ewing is not only one of Alcoa's principal attorneys and local lobbyists but also vice-chairman of the Democratic National Committee. At this point the Truman committee pulled its punches.

I went over the contract between Alcoa and Jesse Jones last week-end and mentioned it in last week's letter because I was naive enough to think the press could hardly ignore the story and would squeeze all the juice out of it before a weekly could get around to covering it. I saw eight or nine newspapermen at the committee hearing on Monday, and I see a good many papers every day, but the only place I saw the story printed was in the Baltimore *Sun,* which ran a short Associated Press account. Until yesterday the only clipping the Truman committee had received on the hearing was from the Baltimore *Sun.* The Ewing angle is political dynamite, but the Republican *Herald Tribune* in New York charitably overlooked it. The New York *Times,* which is for all-out aid to Britain, seems to have failed to see the connection between aluminum and planes. It does not hate Hitler less; perhaps it merely loves Alcoa more. The Washington papers kept mum on the story, although the Washington *Post* on Monday ran a rewrite of an A. P. dispatch saying that Jones would be put on the griddle by the Truman committee.

I think the silence of the press on the matter is as shocking as the inactivity of the OPM. Together they present Mussolini with a fine example of what he calls a "pluto-democracy." They show how little the real controls of the defense program have been changed behind all the recent scene-shifting and shake-ups. This is the kind of thing that rots empires and prepares defeats, and it is time that Mr. Roosevelt woke up to what is going on in his own defense household instead of continuing the grandiose face by which a Stettinius — more responsible than any other man for the delay in expanding aluminum production — is placed in charge of "speeding up" the lend-lease program!

The darkest aspect of this aluminum story is its one bright spot. When

William L. Batt appeared before the Truman committee last May 12, he was able to show by some strenuous arithmetic that the present production of aluminum plus the expansion planned would be just enough by the spring of 1942 to take care of our "direct" military needs. The new bomber programs — which remain headline hashish without aluminum — have since increased those "direct" military needs for the light metal. Four months have been lost, and the only contract signed covers but half the expansion planned. The new aluminum-producing facilities will not be ready by next spring. I learned from Truman committee investigators, however, that the consequences will not be as serious as might have been expected because the lag in aircraft production is greater than the lag in aluminum production. Aircraft production is now expected to hit its full stride by December of 1942 instead of next spring, and aluminum planning is in terms of the winter and spring of 1942–43.

Judging from the testimony last Monday and the contract, what we have to begin worrying about now is whether present expansion plans will materialize in time to take care of expanded plane production in the winter and spring of 1942–43. Unless Alcoa's grip on the OPM and the RFC [Reconstruction Finance Corporation] is loosened, I do not think we will get that aluminum in time. The contract with Alcoa provides for four new plants. One is for alumina, the intermediate product from which aluminum is made. This plant, to be erected in Arkansas, will supply 400,000,000 pounds of alumina a year, or enough to make only an additional 200,000,000 pounds of aluminum. The three other plants are aluminum plants, one with a capacity of 150,000,000 pounds a year, to be built near Massena, New York; the second, with 90,000,000 pounds' capacity, to be constructed "adjacent to deep water" in Washington or Oregon; the third, with a capacity of 100,000,000 pounds, to be set up in Arkansas. That is a total of 340,000,000 pounds of aluminum. No contracts have yet been signed for the rest of the 600,000,000-pound expansion promised in May, or for the additional alumina required to produce the aluminum, or for the additional fabricating facilities necessary. Aluminum ingots don't fly.

The contract is full of loopholes that lawyers will appreciate. No time is fixed for completion of the plants, and there is, of course, no penalty clause. Alcoa merely agrees to "use its best endeavors" to obtain the land necessary for construction of the plants, and it is doubtful whether the sites have yet been picked. The best Jones could say was, "I think the site at Massena, New York, has been picked. I am not certain about

Arkansas. I think the site for the Northwest plant has been picked."
Alcoa agrees to prepare plans, and if the plans are approved by the
government, to complete the work "as soon as practicable." Jones said it
was his recollection that Alcoa thought it would have the plants ready in
less than a year's time. When Hugh Fulton, counsel to the committee,
asked him why that wasn't put into the contract with a penalty clause
attached, Jones said, "I can't tell you." Jones's testimony is a lexicogra-
pher's nightmare. At one point he interpreted the word "shall" in the
contract as meaning "maybe," and at another he said "or" meant the
same as "both." In the construction of the plants Alcoa is not obligated
to exercise "good faith and reasonable care," the usual formula, but
"good faith or that degree or care which they normally exercise in the
conduct of Alcoa's business." The non-lawyer reader may take my word
for it that the second clause would make proof of negligence, much less
bad faith, very difficult. Fulton wanted to know why the term
"reasonable care" wasn't used instead and why the contract said "or"
instead of "and." I quote from the record:

> JONES: ... I don't agree with you that "or" means one or the other. "Or"
>   means both.
> FULTON: "Or" means "both"?
> JONES: Certainly ...

Aluminum is made from alumina and alumina from bauxite. Ninety
per cent of the country's high-grade bauxite, the only kind being used,
is controlled by Alcoa. After the bauxite is purchased, on Alcoa's terms,
the government will still have to ask Alcoa's permission to make alumina
from it in the government's own alumina plant. The contract says,
"When the alumina plant is completed, production of alumina therein
shall be at such rates within its capacity and for such periods as shall be
agreed upon from time to time by Defense [Plant] Corporation and
Alcoa." Fulton asked Jones, "Suppose Alcoa tells you it doesn't agree that
that plant should be operated, even though you have a good many
millions of government money in it? I don't quite see under this contract,
how you could require it to be operated."

> JONES: I suspect you could if you were to try.
> FULTON: Under what provision of the contract?
> JONES: You could do it without a contract. . . .
> FULTON: Why sign a contract where they have a right such as that, Mr.
>   Jones, when you have no right to control and operate the plant?

Why not insert a provision authorizing you to operate the plant if
they don't want to?

JONES: I think we are fully protected. . . .

Under the contract, after Alcoa has permitted alumina to be produced
in the government plant, the government cannot use its own alumina to
make aluminum in its own aluminum plants except at a price satisfactory
to Alcoa. If any alumina is left over, which could be made available to
other manufacturers of aluminum, it cannot be sold except on terms
satisfactory to Alcoa. Alcoa gets a five-year lease on the aluminum plants.
The lease begins either seven years from the execution of the contract or
whenever production reaches 80 per cent of capacity, whichever is
earlier. This allows two years for construction of the plants. Once they
are in operation, production in the government-owned plants is to be at
the same rate as in Alcoa's plants, and under the contract the government
cannot cancel the lease unless production is restricted to less than 40 per
cent of capacity. . . . I wish some Senator would have the courage to ask
Jesse Jones whether this contract was written to defend the United States
or the Aluminum Company of America.

Making Defense Safe for Alcoa, II

∽   ⌒

W HEN G. R. GIBBONS, senior vice-president of the Aluminum
Company of America, was before the Truman committee last
May, he was asked about the famous press release in which Stettinius had
assured the country we had ample aluminum. At the time the Stettinius
statement was issued, Alcoa was already unable to fill orders promptly.
"Reading that release," Hugh Fulton, counsel of the committee, asked
Gibbons, "in the light of what you have testified as to the facts which the
Aluminum Company then knew, if it saw that release, it knew that
release was not correct, did it not?" Gibbons was evasive, arrogant, and
smug. "I might have seen the release," he replied, "and thought it was
quite correct because I might have thought the war would be over in
three months, in which case there would be more than enough
aluminum for civilian needs." He went on to ask a rhetorical question
which reveals the attitude of mind of Alcoa in approaching the problem
of defense. "Suppose," Gibbons asked, "England was immediately
conquered, as it looked very much as though it would be at times, and
the war should suddenly subside, where would we land?" The "we" is
not you and I, who would "land" in a situation where aluminum would
be cheaper and more plentiful than it ever was before, but the
Aluminum Company of America.

It may be that Alcoa feels the same way today. It may be that its
officials have been talking the same kind of "realistic" defeatism to Jesse
Jones. I was told in a responsible quarter that Jesse Jones believes there
may soon be a "negotiated peace," a euphemism for a Nazi victory.
Whether the story is true or not, Jones has certainly played his part in

holding up our aluminum program. Congressman Walter M. Pierce of Oregon, one of the few members of the House with the courage to criticize the RFC [Reconstruction Finance Corporation] head, recently translated the delay into terms of planes. "To date," he said on September 23, "137 days, or 37½ per cent of a year's production, have been wasted in the efforts to protect Alcoa's monopolistic position. On 235,000 kilowatts, this is equivalent to 50,000 tons of aluminum. One light fighter takes 5 tons of aluminum and a bomber 30 tons. This delay is the equivalent of 10,000 fighters or 1,665 bombers." The clatter of pots and pans has helped to distract attention from the dilatory procedure of the RFC and the OPM [Office of Production Management]. The pots-and-pans campaign brought in 11,500,000 pounds of aluminum, which is equal to about one week's production when and if the promised 600,000,000-pound expansion program gets under way.

The war in which millions are bleeding on the Russian plain and millions more await renewed assault in the British Isles is not the war which concerns Alcoa. Alcoa is concerned with "where do we land?" Abroad it has been forced to give hostages to Hitler in the shape of its investments in Norway, Germany, and Low Countries, France, Spain, Italy, and the Balkans. If Hitler wins, Alcoa must do business with the conqueror. It is subject to his reprisals. At home Alcoa must make sure that if we win the war Alcoa does not lose its control of aluminum. The war which is of primary concern to the international Mellon aluminum empire is the war to maintain its possessions abroad and its powers over the precious light metal at home. In the prosecution of this private war Alcoa has had the cooperation of Jesse Jones, of the OPM, and of the War Department. The War Department last year sent a delegation to Secretary Ickes[1] to ask him not to grant Bonneville power to Reynolds Metals, Alcoa's competitor. W. Averell Harriman accompanied the delegation, and War Department engineers have cooperated with Alcoa engineers in picking the sites it preferred in the Northwest. The American people may some day pay a terrible price for a state of affairs in which the defense of their country is subordinated to the defense of Alcoa.

With competing plants about to be financed by the government, how does Alcoa intend to maintain its control over aluminum? The first answer is that it intends to delay the construction of these plants as long as it can. The second, as I showed in my previous articles, is that Alcoa

[1] Harold L. Ickes. Secretary of the Interior, administrator in charge of U.S. fuel resources during World War II.

intends to operate new government plants as a yardstick in reverse. Costs will be so padded as to keep the price of aluminum high, and allow a wide margin of profit on Alcoa's low-cost plants. The third answer is that Alcoa intends to make alumina its second line of defense. Bauxite is first made into alumina, then alumina into aluminum. Two pounds of alumina are required for every pound of aluminum, and Alcoa, with the aid of the OPM and Jesse Jones, will fight to prevent any other company from making the alumina needed for the new 600,000,000-pound expansion program. The contract between Jesse Jones and Alcoa calls for a 400,000,000-pound alumina plant, enough for 200,000,000 pounds of aluminum. The contract provides that alumina made in this new government-owned alumina plant cannot be sold to the new government-owned aluminum plants except at a price satisfactory to Alcoa, and no surplus alumina can be sold to anyone else except on Alcoa's terms. The OPM has recommended the construction of another 600,000,000 pounds of alumina capacity to Jones, and the same provision will almost certainly be in the new contract unless protest is strong. Control of alumina would enable Alcoa to control its new competitors in aluminum.

Alcoa is fighting not only to control alumina but to maintain its near-monopoly in bauxite by hampering the development of methods to extract alumina from our huge alunite deposits in the Northwest and from low-grade alumina-bearing clays in the South. In this it has the cooperation of the OPM and the RFC, and I intend to go into this aspect of the aluminum problem on another occasion. Alcoa is also trying to get the job of building any aluminum plants to be operated by competitors and to pick the sites for these plants. One may reasonably suspect that both the methods of construction and the choice of the site may be affected by Alcoa's own interests. Some of its potential competitors seem to think so, too, and while the OPM claims that it does not care who constructs the new aluminum plants, there was a significant note of annoyance in Bunker's testimony on the Olin Corporation. The Olin Corporation is supposed to be one of Alcoa's competitors under the 600,000,000-pound expansion program. Bunker is the $60,000 a year executive of the Lehman Corporation now dollar-a-yearing for the OPM on aluminum and magnesium.

"So far, I think the Olin Corporation will have to make up its mind whom they want to design that plant," Bunker told the Truman committee. "We came to an agreement in the middle of June that they wanted the Aluminum Company to design and construct that plant.

Since that time, about the first of August, they secured the services of a Norwegian named Sjoeli, and they now feel they would rather have him design it." If the Olin Corporation wants the Norwegian engineer to do the job, why did Bunker say it would have to "make up its mind"? Did he mean "make up its mind" to let Alcoa build the plant? Did the Olin Corporation pick Alcoa originally, or did the OPM suggest that it had better let Alcoa do the construction — or else? That the agreement was not entirely voluntary was indicated by a later passage in Bunker's testimony. "I told him [Olin]," he said, "I had made this arrangement with the Aluminum Company, that if they wished it they could avail themselves of their services on a no-fee basis, for design, construction, and training of their employees. . . . They were delighted." The design and construction of the Olin plant is especially important to Alcoa because it will use alunite in the making of aluminum. Another passage in the testimony indicates that the Olin Corporation was not always as "delighted" as Mr. Bunker imagined with the arrangements made for it by Alcoa.

"You get the picture, Mr. Bunker, as the committee I believe, saw it . . . ," Senator Mead said. "This site [for the Olin plant] near the water was picked out as a very economical site, having in mind shipping facilities and so forth . . . and it was agreed it was an ideal site. . . . Mr. Chadwick [an OPM employee] came out with an Aluminum Company engineer as his adviser, and they didn't get out of the car, they just drove by and vetoed the site, and then Mr. Chadwick agreed it would go over on higher land where it would be expensive to operate, and where probably after the emergency was over it couldn't stand the competition with other competitive companies." Mr. Bunker's answer was cold. "I naturally don't know," was all he said, "whether Mr. Chadwick got in or out of a car at any point because I wasn't there."

Alcoa wants to make sure that the government-owned plants it operates will not be able to undercut its own plants by obtaining cheaper power. Alcoa has a plant at Vancouver where power costs $17.50 a year per kilowatt of capacity. If its new Bonneville plant were established at Cascade Locks, it would get power at $14.50 per installed kilowatt. Despite the most strenuous objections from Secretary Ickes, Jesse Jones a few days ago agreed to allow Alcoa to establish its new plant at Troutdale, Oregon, twenty-five miles away, where power will cost it $17.50 per kilowatt. Either Bonneville or the RFC will have to spend an extra $1,500,000 to $2,000,000 for new transmission lines and other facilities to get the power to Troutdale. These lines will use up more precious copper, of which there is a shortage, and their construction will consume more time, of which there is a greater shortage. Bonneville estimates that it could supply power to a plant at Cascade Locks in six to nine months, but that it may take fifteen months to supply power to Troutdale. Power will cost $300,000 a year more at Troutdale than it would at Cascade Locks. Alcoa comes first, defense second.

I believe the story of the contract between Alcoa and Jesse Jones shows that defense is jeopardized and the security of our country endangered so long as the Houston banker holds the purse-strings of plant expansion. The President will some day bitterly regret the power he has given Jones over the defense program. Secretary Ickes's statement to the Truman committee is a dreadful prophecy we dare not ignore. "When the story of this war comes to be written," he said, "it may have to be written that it was lost because of the recalcitrance of the Aluminum Company of America. It is just as serious as that."

Washington Zigzag

IT GIVES ME GREAT PLEASURE to report that for the last two months no American oil has gone to Japan. This information comes to me from a source which has access to confidential export figures, a source which has been bitterly hostile in the past to our sale of oil and scrap iron to Japan. The same source informs me, however, that we are continuing to ship from 150,000 to 200,000 barrels of petroleum products each month to Spain.

We ought to be able to learn a little from experience. When Japan announced its adherence to the Axis a year ago, Secretary Hull greeted the news with an I-knew-it-all-the-time. Yet ten months passed before we shut off the sale of oil to Japan. If war comes between this country and Japan — and the possibility grows stronger every hour — the Japanese navy will be fueled for many months on American oil, and its guns will hurl shells made with American scrap iron.

It is too late to undo the errors we have made in the Far East, but it is not too late to act with more foresight in Europe. Today's cables bring the report of an interview given the French fascist weekly *Gringoire* by Ramón Serrano Suñer, the atheist who remains Foreign Minister of Spain without arousing noticeable protest from Catholic clerics grieving for "godless" Russia. Suñer again made it clear that Franco is committed to an Axis victory — how could he hope to survive in a democratic world? — and that Spain intends to extend its influence over Latin America. It pains me to report this as news, but it is news which has failed to impress our State Department.

Why do we go on sending our oil to this enemy regime? Is it to keep

Franco from seizing Baku? The crisis in the Far East repeats one of the A B C's of appeasement. Wars are precipitated by a show of weakness, not strength. Japan is beginning to stir because it believes the Soviets are about to receive their death blow. What kept it quiet in the past was not our continued sale of war supplies but its fear that the forces opposing it in the Far East were too strong for a further advance north or south. We nourished an enemy until the enemy felt that it was safe to strike.

Franco is a pipsqueak we are helping to keep alive until the Nazis are ready to turn west again and use Spain as a base of military operations against the United States. Spain today as in Napoleonic times is the natural bridgehead for a Continental invasion. We could appear to the Spanish people as a democratic deliverer rather than as a shabby back-door collaborator with their fascist oppressors. Spain, as the weak spot of Hitler-dominated Western Europe, offers an opportunity for military and political initiative, a chance to show we mean what we say when we talk of building a new democratic order. The Spanish policy, or lack of it, is a reflection of the flabbiness and the disunity on which Hitler feels he can rely for further victories in the west when and if he disposes of the Russians.

We shall not defeat Hitler by making faces at him across the Atlantic, and our War Department is finally beginning to recognize the realities. I am reliably informed that for the first time plans have been drawn up commensurate with the situation that confronts us. A program has been submitted to Secretary Stimson calling for an army of 8,000,000 men, more than 300 divisions, in place of the 1,500,000 men we are training now. If the Russians are defeated, an army of 8,000,000 is a minimum requirement for defense of the hemisphere, and probably too small for offensive operations, if any are possible in Europe. But to equip an army of this size would require a drastic reorganization and mobilization of our industrial capacity. Here again we are still faltering.

It is clear now that the reports brought back by Harry Hopkins from Moscow were much too optimistic. He seems to have thought that Moscow would hold out until next spring. The advance of the German armies again demonstrates that there is no time to fidget and fumble. The British seem to have begun to train men for the offensive too late to take advantage of the Russian campaign to open a new front in Western Europe. Our armament effort is still too low to give adequate aid to the Russians, although their defeat may loose a tidal wave of appeasement in the West that might shake our own democratic system to its foundations.

The financial and big-business influences here which have sabotaged defense and subordinated the needs of rearmament to their own profit and interest will be the first to cry for a deal with Hitler if the Russians go under. They are still a pullback influence on aid to the Soviets, although the President himself sincerely wants to do all he can. An illustration is the hesitancy of OPM [Office of Production Management] circles before the British request for rolling stock, locomotives, and steel to put the single-track trans-Iranian railway in shape for shipments to Russia. The new Labor government of Australia is stripping its own railways of rolling stock to aid the Soviets, but the OPM wants to wait and see if the Russians can hold out. If the OPM waits long enough, the Nazis may make aid to Russia unnecessary.

Mr. Roosevelt is no appeaser abroad, but he is still an appeaser at home. He wants to help Britain and Russia, but he can do so effectively only if he has the courage to organize industry for defense. This involves great political risks, but wars are not won without taking risks. The past week has given further evidence of the extent to which Mr. Roosevelt and the Administration continue to live in a pleasant dream world and to deceive the people about the extent and progress of arms production.

Production is still most notable in the field of ballyhoo. There was the story about our war exports reaching a peak of $155,000,000 in September. This is no record on which to preen ourselves when we think of the gap we must fill between Britain's $1,000,000,000 a month of war production and the New Order's $3,000,000,000 a month. It seems even less matter for self-congratulation in terms of the vast industrial losses in western Russia, for which we must compensate if Soviet resistance is to be maintained. More worthy of attention is the fact that in the past six months our war exports averaged but $40,000,000 a month and the fact that most of the $155,000,000 in September was still made up of goods ordered and paid for by the British before the lease-lend program began.

Tanks are a necessity if the Russians are to continue to fight, but despite the hoopla statements from the War Department that medium-tank production "almost doubled" last month, it will be the winter of 1942–43 before we are manufacturing tanks in any adequate quantity. The "almost doubled," from the best information I can obtain, was an increase from five medium tanks a day to ten. No heavy tanks are in production. Light tanks, the only kind we are turning out in quantity, will be useful for combat only in case of war with Panama or Liberia.

There is a great to-do in the papers this morning because the OPM has "cracked down" on a small Chicago manufacturer for using aluminum to make "juke boxes." What of the automobile manufacturers who still use metals and machines that could be turned to the manufacture of tanks?

December 13, 1941

War Comes to Washington

~～　～~

I FIRST HEARD THE NEWS from the elevator man in the National Press Building. The ticker at the Press Club, normally shut off on Sunday, carried the first flash telling of the Japanese attack on Pearl Harbor. It was a beautiful late-autumn Sunday, the sky clear and the air crisp. At the entrance to the White House a small crowd had gathered to watch Cabinet members arrive. In the reporters' room inside a group was clustered around the radio. I talked to Ambassador Hu Shih by telephone, and he said he felt "really sad" and sounded as though he meant it. The Navy Department seemed busy but calm; the War Department less so. Soldiers in helmets, carrying guns with fixed bayonets, guarded the entrance to the War Department's half of the huge old Munitions Building. They looked awkward and uncomfortable.

The public-relations office of the War Department refused a request for background material on the comparative military strength of the United States and Japan on the ground that since four o'clock that afternoon all information on the composition and movement of troops abroad had been declared a secret. The Navy Department, less strict, was still giving out information already "on the record," thus saving reporters a trip to the Library of Congress. In the Navy Department reference room women employees, hastily summoned from their homes, sent out for sandwiches and coffee and joked about Japanese bombers. There as elsewhere one encountered a sense of excitement, of adventure, and of relief that a long-expected storm had finally broken. No one showed much indignation. As for the newspapermen, myself included, we all acted a little like firemen at a three-alarmer.

The first press release from the State Department spluttered. It said the Secretary of State had handed the Japanese representatives a document on November 26 stating American policy in the Far East and suggestions for a settlement. A reply had been handed the Secretary of State that afternoon. The release declared that Secretary Hull had read the reply and immediately turned to the Japanese Ambassador and with the greatest indignation said: "... I have never seen a document that was more crowded with infamous falsehoods and distortions — infamous falsehoods and distortions on a scale so huge that I never imagined until today that any government on this planet was capable of uttering them." I asked several other reporters at the State Department just what the Japanese had told Secretary Hull to make him so angry. Nobody seemed to know, and the release did not explain. Hull's language was later described by one reporter as being "as biting if not as deadly as his fellow-mountaineer Sergeant York's bullets." It is a long time since Secretary Hull was a mountaineer.

The Japanese memorandum, released later, made it easier to understand the Secretary's stilted indignation. One has to go back to Will Irwin's "Letters of a Japanese Schoolboy" to match this memorandum. "Ever since China Affair broke out owing to the failure on the past of China to comprehend Japan's true intentions," said one of the more humorous passages, "the Japanese government has striven for the restoration of peace, and it has consistently exerted its best efforts to prevent the extension of war-like disturbances. It was also to that end that in September last year Japan concluded the Tripartite Pact with Germany and Italy." The memorandum indicates only the vaguest shadow of any American intention to appease Japan. At one time the President seems to have offered to "introduce" peace between Japan and China and then — I suspect after the visit to the White House of Hu Shih and T. V. Soong — withdrawn it. But the kind of peace the President might have "introduced" could hardly have been to Japan's liking, though the idea may have made the Chinese uneasy. The Japanese memorandum accuses our own government of "holding fast to theories in disregard of realities," of trying to force "a utopian ideal" on the Japanese, and of "refusing to yield an inch on its impractical principles." I hope these compliments were fully deserved.

The proposals made by Secretary Hull in his letter of November 26 were so obviously unacceptable to a government like Japan's that one wonders why we negotiated at all. Japan was to withdraw all its troops from China and not to support any other government there except "the

National Government" . . . with capital temporarily at Chungking." Our War Department is said to have asked the White House for three more months in which to prepare, and it may be that the Japanese were also anxious to delay a crisis. It is suspected in some quarters here that the attack on Pearl Harbor was the work of a minority in Japan fearful of further "stalling." The attack came before the Emperor could reply to the President's personal appeal for peace. If it forced the hand of the Japanese government, it also succeeded in uniting our own country behind Mr. Roosevelt. The reactions of the isolationist press and of Senators like Wheeler are indicative. If Mr. Roosevelt leaned too far in one direction to please the anti-appeasement and pro-war faction, his tactics served to prove to the other side that he had done all in his power to avoid war, that war was forced upon him. Lincoln in the same way hesitated and compromised and sought to "appease" before war came.

We are going into this war lightly, but I have a feeling that it will weigh heavily upon us all before we are through. The vast theater on which the struggle between this country and Japan opens makes the last war seem a parochial conflict confined to the Atlantic and the western cape of the Eurasian continent. This is really world war, and in my humble opinion it was unavoidable and is better fought now when we still have allies left. It is hoped here that the actual coming of war may serve to speed up the pace of production and shake both capital and labor out of a business-as-usual mood far too prevalent. There has been a general feeling that the production problem could not be solved until war was declared. We shall see. It is possible that a whipped-up hysteria against labor and progressives will serve to stifle the very forces that could be used to bring about an "all-out" effort. It is also possible that the coming of war will open the way to greater cooperation in the defense program, to a broader role for labor in the mobilization of industry, to a lessening of attacks on labor in Congress, and to improved morale.

My own confidence springs from a deep confidence in the President. For all his mistakes — and perhaps some of them have only seemed mistakes — he can be counted on to turn up in the end on the democratic and progressive side. I hate to think of what we should do without him, and when I drive down to work early in the morning past the White House I cannot help thinking with sympathy of the burdens that weigh him down. On the threshold of war, and perhaps ultimately social earthquake, we may be grateful that our country has his leadership.

December 27, 1941

The Shake-up We Need

I AM RELIABLY INFORMED that recent events abroad have led our War College to the reluctant conclusion that the cavalry charge is no longer likely to be decisive. It is at least as important to overhaul our social as our military thinking. No official here will admit it in public, and few in private, but what this country needs is more interference with private enterprise. The military-naval revolution which has enabled a coalition of smaller, poorer, and hungrier powers to attack the British, French, Dutch, and American empires with such success is also the reflection of a social revolution, and requires the reexamination of the bromides which ordinarily pass among us for profound truths. When wars are fought with tanks and planes, defeat or victory is decided on the assembly line. We see the relationship between technology and military power, but we have only begun to recognize that technology is more than the fabrication of new weapons. It also includes the way in which we organize our society to produce those weapons, for on that organization may depend the volume of our output, the speed of our production.

In all the talk here of impending shake-ups in defense, too little is heard of the need for a shake-up in fundamental ideas. Without it the effect of substituting Willkie for Knudsen or Wallace for Jesse Jones is likely to be less than miraculous. The war now unfolding marks the end of laissez faire, long honored more in the speech than in the observance, and the fate of free government depends on riding this tide, not bucking it. The root of our troubles, the basic defect of our war effort, the reason for our idle facilities lie in a system of ideas which leads us to regard the proposal to draft machines with horror while we look on the draft of men with equanimity. This is but the war-time reflection of the double standard which normally determines our attitude toward the rights of property on the one hand and the rights of human beings on the other. A society which regards it as proper in an economic crisis to throw men out of work at once but shameful to default on a bond until absolutely necessary is handicapped by its *mores* in mobilizing itself for war. The people who live in it are willing to order a man to risk his life for his country but reluctant to tell a factory owner that he must turn out parts for tanks — or else. Yet in a modern war we can no more depend on the profit motive to gear our economy for an all-out effort that we can depend on the profit motive to fill our army with enlistments at $21 a month and board. Until this is recognized, said publicly, and acted upon, we are headed for one unpleasant military surprise after another.

Just one year ago, in *The Nation* of December 21, 1940, I broke the story of the Reuther plan. Today's papers carry the news that 206,000 workers in Michigan will lose their jobs in the next seven days because no steps have yet been taken to convert automobile factories to defense production. This inability of a great and rich country to gather up sufficient will to mobilize its full energies for war is characteristic of empires in their senility. We are again the victim of want amid plenty, though this time it is a want of armament amid plenty of potential productive capacity. Solution of the problem has been hampered by a succession of complacencies in the capital. The first was the easy assumption that we were unbeatable because we had the greatest productive system in the world. When it began to be realized that this productive system was being largely devoted to a boom in consumer goods, it was assumed that it would transform itself automatically into a vast arsenal if we curtailed the output of automobiles, washing machines, refrigerators, and new houses.

A few months ago, however, officials and others began to see that curtailment alone was no guaranty that facilities made idle by scarcity of materials would be converted to defense production. Smaller industries found it hard to obtain orders from the big business men running the OPM [Office of Production Management] and hard to interest the conventionally thinking army-navy procurement officers in the possibility of turning out armament in factories normally used to produce washing machines. Now I find officials assuming that "December 7 changed all that." The attack on Pearl Harbor should have ended "business as usual," but it did not. To assume that it will without any action on our part is a curious, and comfortable, kind of fatalism. It is well to remember that bombs have been falling on the capital of the British Empire for two years without completely ending business as usual.

The truth is that while men like Stimson and Knox helped the President on the war issue by getting out in front, the top liberals and labor men in the defense setup have been more anxious to avoid fights than to exercise leadership. A fight is now brewing behind the scenes over the scuttling of the Victory Program by Knudsen and army-navy procurement, but at the SPAB [Supply Priorities Allocation Board] meeting at which the program was cut down by some 25 per cent neither Donald Nelson nor Leon Henderson nor Sidney Hillman put up an effective battle. All three have been good influences, but none of them is a fighter. Henderson is more smoke than fire. Nelson shines most by contrast with his fellow-business men. Hillman is able but not inspired or inspiring, and I was glad to see the Tolan committee take a rap at him in its excellent report on the measures needed to mobilize all our productive facilities for war. If Hillman had had the courage to go on the air last fall in support of the Reuther plan he would have looked a hero today. Unfortunately his is not the kind of leadership that will help us find our way to total effort for total war.

It is easy for a newspaperman writing for an independent weekly to talk of the need for interfering with private enterprise. It is hard for these men and other political leaders to do or say anything about it. Our government has political sovereignty under democratic processes, but in the sphere of our economy it is still in the position of a sovereign in feudal times and must deal with powerful economic overlords whose control over the means of public discussion make them formidable antagonists. Public officials who run afoul of these great interests take their careers in their hands, and few can be found to venture a head-on collision with them. Agencies like the Dies committee and the FBI play a valuable role here in keeping the progressives frightened and worried and thus in curbing the most useful forces in the war effort. In this connection I would like to point to Secretary Knox's statement that the most powerful fifth column since Norway operated in Hawaii and to ask why the FBI, with all the vast sums and great power at its disposal, seems to have been so ineffective in curbing it. Maybe if it spent less time tapping wires in an effort to get Harry Bridges[1] and scaring minor clerks in government offices by asking them what they think of communism and what their religious affiliations are, it would have more time left for the kind of detective operations we needed on Oahu.

[1] Militant labor organizer, head of the International Longshoremen's and Warehousemen's Union, West Coast director of the C.I.O. From 1939 to 1955 the Justice Department tried unsuccessfully to deport him to his birthplace, Australia, as a Communist subversive.

PART IV

1942

January 3, 1942

Aid and Comfort to the Enemy

〜〜 〜〜

S O FAR AS I CAN LEARN, the liberation of St. Pierre and Miquelon from Vichy rule by Free French[1] forces was carried out with the knowledge and consent, if not the cooperation, of the British and Canadian governments. Vice-Admiral Emile Muselier spent several weeks on Canadian soil preparing for the occupation. In both London and Ottawa it was felt that the islands, at the mouth of the St. Lawrence, were too important to the defense of the Dominion and the security of transatlantic trade routes to be left to the mercy of our State Department's incorrigible determination to play pat-a-cake with Vichy. The State Department did not consult Ottawa and London before making its agreement to protect Vichy control in Martinique, and Ottawa and London did not consult the State Department before permitting the Free French to restore free government and an anti-Axis regime in St. Pierre and Miquelon. The Free French did not consult the State Department because the State Department had not consulted the Free French, whom it still does not recognize. And it was well understood all around that the State Department, if consulted, would have objected because it does not intend to stop trying to appease Pétain until that aged puppet has outgrown his usefulness to Hitler and the Nazis take over France.

When news of the occupation reached the State Department, it instructed Ambassador Winant to file a protest with the British Foreign Office. Winant, who is no appeaser, assumed that the White House had approved the idea and made the protest. In Washington Samuel Reber,

[1] The French government-in-exile headed by General Charles de Gaulle, which continued resistance to Germany.

the State Department official in charge of French affairs and an appeaser from way back, went in person to protest at the British embassy. He was told that the British knew nothing about the occupation and didn't intend to do anything about it. In the meantime the Foreign Office, through Malcolm MacDonald, jumped the traces of protocol and reached Beaverbrook at the White House. The word which went back to London, after Beaverbrook had inquired, was that the State Department had ordered the protest without first clearing the matter at the White House. The British were informed that the President called in Hull and took the Secretary of State down a peg. Their feeling was that the State Department would be forced to back down on this matter. I am not so sure.

Whatever the outcome, the St. Pierre-Miquelon affair serves notice on the world that the American State Department is now the last stronghold of appeasement. It must also give the impression that our foreign policy is being run in the halfwit fashion that led so many of the Western democracies cheerfully to their doom. On November 24 the Free French delegation in New York released a letter written by the President on November 11 to Lease-Lend Administrator Edward R. Stettinius, Jr., declaring the defense of any Free French territory "vital to the defense of the United States." The invocation of that statutory formula placed lease-lend aid at the disposal of the Free French, and they opened an office in Washington to make arrangements for obtaining materials of war. On December 8, the day after the Japanese attack on Pearl Harbor, the Free French National Committee in London declared war on Japan. This was no empty gesture. In New Caledonia, the New Hebrides, and Tahiti the Free French control South Pacific islands that are now our only remaining stepping-stones to the Far East. Had we backed the Free French, they might have made French Indo-China our base against Japan, instead of leaving it to become Vichy's gift to Japan as a base against the Philippines and Thailand. The Free French are our allies. Vichy is the tool of our enemies. Yet on Christmas Day Cordell Hull, with a stupidity that calls for his removal from office, had the State Department issue a statement sneering at the "so-called Free French navy" and demanding restoration of St. Pierre and Miquelon to Vichy.

I have spent most of the day talking with representatives of the Free French, and I want to report that the Secretary of State's reference rankles. The State Department could not have chosen a better way to undermine the confidence of oppressed peoples everywhere than by its slur, and I think some way should be found to let the world know in decisive fashion that the undemocratic little clique of decayed pseudo-aristocrats and backsliding liberals who dominate the State Department do not speak for the American people. The people of St. Pierre and Miquelon have been dismissing Axis radio reports that we would force return of the islands to Vichy as typical Nazi lies. But to our own "Propaganda Ministry," Colonel Donovan's office for the coordination of information, has fallen the unhappy task of broadcasting to the French people and the French colonies in the past few days the fact that the democratic United States stands squarely behind the traitors who are Hitler's tools in France. How Donovan's division can hope to make effective pro-democratic propaganda in Europe after these broadcasts is a question the White House had better ponder. In North Africa native leaders have already been saying to the Free French, "Why should we take a chance on supporting you when the United States supports Vichy?"

The usual State Department secrecy surrounds this affair, but in the murk one can make out a few main figures. At the top is Cordell Hull with his capacity for yielding one democratic position after another behind the smoke screen of nebulous moral homilies. Too many young lives are at stake for us to be tender any longer with a Secretary of State who favored the sale to Japan of the oil and scrap iron which made possible the bombardment of Manila he now deplores. Lower down, in the bowels of the bureaucracy, is a figure like Reber, in charge of French affairs at the department. Reber received his training at our embassy in Rome under Breckinridge Long and William Phillips, socialite diplomats with strong leanings toward fascism. The rationalizations put forward for our attempts to appease Vichy are much the same as those that Long, Phillips, and Reber propounded for supplying Il Duce with scrap iron and oil for six months after the war began. Behind these figures and their picayune and transparent Machiavellianisms lie forces unsympathetic to democracy and uncomfortable when confronted with popular aspiration. There is also a dangerous under-cover animosity toward the British. In the picture, too, is the State Department's fondness for the Vatican and the Vatican's fondness for Vichy, and the Vatican's old hatred — a hatred it shares with the Fascists — for 1789. The atmosphere is one in which it is much easier to figure out reasons for further appeasement than for forthright and democratic action.

It may be that we must suffer some great and resounding defeat before we cleanse the State Department of the undemocratic bureaucracy which runs it, before we recognize that we cannot hope to muster the peoples of the world in a democratic crusade as long as our foreign policy is in the hands of men whose talk of democracy is made a sham by their actions. If the State Department proves strong enough — to our eternal shame — to force the return of St. Pierre and Miquelon to Vichy, perhaps this betrayal of democracy may at least wake us up enough to force a return of the control of our foreign policy to men more representative of the American people.

WPB, Alias SPAB

〜〽〜 ～✑

THE OPERATOR at the same telephone number says "War Production Board" [WPB] instead of "Office of Production Management," [OPM] but one sees the same dollar-a-year faces in the corridors. On Donald M. Nelson's desk is an elaborate memorandum from Merrill C. Meigs, the dollar-a-year Hearstling from Chicago, proving that we cannot build 60,000 planes this year — or half that many. As, indeed, we cannot so long as men like Meigs hold — continue to hold — the same key positions in the arms-program setup despite successive "shake-ups," each of them little more than a rechristening. I mention Meigs only as an example, but he is worth a little attention on his own. He is top man for aircraft production, and has been since the days when they called it the National Defense Advisory Commission [NDAC]. He was Hearst's publisher during the Chicago strike, is an amateur pilot, and as Sidney Hillman once explained to me, he knows the aircraft people personally. Of other qualifications for this crucial post — energy, imagination, drive — none are visible in Meigs. He is not a production man and he will never be caught stepping on an aircraft manufacturer's toes. There are many more like him in WPB, alias SPAB [Supply Priorities Allocation Board], alias OPM, alias NDAC, and they're still there, despite Nelson's latest reorganization.

If I remember my Anthropology I, certain primitive tribes think a sick man may be saved by changing his name, thereby confusing the evil spirits on his trail. The method has now been tried out again on the arms program. More valuable time — time that means lives — is going to be lost while we slowly wake up to the fact that, as the French say, the more it changes, the more it remains the same. No organization is ever reformed by changing the man at the top or by paper recharting of its bureaus, much less by rebaptism. I'm not going to bother the reader or waste space describing the six new branches into which Nelson has divided the WBP, because I don't think they matter. Just about one month has passed since the last inner reshuffle of this kind. "Calling for a greater degree of industrial mobilization," said the press release, "the Office of Production Management today announced an organization change designed to speed up conversion of civilian industry to war-time production." The details, quite elaborate, have since gone down the drain, but for several days they were the wonder-formula of the Knudsen and Hillman offices. The details of the present rearrangement of internal bureaus will seem as inconsequential a few weeks hence. They approach nowhere near the heart of the problem.

In this umteenth shake-up the President has made the discredited Knudsen a Lieutenant General and Director of Production for the army. The actual placing of the contracts is still in the hands of the army, and my guess is that this will be no honorary post, and that the greatest single bottleneck of the arms program — the automotive genius who knew the automotive industry couldn't be converted — will be firmly planted in army procurement. At the same time, when Nelson pulled the big silk handkerchief off the big silk hat this week, it was seen that Knudsen's fair-haired boy, W. H. Harrison of A. T. and T., was to remain Director of Production in WPB as in OPM. Knudsen and Harrison, as Nelson unnecessarily explained at press conference, will work together. Now I know of no better illustration of what is wrong with the arms program than the testimony of these two men before the Tolan committee on December 22. Harrison was being questioned by Congressman Sparkman of Alabama, and the "division" referred to in the passage I am about to quote is the Division of Production.

> MR. SPARKMAN: Has your division ever made a survey of existing facilities of industry, particularly of the automobile industry, to see what convertible and idle facilities could be used for the production of tanks, airplanes, and other types of equipment?
> MR. HARRISON: Only in the sense that we are looking for specific items. We do then contact and discuss the problem with individual manufacturers....
> MR. SPARKMAN: You never would be called upon, then, to make a survey

that would show you the complete picture as to the convertibility of any particular industry, would you?

MR. HARRISON: Well, up to the present time, sir, we have been taking the individual items and trying to place them, in cooperation with the army and the navy, in those places where it is clear that we would get the quality wanted and in the necessary time, considering, likewise, the price that is involved. But from the standpoint of taking an over-all industry and analyzing and surveying its capacity, no.

A few minutes earlier Robert K. Lamb had asked Knudsen about the methods used to spread work out to smaller business men:

With reference to the small producer, will the procurement officer deal only with prime contracts, so that the subcontractor or small producer will have to come in as a subcontractor for an intermediate subcontractor?

MR. KNUDSEN: Yes, sir; that is right.

DR. LAMB: In other words, he (the small business man) will have to find the subcontractor?

It is the reverse of these methods which must be followed if there is to be any hope of achieving the President's huge arms goals this year. Instead of buying individual items, the government must *organize* industry for production; and instead of relying on the individual small business man to find himself a subcontractor of a subsubcontractor who is willing to give him a small piece of the arms job, production boards must break down the blueprint into bits and pieces and hand them out directly to small business.

From a long talk I had with Senator Truman, who understands the need for this approach to the problem, I gathered that Nelson himself was thinking in these terms. And Nelson indicated as much when he spoke of setting up a one-man boss for each industry to handle conversion. But here again, as in the WPB alias OPM itself, results cannot be obtained so long as the same type of men, dollar-a-yearlings and army-navy bureaucrats, must be relied upon to carry out the orders. Nelson is likeable, intelligent, and well-intentioned, but too trusting. Thus he has handed over Floyd Odlum's subcontracting duties to Harrison, who has the big business point of view, and he picked Edsel Ford's brother-in-law, Ernest Kanzler, as one-man boss of the automobile industry. In these two moves the business-as-usual crowd won precious victories. Odlum was a failure, but he had men around him who couldn't be trusted to keep orders away from little business. His powers are in "safe" hands now. The Kanzler appointment means that the automobile industry will be able to handle conversion in its own way in its own time and eliminates the "danger" of labor participation in management. Yet the secret of reforming the arms effort lies in bringing labor and small business into full participation in the work of production boards in every area and every industry. It will not be reformed by changing one dollar-a-year man for another. Nelson hasn't even changed the dollar-a-year men.

February 28, 1942

Pet Fascists

⌒   ⌒

Oil to Spain. Shipment of oil to Spain, shut off entirely about two months ago when confidential figures on them were published in these pages, may be resumed within the near future. Export-control authorities claim, however, that they now have observers not only at all ports of entry but at all storage points in Spain, that they can prevent any transshipment to the Axis, and that only low-grade oil will be sent.

Hush-Hush. Had the figures on Spanish oil shipments remained undisclosed, shipments would have continued without the new safeguards. Publication of the news made it possible for the Milo Perkins crowd in the Board of Economic Warfare to win the fight for stricter surveillance against the flabbier-minded State Department. Dean Acheson, the Assistant Secretary in charge of export-control matters, and Max W. Thornburg, the department's adviser on oil, seem to have been allies of the Board of Economic Warfare in that battle.

Remedy. The remedy, in the opinion of the State Department, is not to shut off the oil but to shut off the information. There is good reason to believe that the department played a major part in the birth of the Biddle "hush-hush" bill now before the Senate Judiciary Committee. Under the terms of this bill a reporter revealing information declared confidential by any government department would be liable to a $5,000 fine or two years in jail or both. J. Edgar Hoover's friend, Assistant Attorney General Alexander Holtzoff, is to steer it through Congress, but newspapermen here are strongly aroused about it, and the bill can be defeated.

Too Delicate. Acheson, though better than his colleagues on export-control matters, is as bad as the rest of them when it comes to this question of secrecy. He, too, seems to feel that all matters handled by the State Department are much too delicate for public knowledge and discussion, and it was on his urging last year that the Coffee-Gillette resolution for an inquiry into the leak of American war materials to the Axis was killed in committee.

Test Case. The spectacle of our leading diplomats caught with their striped trousers down is indeed a delicate one. An example was furnished this week when Sumner Welles declared Vichy's explanations on North Africa "unsatisfactory." The British have again presented evidence that supplies are going through French African territory to the Axis forces in Libya. Only a few weeks ago A. A. Berle and other officials of the State Department were telling the press that they could find no substance in British complaints and that American observers in North Africa had a complete check on the situation.

Pétain Personally. Like less august mortals, State Department officials are prone to believe what they want to believe, and it is too early to assume that an "unsatisfactory" reply from Gaston Henry-Haye marks the beginning of the end of appeasing Vichy. The State Department feels that it has an ace in the hole because, as was explained to the press, Admiral Leahy can see Pétain personally. Our officials seem to regard this as a great privilege. But reliable reports indicate — not that it matters — that Leahy can see Pétain only in the presence of Darlan or one of the Admiral's stooges.

Progress. When a man does one the honor to receive one personally, it is hard to call him a liar, even in diplomatic language. What if Pétain assures Leahy that no supplies are going to Libya from North Africa? There is good reason to believe that the White House is less gullible about Vichy than the State Department. Even in the department progress is being made. Welles actually granted an audience to Adrien Tixier, leader of the so-called Free French, hitherto cold-shouldered in the department. And it is now admitted by the State Department that Pétain may be a fascist, though it is felt that he is not pro-Nazi. These fine distinctions seem to comfort some people.

Each Its Pet. The British government feels that our government is much too friendly to Pétain; ours that Britain is much too friendly to Franco. Each has its pet fascist. Halifax visited the department during the week to protest against (1) "appeasement" of Vichy, and (2) disclosure of the fact that the British were sending mining machinery to the Rio Tinto copper mines in Spain. Since there is an acute shortage of mining machinery here, and the Rio Tinto mines have long been a source of Axis supply, lease-lend officials were angered by the shipments.

Where Does F. D. R. Stand? Under the Eden White Paper, lease-lend materials or their equivalent cannot be reexported from Britain without American approval. The British embassy here claimed that urgent political considerations, perhaps Franco's empty threat to enter the war, and an agreement between the President and Prime Minister Churchill justified them in making these shipments without further consultation. Consultation was to be avoided because American export-control and lease-lend officials had previously vetoed proposed shipments of rubber and mining machinery to Spain.

The Roosevelt-Churchill Agreement. The agreement, according to the British embassy, was to support the economic life of Spain. Lend-lease is still waiting for an answer from Hull's assistant, Lynn R. Edminster, on (1) whether there is such an agreement, and (2) whether it is broad enough to justify waiving the White Paper and exporting scarce mining machinery to Spain. The State Department's usual technique in handling embarrassing questions of this kind is to delay an answer as long as possible or, providentially, to mislay the letter of inquiry. The department is much more interested in trying to find out how the information leaked.

Gaul, D. C. On the question of appeasement official Washington is divided into three parts. There are people friendly to fascism, particularly of the Catholic variety, who would give Spain and Vichy anything they want, and there are those who are opposed to "appeasement" of any kind, an extremist position but not without support from the events of the past ten years. In between are those who think it necessary to dole out limited quantities of supplies to Vichy and Franco to keep them "from joining the Axis." The President belongs to this intermediate group. The difference between the American and British governments is that the former would give less to Franco and more to Vichy, and vice versa. The difference between the dominant policy in our government and dominant opinion in the State Department is that the latter would like to give more to both.

Machiavellis or Suckers? It may be that this is a very clever policy, or it may be that Hitler prefers to leave the fueling and feeding of unoccupied France and unoccupied Spain to us until he is ready to take them over. Export-control officials may be justified in thinking that they can resume exports of low-grade oil to Franco without danger of transshipment. But Hitler is equally justified in appreciating the tuna sent the Axis by Spanish fishing smacks operating on our low-grade oil. There is another factor sometimes overlooked here. The spectacle of free America dickering fearfully with two-by-four fascist dictators is not the most effective inspiration for a democratic crusade.

March 14, 1942

Dies Helps the Axis

〜 〜

I T IS A PITY that Hitler's Reich does not have a Dies. A special committee of the Reichstag to harass Nazi officials and spread suspicion of Germany's allies could be forgiven the occasional exposure of some notorious democrat. On a purely reciprocal basis the Reich might well go in for a Dies committee of its own in exchange for the growing readiness of our Congress to adopt innovations from Berlin. Saying "Ja" to Mr. Dies has become a habit with the House. Tom Eliot and Vito Marcantonio, the only two Congressmen with the courage to oppose the latest request for an extension of his committee, were cut short with a motion to adjourn. Dies was forced to make some kind of promise that he would "lay off the reds," but no one expects him to keep it. He will soon be helping us to win the war — by summoning Leon Henderson from the task of price control to say whether he was ever a technocrat.

The danger Dies represents is not unappreciated in the House, and a passage in the crafty attack he made on Eliot reflects this. It also illustrates the Texan's ability as a demagogue. He does not allow himself to be forced into a defense position. He knows it is easier to affect people's thinking by association of ideas than by logical argument. These are among the lessons of "Mein Kampf," and Dies showed that he could apply them when Eliot demanded that he explain what he meant when he said, "A fear of displeasing foreign powers and a maudlin attitude toward fifth columnists was largely responsible for the unparalleled tragedy at Pearl Harbor."

Dies's claim to clairvoyance in the Pacific will not bear examination, and he therefore brushed past the question to take the offensive in an extraordinary reply. A stranger to the events of the past few months would conclude from it that Pearl Harbor was bombed by the Soviet Union, that Congress shared the blame by refusing to permit registration of Communists, and that the C.I.O. was somehow responsible for the inability of the Dies committee to prevent the catastrophe.

Dies began his reply by saying that he thought the answer to Eliot's question obvious. He said he was still of the same opinion about Pearl Harbor. "However," he continued, "under all the circumstances, the House of Representatives saw otherwise, and they refused to adopt my amendments." The amendments to which he referred would have required the registration of Communists, but Dies indicated that he bore no hard feelings. "I now believe," he declared graciously, "that the House and Mr. Hatton W. Sumners were wiser than I was to this extent: that I believe that while it is absolutely essential for this committee to investigate and expose Communism, I agree with the great majority of this House that there is no occasion, *regardless of the facts,* to risk antagonizing any other foreign country that happens to be allied with us." The italics are mine. Dies went on to talk of the C.I.O.'s refusal to cooperate with his committee. Goebbels could not have done a more skillful job in poisonous association.

Much in domestic and foreign policy becomes clearer if one studies this passage closely. Dies is no freak in the political skies. He is the embodiment of the forces on which Hitler has relied from the beginning. He is spokesman for those who feel as did the Czech agrarian leader who said, "If the Germans come, they will take half my purse. If the Russians come, they will take it all." His reference to the Soviet Union as a foreign country "that happens to be allied with us" was no slip in tact. The Russians have lost several million men fighting Hitler. We are just on the verge of making the ultimate sacrifice of stopping all production of civilian radio sets next April 22. The relative sacrifices of the allies make Dies's casual reference sting, as it was intended to do. But there are too many men in the War and Navy departments who feel just that way about the Russian alliance.

As important as the foreign are the domestic overtones of the Dies statement. If, "regardless of the facts," one cannot risk antagonizing an ally by investigating communism, the corollary is clear. Not until the Soviet Union is out of the war by defeat or by a separate peace can the war on "Communism" at home be carried on with full vigor.

I have a copy of an open letter recently sent to members of Congress by Walter E. Spahr, professor of economics at New York University and secretary of the Economists' National Committee on Monetary Policy. "It may be doubted," the letter begins, "whether anyone can reliably predict how the United States will emerge from the present war." There is one school of thought, Spahr suggests coyly, "whose members expect that we will emerge as a collectivist state. They point to the large number of collectivists in our federal government and to the power these leftists wield. They believe that the regimentation of this war is being capitalized in every way possible by the revolutionists . . . as a short cut to their desired collectivism." Spahr warns that "a careful watch must be maintained not only over our revolutionists but also over those who clumsily tinker with our economic mechanism." But as long as the Russian alliance holds, the Dies statement implies, there will be difficulty enough in going after Communists, to say nothing of the subversive fellows who merely disbelieve in the gold standard.

The Dies committee survives demonstrations of its errors and of its danger to unity because a majority of the members of Congress haven't really made up their mind whether they prefer to win the war abroad or the war at home. The basic problems of our war effort revolve about the tasks of mobilizing our machines, and educating the masses to the meaning and necessity of the war. The men best suited to the former task are those who have no compunctions about subordinating property rights to patriotism. The men best suited to the latter are those who sympathize with the aspirations of the underprivileged. Both are almost certain to be on the black list of Dies. That is another of the services he performs for the Axis.

Handcuffing Thurman Arnold

〜 〜

TODAY'S ANNOUNCEMENT of the new policy on anti-trust prosecutions is an extraordinary climax to Thurman Arnold's revelations during the past week. Arnold had disclosed the way in which Standard Oil placed loyalty to its Nazi partner, I. G. Farben, above loyalty to the United States. He had shown that the development of synthetic rubber and many other important war materials in this country was stifled by Standard Oil on orders from Berlin. He had revealed, in the top ranks of Standard and its du Pont and Mellon allies, men who appear more interested in protecting their holdings abroad and their monopolies at home than in winning the war. These men and their henchmen are apparently so powerful that, after all these revelations, they can slip the handcuffs on Thurman Arnold. The oil trust is calmly thumbing its nose at the American people.

It seems that the anti-trust laws, not the trusts, have been holding up the war effort. A War Production Board [WPB] official tells me gravely that one War Department compilation showed that an anti-trust prosecution had lost the country 124 days and 23 evenings of the valuable time of one executive vice-president of an unnamed company! The international-cartel agreements on aluminum and synthetics and magnesium and dyestuffs will cost us precious lives and years. Yet here are the President and Attorney General Biddle and Secretary Stimson and Secretary Knox and the unwilling Arnold himself agreeing that prosecution of these and similar trust arrangements may be postponed for the duration because they take up too much of the time of important executives. The country would be better off if we lost all the time of some of these executives. If the officials of I. G. Farben had dared to act like some of the officials of Standard Oil, they would have been in a concentration camp a long time ago, thanking their lucky stars that they hadn't been shot. Here we put up a sign outside their offices, "Do not disturb."

Inquiries into dyestuffs and magnesium are pending. Both are important in the war effort. Are they to be pinched off under the new policy? Either the Secretary of War or the Secretary of the Navy may veto the Attorney General, and the Attorney General can override their veto on a proposed prosecution only by appealing directly to the President. The Secretary of War and the Secretary of the Navy and the men around them were bred in the atmosphere and the service of big business and finance. Some among them have shown a capacity to rise above their background and training that commands confidence and earns gratitude. But these are the exceptions. Even with the best intentions a man cannot altogether shake loose from the habits and preconceptions of a lifetime. Their sympathies, their old friends, their dinner partners, often their own methods in business predispose them toward the very men Arnold has been attacking. If they had possessed this veto power six months ago, would Arnold have been allowed to continue the Standard Oil-I. G. Farben inquiry? I doubt it.

Had Standard Oil come forward after Pearl Harbor and offered to give up its foreign connections and place its patents at the disposal of the country, no one would object to a "let-bygones-be-bygones" attitude toward our anti-trust laws for the duration. But Standard did not do this. It threatened a libel suit when Nathan W. Robertson, one of *PM's* Washington correspondents, revealed that Standard was refusing to pool its patents for butyl along with other synthetic-rubber formulas. It sought by underhanded means to keep its German connections even after we were in the war. Most important of all, Standard went right on stifling the development of war synthetics until Arnold got the goods on it and forced it into a consent decree. Who knows how many other cartel agreements hobbling this country's war effort are still in effect? Since the new anti-trust policy covers investigations as well as suits and prosecutions, War and Navy officials will often be faced with a choice between Arnold's suspicions and the assurances of their old friends and business associates. Is Arnold to be bound and gagged?

I asked a WPB official why the decision to suspend the anti-trust laws had not been made by Donald Nelson instead of by Stimson and Knox. It was felt that it would be wiser to leave the decision with the armed services since the public regarded the War Production Board as dominated by business men. I suggested that the armed services when examined turned out to be as thoroughly dominated by big business men and corporation lawyers as the WPB. The answer very candidly was that the public didn't realize this. One of the sources of this new policy, for example, is a General Walter B. Pyron in Under Secretary of War Patterson's office. Pyron is liaison man between the War Department and the oil industry. He sits in on the meetings of the Petroleum War Industrial Council, a private, not a government, body. Suspension of the anti-trust laws for the duration was one of the main objectives of the council's meeting on March 3 and 4, and General Pyron carried the council's wishes to Patterson. The General was until recently vice-president of the Mellon Gulf Oil Company.

The oil trust which was so anxious to accommodate itself to Nazi business methods, and which now has its men in almost every important agency in Washington, is vitally concerned in bringing about a virtual suspension of the anti-trust laws. It wants to kill off the suit filed by Arnold against the trust in September of 1940. It has already disposed of his Elkins Act suit against its pipe lines with a consent decree so weak that the two attorneys who worked on the case for the government refused to sign it, and one of them resigned in disgust. More important than these suits are the protection of its secret world-wide agreements and connections and the precious patents it holds on the multifarious range of synthetic products which can now be made from petroleum. Oil is becoming a chemical industry, and Rockefeller and du Pont are merging their lordly empires. The consent decree on synthetic rubber leaves with them much of their power over the new synthetics, and the country remains dependent on their good faith and good-will. An Administration determined to let nothing stand in the way of victory would seize their patents under the War Powers Act and purge the government of their henchmen, instead of making them safe from the one weapon the people can use against them, the anti-trust laws.

Gloom and Fatuity

ᔏ᠊ᢇ   ᢏᢦ᠎ᢆ

O N THIS, the first anniversary of the Nazi attack upon the Soviet Union, the atmosphere of the capital is compounded equally of gloom and fatuity. The best opinion here is that Churchill arrived, not to plan a second front this year, but to dissuade the President from attempting one. Rommel has since reinforced Churchill's argument by taking Tobruk and threatening Egypt; the Axis continues to hold the initiative on all fronts. The Navy Department, which seems to have learned little from Pearl Harbor, is busy issuing soothing syrup on the Japanese invasion of the Aleutians. It is now admitted that the Japanese have occupied Kiska, 650 miles west of Dutch Harbor, as well as Attu, western-most island of the chain, but we are assured that the weather on both islands is very bad, "foggy" — maybe the Japanese will all come down with bronchitis and cough themselves to death. Bases in the Aleutians can be used by submarines and planes to raid our shipping if Japan attacks Siberia, or they can be utilized for bombing raids on the Western hemisphere. The Navy Department's light-minded attitude toward this Japanese invasion of our territory is appalling.

This giddiness-in-the-head is not confined to the Navy Department. Pap has been pouring from the press agents of the Administration, the War Production Board [WPB], and the National Association of Manufacturers. The Truman committee on the Guthrie[1] case offers an antidote for the hurrah stories on production, but it will be shelved and

---

[1] Robert R. Guthrie resigned from the clothing and textile division of the War Production Board in March 1942, charging that industry representatives were blocking war production and that the dollar-a-year men diverted materials necessary to the war to their own industries. He repeated his charges before the Truman committee.

forgotten as rapidly as possible. A whole corps of clever propaganda analysts are at work here, listening in on the Axis radio and scanning the Axis press, but few seem to realize that our most dangerous fifth column is complacency and that Washington rather than Berlin remains the most important source of the poison.

The Axis has two principal propaganda objectives. One is to divide. The other is to lull the victim into a false sense of security. The second task, with some encouragement, can usually be left to the victim himself. To paraphrase an advertising slogan, it may be instructive to know the truth, but it's more fun to be fooled. Few here will admit that Tobruk fell, as Manila and Singapore fell, partly because the arsenal of democracy, two years after the launching of the defense program, isn't delivering the goods.

Carefully read and considered, the Truman report on the Guthrie case is the key to the continued setbacks suffered by ourselves and our allies. The arsenal of democracy, as the Guthrie case and the reactions to the report show, is still being operated with one eye on the war and the other on the convenience of big business. The progress made on production so far is the fruit of necessity and improvisation rather than of foresight and planning, and the men running the program are not willing to fight business interests on behalf of military efficiency. Donald Nelson is full of good will and good intentions, but the only battle he has staged since becoming head of the War Production Board was his fight last week to suppress the Guthrie report.

The Guthrie report shows that, months after Pearl Harbor, the men Nelson put in charge of converting the consumer durable-goods industries to war were still trying their best to postpone curtailment of civilian production. It shows that when it came to the test Nelson took his stand with the men of "business as usual" against a business man who seemed only to be acting on the principles Nelson himself was expressing in his speeches. It shows that Nelson and his aides are still trying to palm off curtailment as the equivalent of conversion, although the former is only the first and negative step of the process. It shows that the big-business crowd is as powerfully entrenched under Nelson as it was under Knudsen. It shows that we are not going to get maximum utilization of our resources until there is a shakeup more fundamental than the adding of the new alphabetic alias to the series NDAC-OPM-SPAB-WPB. That shakeup will be effective only if labor, small business, and independent engineering talent are brought into the agencies supposed to direct the mobilization of industry. For the demonstration, and the statements, though some of them were left to implication, the country is indebted to Senator Truman and his colleagues, especially Ball, Brewster, and Mead. They stuck to their guns under pressure from Nelson.

It is important to realize that we are in a very critical period of war production. The shortage of basic materials, which might cost us victory, is itself a victory for the big-business status quo. The shortage of materials has become an excuse for dropping plans to expand basic industries. It has become an excuse for concentrating war output in the new plane, tank, and ordnance plants instead of spreading the work out to smaller-business men. The big-business crowd has succeeded so far in fighting the war its way — with a minimum of conversion, a maximum of new war plants, a minimum of industrial expansion, as much monopoly as possible, and without the dreaded admission of labor into the councils of management. For despite plant committees, labor today has less influence and less voice than ever before in the planning and direction of the war-production program. Yet labor participation is needed more than ever in the basic material-producing and mining industries, for there is no doubt that in the case of many materials the shortage is remediable. We could produce more copper and we could produce more steel if we were prepared to impose overall control and rationalization of production in these industries.

The solution of our problem lies in a more democratic direction of our industrial effort, but the trend is the other way. The next step will be to merge the industrial branches of the WPB in the army and navy, where it will be more difficult than ever for labor to have a voice, where there will be less interference than ever from Leon Henderson's hard-working little crew of all-outers in civilian supply, and where the "dollar-a-year men" can more easily be shielded from criticism. It is harder to spot a big-business man in uniform than in mufti, and Congressional committees are shyer of criticizing "the military." Thus the Truman committee pulled its punches when Undersecretary Patterson intervened last winter to postpone conversion of the radio industry and when the supply branches of the army pleaded for business as usual in the typewriter industry.

The Guthrie report showed how a "plutodemocracy" — to use Mussolini's favorite phrase — mobilizes for war. When the Truman committee last January criticized the dollar-a-year men for their tendency to feather their own nests, Nelson rushed forward not only to defend them but to claim that criticism was interfering with the war effort by making it more difficult to bring more dollar-a-year men to

Washington. A hitherto unpublished story indicates how Guthrie, the maverick, put himself in wrong with the gang the day he was made Philip Reed's assistant. He shocked Reed and WPB General Counsel John Lord O'Brian by announcing that he was selling his stock and giving up his directorship in White Sewing Machine Company because the sewing-machine industry was one of those he would be expected to help convert to war purposes. "You're certainly a rare bird," O'Brian told him — much too rare to last, as it turned out.

October 3, 1942

Capital Thoughts on a Second Front

THERE ARE ONLY THREE PERSONS in Washington who can speak with authority on the question of the second front — the President, General Marshall, and Harry Hopkins. None of the three is in a chatty mood. At the other end of the scale there is a wide variety of "confidential information" of the kind that enlivens the capital's better dinner parties. Even the actual date — several of them — when the second front is to be opened is available. Six weeks ago persons "in the know" had a date in September; gossip has now postponed the second front until the spring.

In between the three who really know and those who merely talk is an area in which a more reliable brand of information is obtainable. There are persons whose jobs enable them to catch the rumblings of the mighty at first or second hand. There are members of Congress whose committee assignments keep them in touch with the main direction of military and diplomatic thinking. There are reporters who specialize in covering a single government department, and who are sometimes willing to pass on what they themselves, for one reason or another, cannot write. In this area, too, talkativeness is in inverse ratio to authoritativeness.

By interviewing a good many people of this kind one can obtain a few scraps of information that have some value. One can also obtain a cross-section of opinion on the second front within official circles. This is useful because it enables one to understand more clearly the men who must make the actual decisions about the second front and the subconscious motivations which flicker dimly behind their elaborate arguments.

The most interesting bit of fact I have picked up, and I think my source reliable, is that the Canadians have spoken up vigorously for an early second front at official military discussions of the problem here. This may help to explain why Dieppe was so predominantly a Canadian affair. It looks as though the British said, "Well, if you're so anxious for a second front, go and try one." On Dieppe itself opinion is divided. Some point to the terrific ratio of losses as an argument for delaying a second front. Others feel that the casualties suffered by the first wave of an invasion must necessarily be high, and that the losses prove only that a large-scale foray is much too costly to be staged at all unless it is fully intended to establish a beachhead and follow it up immediately.

The weirdest notion I picked up came from an important elected official whose work necessitates constant contact with the military. He himself is a man of superior insight, with a courageous and progressive record. He would talk only in general terms, and much of what he said is incorporated in other sections of this letter. One statement he made left me a little breathless. It was an argument against the second front, and I gather that it reflected what he had been told by military men and that he himself did not know whether to be impressed by the argument or to laugh at it. "We've got to keep ourselves in readiness to strike with full force," he said, "wherever the Axis weakens. *Suppose, for example, the Dutch were suddenly to rise against their oppressors, and we did not have sufficient military force to support them.*" If we intend to wait for the Dutch or some other conquered people to take the initiative, we may have to wait a long time.

This chance remark may be unimportant as a clue to official policy, but it is revelatory of mental attitudes. Though both Mr. Roosevelt and Mr. Churchill are men of great vitality who have shown capacity for daring and imagination, they seem to be surrounded by too many men who suffer from spiritual arterio-sclerosis. Behind Anglo-American policy in recent years there has been a constant tendency to play a waiting game, and this out of inertia rather than restraint. Military and diplomatic leaders in too many cases have been men who feared risk, hoped for miracles, were content to wait for something to turn up.

This is not Mr. Roosevelt's temperament nor is it Mr. Churchill's, but the latter is haunted still by Gallipoli[1] and the former dare not interfere too much with his military advisers. Some persons close to the President

[1] In World War I Churchill, then First Lord of the Admiralty, advocated the opening of a second front by means of a landing at Gallipoli, in Turkey. The landing was a disaster and Churchill's reputation suffered accordingly.

feel that he has already gone farther than any predecessor in overruling the generals and the admirals. These persons say this in approval, but they also feel that there is a limit beyond which he cannot go unless he is to shake up whole strata of personnel and not merely override specific decisions.

The President's military and naval advisers may be right in saying that no second front can be opened now. No civilian official of any importance has the temerity publicly to contradict them. The opinion of these military and naval advisers is none the less being evaluated in the light of more general considerations, and in that light their judgment does not inspire too much confidence. The first of these considerations is that this same military-naval leadership in both Britain and America has yet to show any capacity for bold thinking or acting; had it done so, more reliance could be placed on its verdict that the second front is not yet possible. The second is a growing distrust of the established official experts in every field, industrial as well as governmental. The war has deflated one great reputation after another, exploded one solemn and authoritative judgment after another. Some civilian officials resent the tendency to place military matters in a separate and sacred category. They regard these matters as technical questions in the same way that the supply of aluminum, the best way to make synthetic rubber, or the problem of conversion is a technical question. They feel that the "experts" may be as wrong on the second front as their civilian counterparts were on industrial questions. In other fields these civilians see that the best results are being achieved, as in shipping, by fresh men and fresh ideas. They are in no mood to accept the verdict of the generals and the admirals without question.

The second front is, of course, a military problem, but it is also, in many ways, a political problem. Here is one way, as explained by one of the most intelligent observers here, a man who occupies an important position in the government. He is in favor of a second front, and no doubt that colors his reasoning, but here it is: No general or admiral wants to advise an attack that may not be successful and may be fatal to that general's or that admiral's reputation and career. There are circumstances nevertheless in which it may be necessary, for political reasons, deliberately to take a risk that is unwise from a military point of view. This official feels that both the good-will of the Russian people and the morale of the Anglo-American peoples call for a second front. It may be a gamble but sometimes the greatest gamble in a war is not to gamble at all. He feels that the risk may be great but that not to take it is to resign ourselves to years of armed stalemate. Political decisions are involved here, difficult to make against the advice of the military, especially since it would be dangerous to attempt a second-front expedition under the command of persons who felt from the start that it was doomed to failure. The imponderables of will, drive and faith are an army's best regiments, but there is a half-hearted streak evident in sections of British and American leadership. This also is in part political.

It would be doing an injustice to a great many conservatives in the army and navy higher ranks and in the war-production bureaucracy to oversimplify this aspect of the second front. Yet there is some measure of accuracy in the rough observation that the strongest desire for the second front is found among the New Dealers, the least among the big-business crowd. This takes a lot of qualifying. There are a few New Dealers so tangled up in their own emotional and political differences with the Communists that they can't see straight on the war. There are big business men like William I. Batt, W. Averell Harriman, Edward R. Stettinius, Jr., Donald M. Nelson, who sincerely want to do everything in their power to help the Russians, though I don't know how many of them are actually for a second front soon. This is also true among the Wall Streeters so conspicuous in the top civilian layers of the War and Navy departments. In a sense, almost everyone here is for the Russians, even Jesse Jones, though at the Joseph E. Davies reception last week all that Jones could think of to praise them for was that they paid their bills and loans on time.

Vague sympathy is one thing; decisive action another. There is an undercurrent of doubt and hostility which makes itself felt whenever any government agency gets down to brass tacks on a problem of aid to the Soviets. How much risk a man will take, how much sacrifice he will make, depends on how deeply he feels. The survival of the world's one socialist country is a cause most business men and conservatives are supporting, but not until our own country is hit on our own continental soil and our need for all and any allies is apparent to save our own homes will they really become accustomed to this — for them — rather odd alliance. By that time, unless we act more vigorously now, that ally may not be there or may be so reduced in strength as to be ineffective.

I came across an extreme form of reluctance to make sacrifices for the Soviet Union while working on my Russian oil story for last week's letter. Some of the oil men involved put forward the argument, "Why give the Russians our oil trade secrets, when they'll probably make a separate peace soon anyway?" This is wishful thinking of a mad variety:

the same people last fall were saying, "Why give the Russians these processes, they'll soon be licked anyway?" They feel that if the Russians were out of the war, these sacrifices would be unnecessary. As the war grows less and less profitable and calls for more and more sacrifice, there will be more defeatism of this kind in some circles of big business, though in others there will be more genuine patriotism.

Another factor must be touched upon. There is a very small minority of conscious fascists here. There is a somewhat larger group which feels hampered domestically by the Russian alliance. A whole-hearted attack on the American left is impossible so long as even the Communists must be treated tactfully. The Dies gang would like to see Russia out of the war. There are others who, without going too far, are fearful of social changes arising from the war. In an emergency, when quick action and complete decision are necessary, one need only waver a little to be lost. These more or less subconscious waverings play their part here in the question of the second front, as in every other fundamental issue of the war. Only popular pressure can put an end to them. Fight for a second front.

October 31, 1942

Washington's Forbidden Topic

~~~ ~~~

I WANT TO CALL ATTENTION to an extraordinary document
that seems to have been completely overlooked by the daily press. I
refer to the "Additional Comments" of Representative Bender which are
appended to the report on man-power issued by the Tolan committee
last Tuesday. Bender is a Republican Congressman-at-large from Ohio.
He was first elected to Congress in 1938 and only recently became a
member of the Tolan committee. Little is known of him, and that little
gives no indication that he differs much from the average Middle
Western Republican. All "Who's Who" reveals is: "Pres. George H.
Bender Ins. Co.; editor and publisher the *Ohio Republican* and the
National Republican since 1934; mem. Ohio State Senate, 1920–30; pres.
Ohio Fedn. of Rep. Clubs; chmn. Rep. Central Com. of Cuyahoga
County." This certainly smacks of Main Street, and it is as a Main
Streeter that Bender chooses to speak in his "Additional Comments,"
which are really a separate and sharper minority report. "Since the
winter of 1941," he declares, "it has been clear to every Main Street
American that what is needed is a second front in Europe to split the
Axis forces. Spring, summer, and fall have come and gone without a
second front."

Representative Bender's advocacy of a second front is less important
than his courage in being the first public figure here to speak out in plain
language on the deeper issue behind the question of a second front. This
is not whether we are to open an offensive in France next Tuesday or next
month or next spring. The real question is whether we are to plan this as
a war of the United Nations, with a Western offensive geared into the

supply needs of the British, Russians, and Chinese, or whether we are to plan to fight the world alone. The truth is, as every important official here knows, that the President's dominant military-naval advisers are already operating on this latter assumption. The corollaries of this assumption are (1) the addition of several million men to our army, (2) the curtailment of lend-lease aid to our allies in order to outfit that army, and (3) postponement of the offensive until the enlarged army is ready. All three corollaries are already reflected in official action, and informed persons here say that the plan is to stage no real large-scale offensive in 1943.

The Bender report is a hard-hitting six-page summary of the basic man-power, military, and production problems facing us in this war. The full committee report is the ablest and most comprehensive analysis of war needs and war planning ever to appear here, and I hope to discuss it in some detail in my next article. The value of Mr. Bender's "Additional Comments" is that they bring some of the points in the full report into sharper focus. "Our military," Bender says, "have never decided when, where, and with what they are going to fight. For this reason they have not and cannot give to the War Production Board [WPB] and to the War Manpower Commission, respectively, schedules of their requirements for military products and man-power. Without these schedules it has been impossible to plan production, to allocate materials and man-power. And because we have not planned the elements of production, we cannot manage or control the flow of armament. Without such scheduled flow of weapons the military cannot undertake to plan its strategy." The result of this vicious circle is that "we are always on the defensive." And now we are really preparing to dig in on the defensive on a gigantic scale.

Will the reader bear with me while I quote more fully from that passage in which Representative Bender touches upon the capital's most important Forbidden Topic? "At the present time," Bender writes, "the army is demanding a huge increase in man-power." A fantastically high proportion of present production now goes to supply ordinary civilian items for our present army. "When the army is asked," Bender continues, "if it expects to obtain trucks and other equipment in the same proportion to this larger army as it now obtains, no answer is forthcoming." Why do we need an army and navy of about 10,000,000 men? *"The demand by the military for a huge army,"* Bender answers, *"is based in part on the assumption that one or more of our allies will collapse in the coming year.* Upon this assumption, it is then argued that we can rely only on ourselves." Since the Tolan report went to press, Secretary

Stimson has cut his estimate to 7,500,000 men, but a continuation of the present defensive and defeatist strategic thinking will make necessary an army much larger than that, perhaps as large as 13,000,000.

"To equip such an army with training weapons alone," Bender goes on, "would require practically all of our present war production. Therefore, these advocates of a huge army move logically to the next point — the reduction or stoppage of lend-lease shipments to our allies." By assuming the defeat of our allies we are compelled vastly to enlarge the army. By mobilizing a vastly larger army we help to insure their defeat. "When it is pointed out to these advocates of a 13,000,000-man army," Bender says, "that our allies may collapse if we stop lend-lease shipments, they have no answer" — that is, no answer that could safely be made in public.

Behind these defeatist calculations are a complex of considerations and motives. Among them are not merely political dislike for the Soviet Union but considerable elements of anti-British feeling. As deep, if not deeper, than the more obvious anti-Soviet feeling, which wide sectors of our leadership and upper classes have overcome, is a kind of anti-British isolationist-imperialist attitude on the part of some of our foremost military men. An important man in this category is General Brehon B. Somervell, chief of the Services of Supply, the most powerful single figure in war production today and a man who has done his best to cut down lend-lease aid to Britain, the Soviet Union, and China. He feels that we have to "prepare to do this job ourselves."

This kind of thinking would make the Atlantic and Pacific seaboards our first lines of defense. It would cost many millions more in lives and many billions more in money. It means that we would have to defeat the Axis with our men and boys alone instead of with the aid of British, Russians, and Chinese. It would leave them to die in vain rather than as part of a world strategy for victory. "The international implications of army demands for man-power," Bender points out, "are seldom understood. But they are as important as the need to consider man-power requirements of industry and agriculture." It is these broader implications which the dominant military have failed to understand or chosen to ignore. Popular pressure is needed to support the efforts of powerful forces here, including I believe the President himself, to combat this dangerous trend. The moment is approaching when it will be decided whether these are indeed to be United Nations fighting a United Nations war, or each waging its own struggle in desperate and foolhardy isolation.

November 14, 1942

Washington and the Offensive

꒜   ꒜

WASHINGTON, official and unofficial, is as cheered as occupied Europe by the news that our troops are on the march in North Africa. There is a feeling of pleasure that this time we have taken the initiative, that it is the enemy's turn to be surprised, that we have gone into action in the west at last. Not the least of the advantages of the offensive is its tonic effect on morale, and there will be a good deal less bickering as long as we go forward. Other issues suddenly seem to fade into the background beside this new enterprise.

The landings and their propaganda accompaniment were staged with a sense of history. Who could fail to be moved by General Eisenhower's proclamation to the French of North Africa, "The war has entered the phase of liberation"? One imagines the feelings of a listener at a radio in some lonely attic in France who suddenly heard that voice say, "My friends . . ."

The advocates of a second front have been so accustomed to think in terms of a frontal attack upon the French coast that the direction of the new offensive has left some of them uncertain. But there seems to be general agreement among those in touch with the military that though this is not yet a second front it may soon become one, if only because Hitler must make a major reply. If Anglo-American forces succeed in obtaining control of the Western Mediterranean, the way is opened for an attack on Italy or southern France, operations regarded as much easier than an attempt to establish a bridgehead on French Atlantic or Channel beaches bristling with German guns. With this threat at his rear, Hitler can no longer concentrate on the eastern front. It is expected here that the combination of the Anglo-American offensive in North Africa and unrest in France may force Hitler to occupy the rest of the country and that strategic necessities may soon compel him to send troops into Spain.

Provided we follow through with additional forces, North Africa should become a major front. Some eighteen months ago a proposal for a North African campaign, designed to clear the way for an offensive against Italy, was made by General José Asensio, last military attache in Washington of the Spanish Republic. It was presented to our own government through unofficial channels, but there is no indication that it obtained much response. The General and several other exiled Loyalist officers felt that Spain itself would make a poor bridgehead for a Continental invasion because of the ease with which small German forces could hold the few passes through and around the Pyrenees. But they did envisage action against Spanish territory to safeguard the supply lines of a North African advance, and their ideas are useful background against which to form an understanding of coming events.

They felt that the first step should be the occupation of the Canaries, from which German submarines and planes could attack shipping to North Africa, and the second, the envelopment and seizure of Spanish Morocco, which threatens not only water but land communications between the North African Atlantic coast and Algeria. The American forces, by landing on both sides of Spanish Morocco would seem to be in a good position to take it over before the Germans can strike south through Spain. The Spanish troops in Morocco, traditionally reactionary and traditionally pro-German, recruited from adventurers and native mercenaries, are believed to be the only Spanish troops on which Hitler can depend if he moves into Spain. Spanish Morocco is full of German "technicians" who have been preparing since 1936 to neutralize Gibraltar and close the Straits, and it is believed that they can do so easily unless we beat them to the punch. Less well known is the fact that troops from Spanish Morocco, striking south to the valley of the Tazza between the Moroccan border and the Atlas Mountains, could also cut the principal, if not the only practical, land highway between the Atlantic and Algeria. In dealing with this potential threat from the Canaries, Spanish Morocco, and Spain, it is hoped that the actions of our armed forces will be governed by strategic necessities rather than by the illusions which some officials in the British and Foreign Office and the State Department still seem to cherish about Franco.

There are several possible explanations of why we have not already moved against any of these territories. It may have been thought best to land first in French North Africa, establishing an easy base from which to attack the Canaries and encircling Spanish Morocco. It may have been felt that, in order not to antagonize Catholic opinion at home and in Latin America, it was better to leave the initiative with Hitler and let him attack Spain first. There are also those in London and Washington who think Franco independent enough to be dickered with and to be trusted, people who think Franco can be won over to our side. These illusions may be useful to Hitler if he prefers to keep out of Spain for the time being. Spain is thus the exposed flank of our political thinking, as it is of our military advance. Anti-Loyalist antipathies and pro-Franco leanings interfere with the full utilization of the knowledge and experience of Spanish military exiles familiar with the North African terrain and anxious to help. Officers and men are available here and in Mexico for two full divisions of Loyalists. Pro-Franco leanings account in part for maneuvers which leave the initiative in Spain with Hitler. There are forces in the State Department which would like somehow to defeat Hitler while leaving Franco to control Spain, and the twin forces of church and monarchy to rule Italy. They are trying to keep the war as little as possible a democractic crusade, to direct it and the post-war world as far as they can into Metternichian molds.

It is this background of anti-democratic tendencies which makes Secretary Hull's elaborate explanations of past pro-Vichy policy unconvincing. The test of the State Department's sincerity is a new attitude toward the Fighting French. But such an attitude has yet to appear. Fighting French headquarters here last night were a gloomy place, when they should have been jubilant. The Fighting French felt left out of the picture and unwanted; their forces took no part in the landing, and their information from London was that De Gaulle was neither consulted nor informed in advance. While the State Department still looks back with pride on the period when it was collaborating with Weygand, the Fighting French blame the Murphy-Weygand negotiations for the lack of an organized underground in North Africa. De Gaullist work was discouraged by American friendship for Weygand, and the potential opposition was organized around Weygand in the open, where the Germans had no difficulty in smashing it as soon as he was recalled to France. Some State Department officials still put their hope in a "third France" which is neither De Gaullist nor collaborationist, but Frenchmen too milk-and-watery to choose sides in so critical an hour would hardly seem to be very energetic or trustworthy allies.

These unwholesome tendencies in our State Department were never more dangerous than now, when the war has entered a new stage.

One Year After Pearl Harbor

୶୶ ୶୶

LOOKING BACK across the year since Pearl Harbor, the President has much with which to be pleased. The task of mobilizing a fairly prosperous and contented capitalist democracy for war is like trying to drive a team of twenty mules, each stubbornly intent on having its own way. Only by continual compromise with the ornery critters is it possible to move forward at all. Examined closely, by the myopic eye of the perfectionist, Mr. Roosevelt's performance in every sphere has been faulty. Regarded in the perspective of his limited freedom of choice and the temper of the country, which has never really been warlike, the year's achievements have been extraordinary. The curtailment and conversion of civilian industry for war, the peaceful resolution of capital-labor difficulties, the preservation to a remarkable extent of both social gains and civil liberties, the great expansion of arms output, the successful launching of our first major offensive represent stupendous and back-breaking tasks. The President is only a man, with twenty-four hours a day at his disposal, and amid the clamor of criticism, much of it justified, it will not hurt to pause a moment in gratitude for his work in the service of our country.

Someone has said that politics is the art of the possible, and Mr. Roosevelt achieved what he did largely by taking the easiest route; the easiest was difficult enough. He let big business mobilize our economy for war pretty much on its own terms, and established what is in effect a government of coalition with the right. Just as King John had to sign on the dotted line for the barons before they would fight, so the President had to come to terms with the quasi-independent corporate sovereignties that control so much of our productive resources. In criticizing him for this, we must also in fairness criticize ourselves. Had labor and the middle-class progressives been better organized, politically more astute, less divided, more competently led, they would have exerted more pressure in the national tug-of-war. The last Congressional elections were an adequate if rough test of just how much influence the labor and liberal elements have in national and local politics. The things that count are not our speeches or our pieces in the paper but the votes we can muster in Congress in support of the measures we demand. It is easy to identify ourselves emotionally with "the people." At the moment the people are not identifying themselves with us.

The Attorney General is the first public official here to say this publicly, at least by implication. "Is the sentiment of the public," Mr. Biddle asked despondently at Charlottesville last Friday, "really moved by the vision of a better world or is it merely disturbed by anxiety about increased taxation and the threat of unemployment after the war? Do the people of our land fight only to win the war and have it over — or to use the war for great and democratic ends?" The answer of big business had been given at the convention of the National Association of Manufacturers two days before. "I am not making guns or tanks," the president of the N.A.M. said, "to win a 'people's revolution' . . . I am not fighting for a quart of milk for every Hottentot or for a TVA on the Danube." In this the N.A.M. spoke also for the War Production Board [WPB] and for most of our military-diplomatic bureaucracy. Is the answer of the people very different? The Attorney General made it clear that he is afraid that the dominant feeling toward fighting the war is to "get it over." Congress already reflects this desire for "normalcy."

The trend toward the right has gone to ugly extremes "on the hill." In executive committee sessions on the new War Powers bill, the principal objection to the measure was the fear that the President might use it to let in a lot of "non-Aryan" refugees after the war was over. The old slur about the Jew Deal has made a covert reappearance. Sumners of Texas on the floor of the House Wednesday attacked New Deal administrators as "this bunch of people who . . . do not much more than get into this country before they are trying to tell us how to run this government." It would be a mistake to identify "Send 'Em to the Electric Chair" Sumners with the voice of the American people, but there are enough like him in the Democratic Party and in Congress to cheer the Axis and bedevil the Administration. The one part of the war machine generously left to New Dealers is that in which they are certain to become unpopular — the political-suicide assignment of price control and rationing. Sumners and his kind are making the most of it to set the farmer against the New Deal. Wait till they get started on how Lehman is taking food from Americans to feed foreigners!

Coffee of Nebraska thought the Sumners speech "wonderful." Cox of Georgia rose to suggest that perhaps the time had come to break away from party lines in order to get rid of these "carpetbaggers." Rankin of Mississippi and Hoffman of Michigan joined in, unrebuked, though next day Hook of Michigan gave Hoffman a drubbing in debate. Hoffman suggested that Congress set up a new committee to investigate the Marshall Field publications, the left and liberal weeklies, and the Washington *Post* for attacking Congressmen of this odorous variety in the last campaign. Hook threw Hoffman into confusion by asking whether this meant that the latter had lost faith in the Dies committee. Hoffman replied lamely that Hook and others had criticized the Dies committee so much that "they now have too big a job on their hands to handle all this."

As Congress moves right, the Administration may move with it, if only out of necessity. The precarious course of the Panama agreement through the Senate last week showed how dependent the President and his party leaders are on right-wing Democrats. The debate and the vote were a foretaste of what is coming when we begin to make the peace. The power of a Cordell Hull, who can swing Southern votes, is likely to increase, that of a Henry Wallace to wane, as the drift continues. In a sense we are already losing the peace more rapidly than we are winning the war, for the shape of our society is being determined by the undemocratic and monopolistic fashion in which it has been mobilized for war production. This trend will only be reversed if the Axis staying power proves much greater than, in the present optimistic mood, is now expected.

Is the outlook for the liberals hopeless? Not at all. The pendulum now swinging away from social reform will swing back. At present, in the full flush of boom employment, after twelve years of the New Deal, the country is ready for a change, and 1944 may see a right-wing Republican elected. The reaction is likely to go too far. Workers and farmers will not easily give up what they have won through Mr. Roosevelt since 1933. The idea of social security is too potent to be stifled. The Republicans must either submit to these currents or go under in trying to combat them. The immediate outlook for progressivism is dark, but it has been dark before, and it is some comfort to know that its future is nowhere near as bleak as Adolf Hitler's.

December 19, 1942

The Anti-Wallace Plot

〜 〜

T HANKS TO THE VIGOROUS POSITION taken by Vice-
President Wallace and Milo Perkins before the Senate Banking and
Currency Committee, the Danaher amendment to restore the power of
Jesse Jones over the purchase of critical materials abroad has been
blocked. After the hearing, which was held in executive session, Senator
Wagner, the committee's chairman, asked Senator Danaher, "What do
you think of your amendment now?" "Don't call it my amendment,"
was the aggrieved reply. The Senator from Connecticut, who is not a
Republican of the diehard variety, has been apologizing to friends that
this was a party measure handed him by the minority leader, Senator
McNary.

Last spring, with elections coming on, the Republicans were virtuously
critical of Jesse Jones's handling of rubber and his unfairness to small
business. Now, with the elections past, the minority party and the
Administration's most powerful officials have been plotting to overrule
the White House executive order of last April 13, which shifted final
authority over stockpile purchases from Jones to Wallace and the Board
of Economic Warfare [BEW]. The order was issued when Jones's
stinginess and procrastination became too obvious to be overlooked by
the President, an experienced overlooker where Jones is concerned.
According to one report, Jones had spent only $3,000,000 of a
$500,000,000 fund given him by Congress a year and a half earlier for the
purchase of badly needed war materials. I cannot vouch for the figures;
much of what Jones and the RFC [Reconstruction Finance Corporation]
do is a military secret. The impression conveyed by the figures, however,

is certainly correct; yet McNary indicated that if the Danaher amendment were adopted he would also seek to restore Jones's power to veto proposed expenditures by WPB [War Production Board], the Maritime Commission, the Petroleum Coordination, and the Rubber Director. This would be worth several divisions to our enemies. "But Jesse," Donald Nelson was once heard to exclaim despairingly on the telephone, "there's a war on." Jones would rather lose a battle than a haggle.

Fortunately the Texan is so accustomed to the hat-in-hand humility of applicants for loans as to be thrown off balance in encounters with mortals who do not need to borrow money from him. He gets as flustered in a fight as the town banker jostled by the town drunk. Last winter he was so upset by a critical editorial in the Washington *Post* that he punched its publisher in the eye. Lately he has become a constant contributor of protesting letters to the Washington Merry-Go-Round, an unprofitable occupation. In his private appearance before the Senate Banking and Currency Commission two weeks ago Jones made the lordly error of neglecting to brush up on his facts before inciting its members to riot against the BEW. His characteristic mixture of insolence and ignorance might have succeeded if Senator Wagner had not insisted that the committee hear the BEW's side of the story. Jones's picture of how the BEW and its director, Milo Perkins, operate turned out to be so childishly and patently untrue that Jones's Senate supporters felt that he had left them out on a limb.

Jones charged that BEW expenditures were not audited. Perkins showed that all actual spending, though under BEW directives, was by the RFC and that the RFC knew where every nickel went. Jones pictured Perkins as a one-man director. Perkins showed that the Board of Economic Warfare, containing top representatives of State, Treasury, War, Justice, Navy, Agriculture, Commerce, WPB, Lend-Lease, and Inter-American Affairs, meets at least every two weeks for a full discussion of its activities. The board differs considerably from the hand-picked boards of yes-men who run the RFC and its subsidiaries. Jones complained that the executive order giving the BEW and Perkins power to direct RFC expenditures for critical materials was unprecedented. Perkins showed that it was, comma for comma, the same as that which freed Nelson from financial dependence on Jones. Perkins pointed out that he had only used this power three times. Wallace interrupted to say that Perkins should have used it more frequently. "In the future," the Vice-President said, "let's have more fights and fewer shortages."

It would be a mistake to believe that the attempt to hamstring the

BEW is over. It would also be a mistake to believe that this is merely a conflict between Jones and the BEW. Behind Jones is the State Department, and behind the State Department are those forces, clerical and capitalist, which have no intention of letting this era become, in Wallace's phrase, the Century of the Common Man. Only a few weeks ago mining interests which operate in South America held a private powwow to discuss means of combating the labor and health clauses which the BEW has begun to put into all contracts for the purchase of supplies in Latin America. There is a good practical argument for these clauses, and the Senate Banking and Currency Committee found it impressive. But the mere fact that they will enable us to obtain more war materials is not enough to down the horrid suspicion that these clauses may also help to create a more decent world.

Not that the BEW is a particularly radical organization. Its export office is headed by a former General Motors executive, its import office by the former operating head of a big New York importing house. But the BEW is Wallace's original idea; as its chairman he has power to overrule the other Cabinet members who sit on it. The BEW reflects Wallace's progressive and humane outlook, which happens also to provide a very practical approach to the problem of increasing Latin America's output of badly needed materials. Whether in the rubber-bearing jungle, in the mine, or on the plantation, Latin American production is hampered by bad and unhealthy working conditions. Months ago Department of Agriculture agents in Brazil were warning that Adam Smith economics would not work in the jungle, that a mere increase in the price of rubber would not necessarily increase the output of latex, that the key lay not so much in higher prices for the owners of vast jungle lands as in assuring native labor of decent food, fair play, and quinine. Rubber, though the most dramatic example, is not an exceptional case. The widespread silicosis which interferes with maximum production of tin and copper in Latin America is another example of the need for social reforms to combat a shortage of materials. This New Deal approach is, of course, foreign to the State Department. I am told that in Bolivia, where the Congress recently passed a law to combat silicosis, the American ambassador brought pressure on the President to veto it.

Contrary to popular impression, Latin America has some of the world's most advanced labor and social legislation. In the past this legislation has been kept innocently confined to the statute books. In most Latin American countries powerful American and British corporations, with the backing of State Department and Foreign Office, have been able to ignore these laws, though they occasionally pay fines, like the madams in a red-light district, to help the police keep up appearances. Now another agency of the American government, the BEW, is inserting in raw-material contracts clauses requiring contractors to obey all labor and social laws and also to embark on specific programs for the improvement of health and sanitation. The cost of these is borne directly or indirectly by the BEW, but the companies operating in Latin America are thinking ahead to the peace. Can the old conditions be restored after the peon has had a taste of better things? Will labor costs go up permanently? True, a higher standard of wages and living for the Latin American masses would also provide a better market for the North American exports, but that horizon is too broad to fit into the bookkeeping of United Fruit or Anaconda Copper. The State Department has accepted these labor clauses, but Jones could put a stop to them if his old power over BEW expenditures were restored.

The BEW has also been annoying the State Department in North Africa. Recently, at a State Department meeting, with BEW representatives present, A. A. Berle accused the BEW of causing the death of American soldiers by holding up certain shipments to Africa. Dean Acheson on that occasion defended the BEW. Berle said he had a letter in his pocket from an American general to prove his statement, but failed to produce the letter when challenged. Inquiry brought a denial from military authorities, who praised the BEW's work in North Africa.

The BEW seems to have objected not to dealings with Vichy but to letting Berlin profit from such transactions. The existence of the BEW meant that an independent and progressive agency of the government was in a position to know what was going on. The facts it made available to inner Administration circles did not reflect credit on either the astuteness or the efficiency of our diplomats.

Vichy promised us not to ship molybdenum or cobalt from North Africa to Germany, then made a deal to send 3,000 tons of cobalt ore to the Reich, enough to cover Hitler's deficit in this essential material for the production of synthetic oil. On one occasion Vichy dispatched a destroyer to scare off a British submarine that tried to stop a shipment of cobalt in a French ship. Shipments of American oil to North Africa under the Weygand-Murphy agreement of February, 1941, were used to produce minerals for the Reich and to replace oil sent to Libya. The French embassy in Washington at one time admitted deliveries of 3,600 tons of lubricating oil, motor oil, and aviation gas from North Africa to the Axis forces in Libya. In some cases American supplies went directly to Rommel. By March, 1942, the situation was so bad that Leahy informed Pétain that the United States was discontinuing shipments because Vichy had broken its promises by sending food, fuel, and trucks to Libya. In June the State and War departments wanted shipments resumed, but only of food. As late as August Murphy reported that Vichy was ready to supply no more cobalt for export, except to Germany. There was criticism by the BEW of the way food, cotton, and sugar were distributed in North Africa. One United States consul reported that distribution and propaganda work were so poor that Arabs often thought the goods they were getting were of Portuguese or German origin.

The State Department wants no surveillance by progressives, especially when, as in North Africa today, we begin to mold the future shape of Europe. So long as the BEW controls exports and imports it may feed and supply populations unwilling to accept State Department decisions on their destiny. The BEW must be got out of the war before peace comes, lest the old order for which the State Department stands be endangered. The Metternichs are ganging up on the BEW because the BEW is Wallace, and Wallace is the champion of the common man.

December 26, 1942

The Loss of Leon Henderson

HOW WELL Leon Henderson served the people of this country will become more apparent as the new Congress, on a reactionary rampage, forces a general loosening of anti-inflationary regulations. Up to now, thanks to Henderson's integrity and courage, and despite the power exercised by special economic interests in our political life, we have done a better job than any other capitalist country in fighting inflation. The loot of Europe has tended to hold German prices down; Lend-Lease has helped maintain supplies in Britain. We have managed to hold the advance in the cost of living to less than a fifth of the advance that occurred in the First World War, although a much larger share of our productive capacity is going into war production and war exports. This is a magnificent achievement, and it is the more remarkable because up to last May Henderson had no real power over any prices and has never had adequate power over farm prices.

The clamor of the press against Henderson is no real index of the public's attitude toward him, but no man can expect to be a price administrator in war time and win popularity contests. Henderson's fate deserves a place in the meditation of philosophers. By fighting inflation he was serving the general interest but antagonizing a long list of special ones. These were not limited to what we are accustomed to call "the interests." The steel industry knuckled under to Henderson on prices at a time when he had only the power of bluff and bluster. It was the farm bloc and labor which proved his undoing — the former by a frontal attack, the latter by the inability of the rank and file to work up much enthusiasm for a man who was holding down their wages, albeit for the best of reasons. He had to step on everybody's toes in order to protect everybody from runaway prices. The pain inflicted was immediate, the danger comparatively distant. Everybody seemed to feel the hurt of his own special interest more deeply than the benefit to the general interest in which all shared.

There are many reasons for Henderson's resignation, but none of them would have mattered had it not been for the last elections and the next Congress. His eyes are bad and his back needs treatment; these ailments, though genuine enough, come nevertheless under what Freud might have called the psychopathology of politics. There is nothing wrong with him that a New Deal victory and two weeks in a health resort could not patch up. The President did not ask for his resignation but must have been relieved to get it as he prepares to deal with the new Congress. A new face is a good thing at any time in so unpopular a post as that of price administrator, and to the White House it must have seemed all the more necessary at this time. Henderson resigned after asking the advice of Byrnes.

Henderson's unpopularity in Congress was based on two things. One was that he had the spunk to say no to requests for special favors. These requests came from progressive as well as reactionary members of Congress anxious to "take care of" industries and persons back home. The other was that, whether from ineptness, excessive political purity, or naivete, or possibly all three, he allowed price-control jobs and machinery to fall largely into the hands of state political machines. These were often anti-New Deal and in many cases Republican. In some strategic areas in the last election the OPA [Office of Price Administration] patronage and machinery helped to defeat New Deal candidates. These practical considerations rather than the use of logarithmic computations in questionnaires turned Congress against him. If Henderson had "played ball" he could have used differential calculus in fuel-oil rationing and still found defenders on the Hill.

Henderson's retirement is part of the general movement away from liberalism. He has led a precarious existence since his appointment to the Defense Commission in May 1940. He has made his compromises, but on every basic issue he has been firm — and right. He led the fight in 1940 for expansion of steel, aluminum, and other basic materials. He led the fight in 1941 for curtailment and conversion of civilian industries. Had he been in a position to run, rather than merely to needle, the defense program, we should have been far ahead of where we are now in war production. Around him, in the price administration and the civilian-supply division of the WPB [War Production Board], were the ablest and most devoted group of New Dealers and progressive business men in Washington. The only field in which they had authority was prices, and there they did a good job. Henderson's resignation marks the second phase of the New Deal retreat, as the alliance with big business in May, 1940, marked the first. Both have their political logic, but the time may rapidly be approaching when the President will have to stand and fight. When that time comes, Henderson will return to the high position he deserves.

I had intended to devote this week's letter entirely to Henderson's resignation, but late tonight, from a trustworthy source, I received some information of importance on the supposed revolutionary plot uncovered in Bolivia. The "revolt" so happily stifled by the imposition of martial law seems to have had a good deal more to do with the shortsighted social policies of our State Department and diplomatic service than with the machinations of Nazi agents. In last week's issue I reported that I had heard that the American Minister to Bolivia, Pierre Boal, was trying to persuade the President of that country to veto a silicosis-prevention law. It appears that this law was only part of a general labor code which was before the Bolivian Congress. The imposition of martial law prevented the code from coming to a final vote, a fact discreetly omitted by the official reports from La Paz.

The demand for the passage of the general labor code was one of the causes of a strike in the tin mines, which was also crushed by the declaration of martial law. The code would have provided, among other things, for collective bargaining, freedom of organization, minimum wages, and payment of wages every fifteen days. This final provision is the best commentary on the labor conditions prevailing in Bolivia. Actually the miners are kept in a kind of peonage. As Mr. Boal is said to have put it recently in a five-page cable to Secretary of State Hull, "They are now paid tardily deliberately in order to maintain them on the job and to give them a stake in their next month's pay." This was a delicate way of saying that if the miners were paid late and irregularly they went into debt, and that if they were in debt they had to keep on working. Our minister went to the President of Bolivia on behalf of the mine owners to prevent the passage of this labor code, although with the high prices we are paying for Bolivian tin the Patino interests can well afford to pay the miners better wages. Hull's reply to Boal's cable is reported to have given discreet support to the latter's anti-labor activity. For the sake of Good Neighbor relations, some Congressional committee ought to put the State Department on the griddle in this affair and show Latin America we mean what we say in our speeches.

PART V

1943

Dies and the Backbone Shortage

TWO THINGS STAND OUT from last week's debates in Congress on the Dies committee. One is that we have in Dies a very able demagogue who is laying the foundations for a powerful post-war fascist movement in America. The second is that there would be a good chance of defeating him if the Administration had the courage to provide the fight against him with some leadership. Unfortunately the White House seems to be as weak and half-hearted in its domestic as in its foreign policy. The same irresolution that permits a French fascist and anti-Semite to be installed as Governor General of Algeria was scandalously evident on the home front during the past week. Presumably we are engaged in a war against the Axis. Yet a group of diehard isolationists in Congress was strong enough to force the Attorney General to remove William Powers Maloney from the prosecution of the case against the thirty-three alleged seditionists, and a leading member of the President's own party was permitted unrebuked to condone anti-Semitism on the floor of the House of Representatives.

It is true that the President has named an official committee to handle "complaints of subversive activity" by federal employees, and this will be of some puny help in combating Dies. But it is essentially defensive action, and it meets Dies on his own well-chosen ground. To pretend that this is all a serious hunt for Communists is to play into the hands of Dies; even the bitterly anti-Communist *New Leader* maintains that only eight of the thirty-eight officials named by Dies are really Communists. Recent utterances from Berlin show that fear of communism is still the Nazis' chief hope of a negotiated peace. To allow the Dies committee to go on operating is to give Goebbels a sounding board in our midst and to permit American fascism to organize itself at home while we fight the fascist Axis abroad.

The new theme song of the anti-democratic forces in this country is "bureaucracy." Suddenly one hears it echoed on every side as though some smart publicity man had arranged the chorus. When Dies spoke of "a new philosophy which in one country is communism, in another fascism, in another country Nazi-ism, and in another country bureaucracy," he was hitting straight at the New Deal. When Dies said on the floor that the fight against this new philosophy was "more important than the conflict between rival armies" and then changed from the *Congressional Record* to "of almost equal importance with the conflict between rival armies," he was making a confession. He was afraid of his own little slip of the tongue, of the revelation that the war Martin Dies is really interested in fighting is the war against democracy at home.

Unlike the Administration, Dies is rarely on the defensive. One of the few instances in which he has been forced into this position occurred last week when the Texan remarked on the floor of the House: "There have come repeated demands that this person or that person be branded as pro-fascist or pro-Nazi simply because he expressed anti-Jewish views." This is the nearest Dies has come to explaining why some of his committee's best friends are Axis agents. Hitler himself could not have surpassed the demagogic sleight-of-hand with which Dies defended himself against his accusers. "I do not hold," he said, in another passage which he himself later expurgated from the *Congressional Record,* "with those who condemn anyone on account of the misdeeds of some people in that [Jewish] race, but there is no law against a man's denouncing the South. God knows I have heard Southerners denounced as viciously in certain quarters of this country as I have ever heard Jews denounced." This may be a non-sequitur to intellectuals, but it was an effective appeal to wounded Southern pride. Dies went on to explain that anti-Semitism is not necessarily fascism and to identify fascism itself with "people who believe in simple, fundamental Americanism, people who believe in preserving our Constitution, people who believe that America shall not fall a victim to maudlin internationalism." One does not answer a speech of this kind by appointing another committee to investigate communism!

Despite the cheers for Dies on Monday, the debate on the floor of the House Friday indicated that he is not unbeatable. The House voted 153 to 146 Friday against a motion which would have barred from public employment the men Dies had named as communistic on Monday. The real issue in the debate was well stated by a Dies supporter, Gifford of Massachusetts. "Almost the entire membership of the House rose and cheered the gentleman from Texas the other day," Gifford said. "Certainly we seemed to have approved his findings. Am I today to be told that each case must be proved before each and every member of the Committee on Appropriations before the findings of the gentleman from Texas and his committee are accepted?" The issue was, indeed, as the exasperated Gifford saw it, a question of confidence in Dies. One conservative Congressman after another, men of both parties, from North and South, rose to attack the motion, to defend from their own knowledge one or another of the men Dies had smeared, and to declare that they would not condemn these men without evidence. But if the Dies committee, after all these years of activity and the expenditure of half a million dollars, cannot marshal enough evidence to impress anti-Communists like Dirksen of Illinois and Tarver of Georgia, it is highly vulnerable.

In this, as in other matters, the Administration underestimates the intelligence of the American people. An examination of the press, as of Friday's debate, will show there is enough sense of fair play, of devotion to basic American ideals, and of the realities of the war to overcome the red bogy even on the right. Keefe of Wisconsin, Folger of North Carolina, Ludlow of Indiana, like Hobbs of Alabama in the earlier debates over David Lasser, reflected the strength of the basic traditions we all share. "I am not willing," said Case of South Dakota, "to condemn thirty-eight men and women in thirty minutes on ex parte presentation without even a specific statement on each one of the individuals concerned. We are supposed to be fighting a war to sustain the Anglo-Saxon idea of justice." And O'Connor of Montana did not speak for himself alone when he cried, "Suppose these men have had communistic leanings? Who in the name of God today are stopping bullets that would be killing our boys? ... Who are we fighting — Russia or Germany?"

Dies could be beaten if there were available but a little more courage and leadership. Brave young Will Rogers rose on the floor to register his dissent Monday after Dies spoke. Ickes, who has more spunk than the rest of the Cabinet put together, replied to Dies with a scorcher. James L. Fly of the Federal Communications Commission stood up like a man before the House Appropriations Committee in his defense of Frederick L. Schuman and William E. Dodd, Jr., against Dies committee charges. Unfortunately, elsewhere in the New Deal the critical shortage is backbone.

The Charming Mr. Baruch

BERNARD M. BARUCH, who has been building up his personal influence for months from a suite in the Carlton, is expected to return to power as a result of the renewed battle which has broken out between civilian war-production authorities and the armed services. This growing influence has many sources. Baruch is shrewd and charming. He likes people. He has money. Several Southern Senators and Director of Economic Stabilization James F. Byrnes are beholden to him for past campaign contributions and also for his good advice and friendship, for Baruch is no ordinary fat cat of politics.

Baruch gets along equally well with conservatives and New Dealers. He is consulted by Cordell Hull and he is consulted by Ben Cohen. He has more understanding of social issues than is common in one of his class and background. But while he does not pander to the vulgar prejudices which pass for political thinking in some section of Wall Street, he is safe enough by their standards, as the Baruch rubber report showed. Whether or not the Standard Oil crowd took him into camp, they certainly got what they wanted from him. He may not have been as gullible as Conant or as complaisant as Compton, his colleagues on the rubber board, but he went along. The reward for Baruch was the kind of favorable publicity the press reserves for those who serve its ultimate masters. For Baruch, it was a glorious return to the spotlight, and his vanity is commensurate with his ability, which is admittedly great.

Why do so many people consult Baruch? He has been around for a long time and knows the ropes. He has sense. He is *simpatico*. He has a capacity for smoothing out ruckuses, a valuable talent in a town as full of them as Washington. He knows how to handle the press. The picture he has built up of himself is that of a contented old man feeding the squirrels from a bench in the park opposite the White House and occasionally running into old friends who stop to chat a while with him. This is a masterpiece of public relations. When Cissie Patterson's sheet disturbed this idyllic picture with the story of the big dinner party for Hopkins, Baruch hastened to wipe out the nasty story with a $1,000,000 contribution to war charities. And judging from the way he is now treated in the *Times-Herald,* he must have Cissie eating out of his hand.

It is my impression that Mr. Roosevelt does not like Baruch. They are too much alike; both are charmers. Mr. Roosevelt feels about Baruch as a young married woman does when her mother tries to help her by showing her the right way to handle a maid or a baby. He resented Al Smith's attempt to "help" him when he first succeeded Smith as Governor, and there is reason to believe that he has been irked by Baruch's burning desire to show him how *really* to run a war. Baruch's vigil in the park across the way may have been a boon to the squirrels, but it was an annoyance to the President. It was a kind of humble picketing — "Mr. Roosevelt is unfair to elder statesmen."

Now it looks as though Baruch's moment had come. The Under Secretaries of War and the Navy are furious with WPB [War Production Board] Chairman Nelson for dismissing Vice-Chairman Ferdinand Eberstadt and giving full scheduling powers to Vice-Chairman C. E. Wilson. The army-navy crowd are powerful and united; and the President will have to do something to appease them. His usual method of dealing with these intra-Administration squabbles is to set up a new super-board, and the indications are that there will be a new one, with Baruch as top man, on production. The army and navy supply chiefs would like Baruch in that job because his conception, like theirs, is that the civilian agencies should concentrate on materials and leave procurement and scheduling to the military and naval supply service. Baruch is satisfactory to big business because he is a strong believer in leaving a major part of war production to the industry committees. But he is also smart enough to make considerable concessions to labor, perhaps also to work out a compromise under which Wilson would have enough power over scheduling to do his job.

This current quarrel can easily be over-simplified and over-dramatized. It is only superficially a military-civilian struggle. Only 9

percent of the men in the War Department's services of supply are
regular army officers; the rest are business men in uniform. It is a clash
between two groups of big-business men, one linked with the military
bureaucracy, the other somewhat tenuously allied with New Dealers
and labor. I think it would be unfair to accuse the military crowd of
bad motives. They fear interference with their supply programs if
Wilson actually digs down into the job of scheduling, for to schedule he
must rearrange contracts, and in rearranging he will be passing on
whether we need this gun more than that tank. It is easy to understand
the desire of the military to keep the supply program in their own
hands. Unfortunately, when a $260-billion war order is suddenly
imposed on an economy which never generated more than $80 billion
worth of income a year, the whole structure must be tightened up if the
job is to be done. I have a great deal of respect for Wilson and believe
that he is right in this dispute, but I should like to see it peacefully
resolved, for the Under Secretaries of War and Navy also command
respect and consideration.

Nelson, a very weak man, fired Eberstadt and delegated all power to
Wilson from fear as much as from conviction. He felt that Eberstadt and
the army-navy crowd were out to get his job, and he is staking his future
on Wilson. Wilson started out to break the bottlenecks in the war-
production program. These bottlenecks are in items which go into the
final manufacture of many different war materials. But to get more
aluminum extrusions for aviation, he found that he needed power to
rationalize and schedule aluminum production. This is not popular with
the aluminum industry. And to get maximum production of aviation,
Wilson found that he had to go to the other end of the process and try
to change army-navy specifications. Obviously escort vessels can be built
more quickly if you concentrate on one type instead of six, but at this end
he stepped on the toes of a lot of admirals. It seems to me that the size
of the program and its urgency point to the need for centralizing full
control of the program in one man's hands, and that man a civilian. For
only a civilian can mediate between army and navy.

In my opinion Eberstadt represented too completely the Wall Street
monopolist point of view to do an all-out job, and his dismissal by
Nelson was all to the good. But labor and liberals cannot stop short at
supporting Nelson and Wilson and working for the Tolan-Kilgore-
Pepper bill for a streamlined civilian-headed war agency. Wilson will
find it much easier to break bottlenecks, to force through emergency
methods and the use of emergency facilities in making components, if

instead of depending on industry committees as he now does he also has the help of labor and small-business committees. For a fight between big-business men is not likely to result in a more democratic war-production program, and if we are to meet this year's goals we need the fullest help from small business and labor as well as from big business.

Thurman Arnold and the Railroads

I HOPE TO BE ABLE to take the time soon to make a study of the work Thurman Arnold did as head of the Anti-Trust Division of the Department of Justice. I can only record at this time the regret that most progressives here feel over his retirement — for that seems the word for it — to the bench. His division was one of the last places in Washington where the old fighting New Deal spirit still survived. Almost everywhere else one sees the big-business crowd in power.

Arnold is a very odd character, and there is no telling where he will end up politically. He is mercurial, not too profound, thoroughly opportunistic — distinctly a populistic middle-class radical who might even end up on the far right. I should like to emphasize the word "might" because it would be unwise to draw too logical conclusions from some of Arnold's weirder ideas. It is just as possible to imagine him a fervent anti-fascist in a period of crisis. For he is courageous, generous, and warm-hearted, equally removed from the poles of bigotry and milk-and-water liberalism.

The Anti-Trust Division is the battered citadel of a romantic lost cause, usually betrayed by its own nominal leaders. It contains some of the most devoted and hard-working officials in the capital. There are men in it with an extraordinary and detailed knowledge of the industries under their supervision, men who could make many times their government salaries if they chose to serve the monopolies they have fought. It is a tribute to Arnold that he won the devotion of these men. He won it by putting up a better battle against monopoly than the Anti-Trust Division had ever been able to wage before.

I need hardly add that this battle was fundamentally as ineffective as Arnold's evangelical efforts to persuade a middle-aged, paunchy capitalism to leap back into the competitive scrimmages of its youth. Neither legislation nor lectures will cure its economic arterio-sclerosis, and the war has both speeded up the growth of monopoly and weakened such countervailing forces as the anti-trust laws. Today the WPB [War Production Board], the War and Navy departments, the Office of the Petroleum Administrator for War, and large areas of the BEW [Board of Economic Warfare] are run by business men and lawyers who have devoted much of their activity to violating the anti-trust laws. Little wonder that they proved powerful enough, first, to force weak consent decrees on Arnold, then to shut off one scheduled prosecution after another, and finally to promote Arnold to the bench.

A complaint one hears against Arnold from the fuddy-duddies — the ex-liberal careerists and picayune opportunists who are rationalizing the appeasement of big business — is that Arnold "talked too much." By this they mean that Arnold, when forced to take a consent decree or to stop a prosecution, often let the inside story leak to the press or to a Congressional committee. The fuddy-duddies regard this practice as somehow ungentlemanly, indecent, and improper. Apparently the facts of life, the actualities of economics, are too delicate for the ears of common folk. The same gentlemen who spout about democracy on minor provocation resent Arnold's habit of taking his cases to the people. Had it not been for Arnold's refusal to act according to the *mores* of our better social clubs, the facts of the Standard Oil-I. G. Farben cartel would have been safely buried with the consent decree instead of spread on the record of the Truman committee and broadcast in the press. Arnold fought the hush-hush policy that more and more pervades the capital and prevents disclosure of the facts.

The anti-trust laws seem to have a beneficial effect, in one way at least, upon the courts. We owe Chief Justice Stone of the United States Supreme Court to the Aluminum Company of America. Alcoa, according to a familiar story, preferred to have Coolidge put his Attorney General on the bench to having his Attorney General put Alcoa in the dock. It is difficult to determine to which monopoly we owe the new Circuit Court justice, Thurman Arnold. The honor seems to go to the railroads of the United States and to their friend, that tired radical, Joseph B. Eastman, director of the Office of Defense Transportation. For Arnold's last major venture before being kicked upstairs to judicial honors was his attempt to take on that twenty-six-billion-dollar giant, the American railroads. Little of the story of that last battle has leaked to the press, though we shall hear more of it one of these days from Congress.

Arnold has had twenty-one anti-trust cases shot out from under him by the arrangement of last spring whereby the corporation lawyers and bankers who man the offices of the War and Navy departments are permitted to suspend the anti-trust laws for the convenience of themselves, their ex-clients, and their friends. Among these cases are no fewer than five against the du Ponts and two against General Electric. All but one of them are criminal, not civil, cases. In all but two instances the prosecution was stopped after indictments were obtained. These indictments act as a considerable deterrent. Recently the Secretaries of War and the Navy have begun to stop investigations before indictments can be returned. One such case was the inquiry into the Hawaiian pineapple industry. The other involved a group of three indictments prepared against the Illinois Freight Association and the Central States Motor Freight Bureau. These were to be the beginning of the first major attack on the greatest monopoly in this country, the growing monopoly in transportation — on the methods whereby the railroads fix not only their own rates but impose uneconomic and non-competitive rates on the movement of goods by air, water, and highway. The investigation was stopped at the request of Eastman, with the approval of Under Secretaries Patterson and Forrestal.

A letter to Attorney General Biddle by Secretary of War Stimson and Acting Secretary of the Navy Forrestal throws new light on the curious procedure now being followed in anti-trust cases. It reveals that drafts of the proposed indictments were presented by the Anti-Trust Division to the Secretaries of War and the Navy before submission to the grand jury in Chicago, and that this was done "in pursuance of an arrangement made at a conference held in your [Biddle's] office." The War and Navy departments, and Eastman, prevented the proposed indictments from ever reaching the grand jury. War, Navy, and Eastman were willing only to permit prosecution of labor leaders and others who were alleged to have used a strike to coerce a motor carrier to increase its rate. Arnold and Biddle refused to do this. They objected that the basic conspiracy was to enforce fixed and non-competitive rates, that the strike was only one of the means used to enforce these rates, and that "it would not be possible to draw an indictment which contained only the means used and did not describe the basic plan." This readiness to prosecute labor rather than capital under the anti-trust laws is worth noting, though it is hardly a new phenomenon.

The situation in transportation today may be visualized if one imagines what it would have been like a century ago had the canal-boat companies possessed the financial means and political power to control the railroads. The railroads have become a gigantic racket in which a group of financial and managerial insiders enrich themselves at the expense of the properties in their care and the shippers these properties serve. Ostensibly their rates are fixed by the Interstate Commerce Commission [ICC]. Actually they fix their own rates through rate associations declared illegal under the anti-trust laws in 1897 but still going strong. Powerful shippers have their own ways of getting around these rates, but the weak have only the costly recourse of an appeal to the ICC and the courts. Regulation by these processes may be compared to an attempt at finding one's way through a Brazilian jungle with the aid of a handbook on Swedenborgian theology. On the one hand, we have a hopeless maze of nearly half a million freight rates fixed by private associations. On the other, we have a highly metaphysical system of government regulation which attempts to check the tariff on prunes from Santa Clara by reference to the lofty, if subtle and arid, concepts of fair return on the fair value of the railroad property used. The resultant controversies would have delighted the medieval philosopher, though they are well calculated to bewilder and discourage the shipper.

In our society, the gravitational pull exerted by huge masses of capital inevitably forces into their orbit the agencies set up to regulate them. This is what happened long ago to the ICC, which has not only permitted the continued operation of these private price-fixing associations but has enabled the railroads to reach out for control of waterways and highways. The railroads have been allowed to drive water-carrier competitors out of business by discriminatory rate practices and to obtain ever greater control of competing bus and truck lines. This development tends more and more to deprive the public of the benefits of these cheaper forms of transportation and to enable the railroads to maintain obsolete methods free from the healthy prod of competition.

More important to the future of our society is the control exercised by the railroads over aviation. The Anti-Trust Division was preparing to take action against the contract by which the Railway Express Agency controls air freight. Under the agency's contract with the air lines, air express rates cannot be less than twice the rail rate, but they are actually held at five to seven times the railroad rates. Yet according to Grover Loening, technical consultant of the War Production Board's Air Cargo Plane Committee, cargo planes today can be run at 8 to 10 cents a ton mile as compared with rail rates of 10 to 15 cents a ton mile. To stifle the development of air transport is to stifle development of national defense.

A mass of facts on uneconomic railroad practices was gathered by the Anti-Trust Division in preparing the railroad cases. It will take a Congressional investigation to bring them to light. The railroads, fresh from their victory over Arnold, are now preparing to ask Congress to free them from the restrictions imposed by the anti-trust laws, the Panama Canal Act, and the Transportation Act of 1940. They want the right to bring water carriers and trucks under common ownership, to place air transportation under some agency, like the ICC, which the railroads control, and by these means to saddle uneconomic rates upon the nation's industry and agriculture. We see here the use of political power to maintain and expand economic privileges. This is as far as possible removed from classic conceptions of the free market. If we had good sense, we would take the railroads over now, end their war profiteering, and increase their efficiency. The railroads, as Arnold's elevation to the bench indicates, are — with their brother monopolies — taking us over instead.

Planning and Politics

꿈꿈

THE SO-CALLED American "Beveridge plan"[1] submitted to Congress by the President has been lying around the White House for some time. It is in two parts. One deals with security, work, and relief policies; the other with post-war planning. The first, a tome of 640 pages, was actually delivered to the President three days before Pearl Harbor. The second, a literary quickie of but 50,000 words, was sent to the White House a year later, on December 16, 1942. Thus one had been on his desk for fifteen months and the other for three when the President finally passed them on to Congress.

Mr. Roosevelt is a master of publicity, and it is interesting to speculate on his timing. The moment chosen by the President for the submission of this plan served to distract the press and Congress from Admiral Standley's quaint attempt to better our Russian relations by kicking the Soviets in the teeth. In longer perspective, as has been widely enough noted, the release of this post-war security program in the wake of the President's first copy trial balloons opens the 1944 campaign. The report may also serve several functions in Mr. Roosevelt's strategy for dealing with an unusually cantankerous Congress. The President is said to hope that Congress will overplay its hand, and this report may goad his opposition to greater follies. The report effectively contrasts the President's large and historic aims with the picayune and querulous fault-finding and scandal-mongering that is the principal characteristic of the bi-partisan anti-Roosevelt bloc in Congress. Mr. Roosevelt has set the

[1] A report prepared for the British government in 1942 by the economist William H. Beveridge. It proposed a social security system "from the cradle to the grave" for all British citizens.

stage for a campaign far more momentous than his two past triumphs — the original fight to enact the New Deal and the struggle to force its acceptance by the Supreme Court.

Some of the right-wing papers, with a kind of senile glee, assume that the President's plan is already buried. They drew comfort from the fact that it has no chance of being enacted at this session of Congress. They believe it will be safely interred by the coalition of conservative Democrats and standard-model Republicans which dominates the new special Senate Committee on Post-War Plans set up under the chairmanship of Senator George. They are entitled to the pleasures of self-deception. Roosevelt's strategy, in fact, depends on opposition. The George committee is made to order for his purposes. Mr. Roosevelt wants to be able to go before the country — and the armed forces, which will vote by mail — in 1944 and say, "I offer jobs and security. My opponents offer joblessness and insecurity." This is not a program which can be beaten by calculations as to budgetary cost or appeals to the virtue of private enterprises. Hoover fashion, American politics will revolve around this program for a good many years to come, and it can be defeated only by a new type of demagogy in which fascist-style politicians will seek at one and the same time to outbid the President and to confuse the issues by appeals to the crasser forms of prejudice. Just as fascism in the Reich had to pander to the fundamental socialist outlook of the German people, so in this country it must hide not only behind appeals to American feeling for liberty but also behind promises to satisfy a newer and equally deep, if not deeper, desire for security.

It is an indication of the President's stature and genuine vision that he has gone beyond the necessities of social politics in submitting this program. It would have been enough, politically, to promise cradle-to-the-grave security, along the lines of the Beveridge plan in England. To have stopped at that point would have been in accord with one of the basic tendencies of the New Deal. This is the tendency to solve our economic problems by cutting down real wealth and increasing real costs. Wealth is plowed under to provide the scarcity necessary for the profitable operations of the privileged, property-owning classes, business and agrarian, while costs are raised to provide doles to placate the underprivileged. The New Deal has never had the courage in the past to put idle men at idle machines to produce the means to feed and clothe themselves. This larger economic sanity has been beyond the realm of the political possibilities within which it had to operate as a middle-class reform movement. But a grandiose dose will not solve our problems, despite the naive theory — which runs back from Keynes to Sismondi — that our economic society is a kind of gigantic poker game which can be kept going by periodically redistributing the chips of "purchasing power." Nor is "Beveridge planning" a worthy goal for our youth, which must strive to release the great creative possibilities which still lie stifled, for all our past achievement, in the American land and people.

It is at this point that one notes the striking difference between the first and second report sent to Congress by the President. The bulky report on Security, Work, and Relief Policies takes only faint and tentative steps toward the broader horizons of the Post-War Plan and Program. The germ of the second report is in the call of the first for "increasing emphasis upon policies aiming at the prevention of economic insecurity through a fuller utilization of our productive resources, including labor...." But in the main the first report is only a comprehensive social worker's approach to our economy, deriving from the grimly realistic but defeatist and socially bankrupt premise with which its findings open. "The American people," the report begins its final summation, "should base public-aid policy upon the acceptance of the following facts: (1) The need for public aid will be both large and persistent for some time to come...." Though I have not read the entire 450,000 words of this report, I do not think it does more than touch timidly on the basic principle that we can preserve neither our natural nor our human resources merely by letting the idle rake the leaves away from the unsightly edges of the profit system.

What is little more than implicit in the earlier report achieves explicit statement and bold development in the second, which bears the marks of its war-time origin. "Our peace aims," says an opening statement which finds only a perverted reflection in the conduct of our diplomacy, "are war weapons which in the end may determine the outcome of the military struggle in which we are now engaged." Freedom from Want has hitherto had an ambiguous exegesis, reflecting Cordell Hull's anachronistic Manchester liberalism; it was originally translated by the President into "economic understandings which will secure to every nation a healthy peace-time life for its inhabitants." Here Freedom from Want is expanded into a new Bill of Rights, all of which may be derived from the first, the "right to work," *usefully and creatively* through the productive years." The italics are mine, but the emphasis pervades the entire report.

The report on Post-War Plan and Program has a two-fold purpose. It aims first to outline a program for the orderly transition from a war-time to a peace-time economy, and secondly to sketch the broad outlines of a plan for development of an expanding economy through the cooperation of government and private enterprise. Both purposes are likely to arouse opposition from the larger private units in our economy. So far as the program for economic demobilization is concerned, it provides, among other things, for aid to smaller business units, for free access by business "to the use of both old and new materials and processes unhampered by misuse of the patent system," and for vigorous enforcement of labor legislation in a period when standards will be endangered by the laying off of many workers. Measures of this kind are unlikely to be popular with those who stand to gain the most from a disorderly demobilization and deflation in which financially weaker businesses may be gobbled up, new monopolies established, and the bargaining position of labor weakened.

In dealing with the second purpose of this report, to achieve an expanding national economy, we enter for the first time into the realm of genuine social security, into the field of measures designed to effect the security of our society as against makeshift measures to protect the security of individuals. What is envisaged in the report is not socialism but that kind of mixed state in which alone capitalism can hope to remain progressive. The report looks toward work programs that would increase the nation's wealth by developing its resources of soil, water-power, and transportation; toward the kind of governmental interference that would clear obstacles to genuine private enterprise in business; toward government partnership in certain basic fields; and toward government intervention to maintain useful productive employment where these other measures fail to maintain it. It is impossible here to dwell in detail on the National Resources Planning Board's specific suggestions, but they represent a rich, diversified, and flexible program, free from dogmatism or arid theory.

From the standpoint of business as a whole, it would be far better to accept a measure of social planning and governmental partnership in the maintenance of employment than to bear the heavy tax costs involved in a high level of joblessness. But business is deeply anarchic in its instincts, and the bigger businesses have usually preferred either a dog-eat-dog policy or an unprogressive freezing of the economic status quo. The danger in this program, as in all planning under capitalism, is that it may become a means whereby the monopolies and the combines use the political power and financial resources of the state to solidify their own power. The most obvious example of this danger is in the board's proposal for a National Transportation Agency which would regulate all means of transportation and have access to public funds for improvements. The railroads, which have learned from the ICC how easy it is to control a public regulatory body for their own purposes, would like such a setup as a means of curbing compensation from truck and plane and as a way to tap the Treasury. As the largest aggregation of capital in the field, the railroads would ultimately dominate the agency, as they do the ICC.

There are similar dangers in the proposal for mixed corporations in fields like aluminum and synthetic rubber, where government "could participate in the selection of . . . business units which are to continue to operate in these industries." But the situation could hardly be worse in these fields than it is today. Posterity may look back and see the Roosevelt plan as a mirage, but if it does, the fault will be ours. Our task is not to ponder the spectacle from mountain tops but to do our duty by the future by fighting to achieve as decent a society as we can. Laissez faire capitalism is dying, and it is up to this generation to see whether the new controls will be democratic or monopolistic. Given the deep desire of the people for security and freedom, the outcome is not a foregone conclusion. The President has launched out on the greatest battle of our time.

April 24, 1943

Relaxing Too Soon

❧ ❧

A CURIOUS ATMOSPHERE is visible in the world of business. Though we are as yet only ankle-deep in the war, the impression is growing that the job of war production has passed its peak, and that we can now begin to think of a return to greater civilian production. The service-equipment division of the War Production Board [WPB] has prepared a plan for resuming the manufacture of office machinery. The WPB has issued an order easing its prohibition against the use of steel for non-essential purposes. Manufacturers may use stocks of partially or wholly fabricated steel parts in the production of a wide variety of gadgets ranging from electric hair-curlers to shoe buckles. Trade papers began to talk last fall of the possibility of obtaining materials for renewed civilian output, and the same sort of speculation has now reached the daily press. The financial section of today's New York *Times,* for example, carries no fewer than three articles on the prospect of greater civilian output.

William J. Enright, who covers business circles for the *Times,* says "war agencies intend to start the reconversion of industry to the production of essential civilian goods by the end of the summer." Kenneth L. Austin, who reports on finance and heavy industry, declares New York and Washington are hearing "forecasts that the supply of steel for military, naval, and shipbuilding needs soon will appear to have been more than amply covered, and...metal will be available for non-essential civilian needs within the next six months or less." C. F. Hughes, who writes the enlightened and well-informed Merchant's Point of View for the *Times,* reflects widespread opinion at the capital when he says, "In guns, bombs and shells, motor vehicles and tanks we have already produced more than enough for any reasonable requirements of [our] armed forces or those of our allies."

This feeling that the job of war production is in its declining phase has found expression in the ranks of both capital and labor. Walter D. Fuller, president of the Curtis Publishing Company and chairman of the executive committee of the National Association of Manufacturers, said here last week that the country was suffering from overproduction of certain types of war materials. Fuller declared that we had built up a sufficient backlog of weapons to justify more emphasis on civilian needs. Philip Murray, president of the C.I.O., told the Institute of Women's Professional Relations that the United States is confronted with mass unemployment because we have produced more war materials "than the United Nations can use or the United States can transport." He was unwise enough to speak of difficulties created by "a mad desire to expedite war materials."

There are many parts of the earth in which talk of this kind must make painful and puzzling reading. Our men in the Southwest Pacific are not suffering from an excess of supplies. Australia is worried about a possible Japanese offensive. Last year's widely ballyhooed offensive in Burma has subsided, for lack of material, into the faintest kind of nudge. The Chinese, who have done more with less than any of the United Nations, must think us mad. Our French allies in North Africa, from latest reports, are still using outmoded equipment. The Soviet Union, still the only nation fighting Hitler on a major scale, continues to look for a second front, a military enterprise that will require huge amounts of material if it is to be successful. Granted that we may be producing more than we need on the present scale of our operations, granted even that in some items we have produced enough for any scale of warfare, is it possible that in the over-all picture we have reached a stage where we can relax and turn back to more normal production?

There is evidence that even on the present scale we are still far from the point where we can begin again to make gadgets. Expansion of steel-making facilities is behind schedule and is being curtailed on the general view that we now have enough steel not only for war but for more civilian output. Yet WPB [War Production Board] Chairman Donald M. Nelson said last week that ordinary carbon steel had now become our most serious bottleneck. Production for the third quarter of this year, according to Nelson, will be only about 14,450,000 tons. The demands of our various military and lend-lease agencies and essential civilian supply for that quarter total 20,830,000 tons. There is a deficit of more than 5,000,000 tons, or 25 per cent.

The full significance of those figures becomes more apparent if we recognize that the President's Victory program of January, 1942, has been quietly revised downward not once but several times. "The earlier question of whether we would need eighty billions in war output this year," C. F. Hughes writes, "is on the way to being answered with a flat 'No.'" The phrase "on the way" is an understatement. Except in shipbuilding, even in aircraft, we not only are failing to meet those goals but have reduced them. In this connection I should like to call attention to an authoritative article on the Army Supply Program by Major General Lucius D. Clay in the February issue of *Fortune*. Major General Clay is assistant chief of staff for matériel in the General Staff Corps. His article is extraordinary reading. It shows how long the War Department waited before drawing up plans for an all-out effort and how soon it relinquished them.

"Immediately after Pearl Harbor," General Clay writes, "the Supply Division of the General Staff recognized the necessity for the revision of the Army Supply Program for all-out war. By early February it had completed the first Army Supply Program for this purpose." The Pearl Harbor mentality seems to have dominated the General Staff as well as the commanding officers in Hawaii. General Clay says this first program "was based on the mobilization rate and the composition of troops deemed desirable at that early stage of war, and it included large quantities of matériel that our allies had ordered or requested the year before." This first program called for $62 billion in supplies "through the calendar year 1943" or $31 billion a year in 1942 and 1943. This was reduced, according to General Clay, to $45 billion in April, 1942. Later it was reduced again, to $38 billion. In November, 1942, it was further reduced — to $31 billion. "For 1943," General Clay reports, "our problems in materials and facilities appear to be solved — *to the extent that objectives have finally been brought within the limit of available supplies and facilities*" (my italics). The production problem was solved by reducing the production program! It is measured by these reduced goals that we now have "overproduction of war material." It is on the basis of these reduced goals that plans for expanding production in steel and other basic materials are being curtailed and the resumption of non-essential production is planned. The monopolies which fought expansion have succeeded in cutting the war effort down to size, and "business as usual" is again raising its head. This is a dangerous tendency, which may yet prove costly in terms of lives.

July 10, 1943

Why Wallace Spoke Out

〜 〜

ET NO ONE call Henry Wallace an ineffectual dreamer. He has
just won his second victory in six months over Jesse Jones. In this
town, which worships "toughness" but usually mistakes the loud-
mouthed for the strong, that is an achievement. For no other single
figure here, unless it be the President himself, wields more political
power than the arrogant banker from Houston, Texas. Last December
Wallace went before the Senate Banking and Currency Committee and
persuaded it to abandon an amendment which would have restored
Jones's power over the purchase of critical materials abroad. Danaher of
Connecticut carried the ball for Jesse then, but "Don't call it my
amendment" was Danaher's aggrieved comment after the hearing. This
time Jones's tool was McKellar of Tennessee, with an amendment which
would have given the RFC [Reconstruction Finance Commission] a veto
over purchases by the Board of Economic Warfare [BEW]. The Senate
Appropriations Committee decided to abandon the amendment after the
Vice-President let loose with a scorcher.

McKellar opened his campaign with a pathetic picture. "Mr. Jesse
Jones," he said to the Senate on June 4, "testified a day or two ago before
the so-called Economy Committee that Mr. Milo Perkins absolutely ran
the entire establishment of 2,620 employees; that his word was law, even
over him, Mr. Jesse Jones. . . ." The establishment referred to was the
Board of Economic Warfare. The despotism, were it but true, would call
for bell-ringing. Until now, nobody's word has been law for Jesse Jones,
except perhaps that of a second vice-president of Standard Oil, Aluminum Company of America, or Bethlehem Steel. If it were not necessary

for *someone* to obey the White House injunction against intra-Administration feuding, the President might have been lambasting him publicly long ago.

It is true, as a weary New Dealer told me recently, that "nothing in this town is so easily ignored as a White House directive." No one has been so brazenly successful in ignoring them as Jesse Jones. As early as the fall of 1940 the President instructed Jones to finance a power line which would have made New York City's idle power available to war plants in upstate New York. Consolidated Edison preferred to leave this power idle rather than risk the possibility that the same line would bring cheap St. Lawrence power to the metropolis after the war was over, and the Aluminum Company was afraid the line would encourage public development of the St. Lawrence. The line has never been completed. In August, 1940, with the President's approval, Emil Schram, then head of the RFC, promised the Bonneville Power Authority and a group of public-power authorities in the state of Washington a $70,000,000 loan to buy the Puget Sound Power and Light. The company was heavily over-capitalized, $17,000,000 in arrears on its preferred dividends, and lacked credit for the expansion of facilities to supply additional power to the new war industries of the Northwest. But this extension of public ownership was opposed by power interests, and though the President and Secretary Ickes prodded Jones for more than a year, the promised loan has yet to be granted.

I cite these facts to show that the differences between Jones and the Vice-President cannot be attributed to the latter's temperament, which happens to be mild; Jones would try the patience of a St. Francis of Assisi. No one else in Washington except the accomplished bureaucrats of the State Department has gone so far in perfecting the art of governing by *not* doing things, by mislaying documents, overlooking directives, and forgetting to sign checks. This last has been Jones's forte since the President on April 13, 1942, placed the acquisition of strategic materials in the hands of the BEW, with full power — on paper — to direct the RFC to make the necessary expenditures. The procedure is for the War Production Board [WPB] to decide what critical materials are needed, and how much. The BEW negotiates the contracts. The RFC at the BEW's direction is supposed to arrange the actual purchase, transportation, and warehousing. This is what the RFC, when the royal whim dictates, forgets to do.

The Board of Economic Warfare was established on July 30, 1941. The executive order of April 13, 1942, was long overdue, as one

Congressional investigation after another has demonstrated. The Vice-President's vigorous statement provides a bill of particulars on what Jones had succeeded by that time in not accomplishing. The OPM [Office of Production Management] had asked for 3,000 tons of beryl ore, which is used as an alloy with copper. Jones had made one contract for 300 tons; none had been delivered. The OPM had recommended the purchase of 178,571 tons of castor seeds, which provide a hydraulic fluid for war machines and a protective coating for plane motors. None had been purchased. The OPM asked for 2,500 tons of cobalt, which strengthens high-speed cutting steels. By April 13, 1942, Jones had contracted for the purchase of 159 tons. The OPM wanted 6,000 tons of corundum from South Africa with which to grind glass and lenses for military purposes. No purchases were made. We are dependent on the Far East for vital fats and oils. In October, 1941, the OPM recommended the purchase of 30,000 tons. In November the figure was raised to 208,000; in January, 1942, to 308,000; in February, to 317,499. By April 13 the RFC had contracted for 2,200 tons of one type of oil; none had been delivered. "For all practical purposes," the Vice-President said, "virtually nothing was done by Mr. Jones to build a government stockpile of fats and oils even after Pearl Harbor, when the Japs were conquering the Far East." Jesse was still waging a sitzkrieg.

Palm oil is essential in making tinplate. The OPM before Pearl Harbor asked for 30,000 tons. Amount purchased by the RFC four months after Pearl Harbor: none. The RFC had bought no flax, though the OPM had recommended the purchase of 6,500 tons. It had bought only 1,210 tons of jute in India, though the OPM wanted 80,000 tons. Sisal twine is essential in harvesting crops. The OPM wanted first 100,000 and then 250,000 tons; Jones has bought about 33,600 tons. Tantalite, one of the most urgent of strategic material needs, was the subject of a flurry of correspondence before Pearl Harbor among the OPM, the State Department, and the RFC. The purchase of 1,000,000 tons was recommended; none was bought. Zirconium is essential in making flares, signals, tracer ammunition, and blasting caps. Three months before Pearl Harbor the OPM urged the purchase of "reasonable amounts" in Brazil. Four months later: no contracts to purchase had yet been made. As in most items, Jones seemed to think the reasonable amount was none at all.

No one with imagination and a sense of responsibility to our fighting men can read the Wallace statement without a sense of agony. For Jones has continued to be the biggest single bottleneck of the war program since, and despite, the April directive. The day after it was issued General MacArthur wired Washington that 2,000,000 seeds of the Far Eastern cinchona had been brought out of the Philippines on one of the last planes leaving for Australia and "must be planted *without delay.*" Cinchona produces quinine, and malaria was a more deadly foe than the Japanese on Bataan. It was proposed to plant the seeds in Costa Rica. It was not until late January, 1943, that the RFC would finally agree to provide some funds for this project. It will be 1946 before any quinine can be produced. The months lost are lives lost. "For all the full power the President has given the Board of Economic Warfare over imports," Wallace said, "we are helpless when Jesse Jones, as our banker, refuses to sign checks in accordance with our directives." If only our enemies had a Jesse Jones, too!

All the vices the worst Congressional ranters attribute to what is left of the New Deal are exemplified in Jones and the RFC. Nowhere will one find a more lush growth of bureaucratic evils; nowhere is there more red tape, nowhere more irresponsibility. Nowhere else has post-war planning — in the sinister sense — so interfered with the war effort. Jones is dominated by the petty ambition of a petty banker's mind — to show a profit on the books of the RFC when the war is over. His great fear is lest RFC operations interfere after the war with business as usual and monopoly. The war itself is incidental and peripheral in his thinking. His arrogance flows from his power; his power from the possession of the greatest money bag in history. Many members of Congress, eager to dip into its bounty for their constituents, are his flunkies.

That the Vice-President has had the courage to expose and attack this millstone around the neck of the war effort should make every decent and patriotic American grateful. That the Vice-President succeeded in killing off the McKellar amendment, as he did the Danaher amendment before it, testifies encouragingly to the existence of a substratum of good sense and non-partisanship in the Senate. But if Jones and his reactionary Southern friends have their way, Wallace will pay for his temerity with the Vice-Presidency. They want the nomination for one of themselves in 1944, and they want Wallace's political scalp.

The first vehicle chosen for the attack is the Byrd committee, which, after meekly accepting Jones's refusal to let it look into the books of the RFC, is now dutifully to be let loose on the BEW. Jones's own reply to the Wallace statement is of interest only to the student of semantics; it rests on over-all figures as to his "commitments" and what he "initiated."

There is always a big gap between Jones's commitments and his actual expenditures; the latest report of the RFC subsidiary which buys up certain commodities to keep them out of the hands of the Axis shows an impressive total of $226,000,000 in authorization — but only $30,000,000 in actual disbursements. Jones cannot afford the investigation on which he loudly insists, and must take the offensive. In that offensive he will have strong support in Congress and even stronger support in the press. For Jones may be staking his future on his attack upon Wallace, and the future of big business is tied up with Jones. His Defense Plant Corporation owns $7,000,000,000 worth of facilities in the aviation, aluminum, synthetic-rubber, magnesium, steel, machine-tool, automotive, radio, and mining industries. And their post-war disposal must be kept in safe hands. On the bargain counter of a post-war deflation, these facilities will lay the basis for fabulous private fortunes. In New Dealish hands they would be a threat to monopoly. "We do not have anybody in our organization," Jones boasted to the House Appropriations Committee in February, "that has any queer ideas." Big business dare not let so sound a thinker go down the drain, whatever comfort his small-mindedness may bring the Axis. Thus, Jones and Wallace not only symbolize the best and worst tendencies in the war effort, as in American life, but are the focal points of the forces striving for mastery of our post-war future. Not only the lives of many in the field but the kind of America to which they will return depends in large part on the outcome of this struggle between the small-town Texas banker and the farmer-idealist from Iowa.

Wallace Betrayed

$\sim\!\!\frown$ $\frown\!\!\sim$

F RANKLIN D. ROOSEVELT has again run out on his friends. The letters to Wallace and Jones are a repetition of the "plague o' both your houses." In 1937 this craven tactic drove from progressive ranks one who might have been America's ablest labor leader instead of the dark menace that he is today. In 1944 it will probably cost Henry Wallace the Vice-Presidency, the New Deal its most promising leader. When the firing grew hot in the Little Steel strike, Roosevelt turned impartially on the workers who believed in him and those who shot them down. Now, smugly even-handed, he equally rebukes the loyal and the disloyal, the lieutenant who risked his political future for the war effort and the lieutenant who sabotaged it. Justice itself could not be more blind.

No one would gather the true state of affairs from the President's complacent epistle of July 15. Until April 13, 1942, power over the importation of strategic materials was divided between Jones's Reconstruction Finance Corporation [RFC] and Wallace's Board of Economic Warfare [BEW]. On that date the President issued a directive placing full power in the BEW and instructing Jones to provide it with the necessary funds on order. Jones has ignored and disobeyed the Presidential directive. Instead of enforcing his order, the President decides to punish both men, the one who was carrying out instructions and the one who was violating them. This may be the comfortable way out, but it is not good administration.

Jones had gone to the Senate Appropriations Committee for an amendment by McKellar which would have restored by law the veto over material imports which was taken from Jones by Presidential directive. Jones was thus in the position of going over his chief's head to Congress. So serious a challenge to the President's authority called for summary action if White House instructions were to be taken seriously in the future. Jones is a powerful man, but the President, if he took his courage in his hands, is more powerful. A fight between them might hurt Roosevelt in 1944, but Roosevelt could ask for Jones's resignation as Secretary of Commerce and Federal Loan Administrator, and my guess is that in a showdown the Texan would knuckle under rather than relinquish a potent national position he might never recover. Roosevelt chose weakly to overlook Jones's insubordination.

What the President, with all his power, feared to do, the Vice-President accomplished. The political reasoning that led the President to acquiesce in the flouting of his authority applied with greater force to the Vice-President. By Roosevelt standards Wallace should have quietly accepted the McKellar amendment and knuckled under to Jones. What Wallace achieved by a brave and outspoken discussion of the facts is the best answer to the defeatist strategy of the White House. When the Senate Appropriations Committee voted down the McKellar amendment, it showed that Jones could be defeated in Congress and that appeasement was not the political necessity it is represented to be in White House apologetics. Wallace was fighting Roosevelt's battle as well as his own. The blow that struck him down was not Jones's but Roosevelt's, and the President chose to run away, not in the heat of battle, but in the flush of victory. The President has never shown less courage.

From several sources, a few days before the President betrayed Wallace, I heard that Speaker Rayburn wanted the Vice-Presidential nomination in 1944 and that the Texas delegation was trying to convince the White House that the Wallace-Jones dispute was an ideal occasion "to get rid of Jones" by sacrificing Wallace. But Jones emerges from this affair with little, if any, diminution of his power and with his prestige at the Capitol enhanced. Everybody knows the President cannot be relied upon to support a subordinate who becomes unpopular or suffers a defeat. Apparently he cannot be relied upon to support one who is victorious. If Wallace was let down by Roosevelt after twice defeating Jones in Congress — the Danaher amendment last December would have accomplished the same purpose for Jones as the McKellar amendment in June — if the President will not stand up in victory for the man he himself picked in 1940 to be his successor, will any lesser official in the future dare flout Jones's wishes, even when Jones himself is flouting the President's?

What rankles most in the President's action is its specious air of fairness. Both Wallace and Jones are to be punished for violating the President's instructions by engaging in an "acrimonious public debate . . . in the public press." But those instructions against intra-Administration quarreling — overlooked by the President in a whole series of cases — permitted subordinates to speak freely before Congressional committees, and Wallace was answering false allegations made in testimony before the Senate Appropriations Committee. It was Jones who violated the agreement reached at the White House conference with Byrnes and Wallace by rushing into print with an attack on Wallace. It was Jones who ignored the President's wish that there be no Congressional investigation of this affair. It was Jones who arranged for an inquiry by his friend Senator George and the Senate Finance Committee and tried to stir up another inquiry in the House. Here again the innocent are punished with the guilty — ostensibly.

Actually only the innocent are punished. The BEW alone is abolished; not the RFC. Jones's friend, Leo T. Crowley, becomes head of a new Office of Economic Warfare [OEW]. He does, indeed, take from the RFC those subsidiaries engaged in importing materials, but these subsidiaries remain dependent on Jones and the RFC for their funds. Byrnes is given final authority over imports in line with policies laid down by Hull. Thus a right-wing quadrumvirate — Crowley, Byrnes, Hull, and Jones — take over from Wallace and Milo Perkins. In Rayburn or Byrnes the President may think he has a running mate better suited to the political climate of 1944. But he has struck a blow, through Wallace, at all that he himself has represented in the minds of the masses. Leon Henderson, Thurman Arnold, Henry Wallace — this is the roll in recent months of the men Roosevelt has sacrificed to the right. The man who created the New Deal seems intent on destroying it before he leaves office in his flaccid retreat before the bourbons of his own party. Isn't it time for labor and the left to look around for new leadership? Newer men, notably Wallace and Willkie, are providing a courageous idealism that contrasts more and more hopefully with the appeasement policies Roosevelt is steadily pursuing in both domestic and foreign policy.

How Washington Reacted

〜 〜

WASHINGTON'S REACTION to the fall of Mussolini was curiously apathetic. Secretary Hull appeared nervous lest he say the wrong thing at Monday's press conference, and afterward the press attachés even asked me — and I am not the most popular of correspondents at the State Department — how I liked the conference. There was an unusually large turnout to hear what the Secretary of State of the world's foremost democratic power would have to say of the fall of the world's first Fascist dictator. Perhaps the most significant observation that can be made on the conference is that Hull seemed ill at ease.

Kingsbury Smith, the Hearst I. N. S. correspondent, who looks like an Italian count but is said to hail from Missouri, took his accustomed place in the front row and opened with the prescribed question: Did the Secretary of State care to make any comments on developments in Italy? Secretary Hull replied that he had long been convinced that fascism carries within it the seeds of its own destruction. The very timely and appropriate ending of Mussolini, he thought — direct quotation is permitted only by special permission and on special occasions — was the first major step in the early and complete destruction and eradication of every vestige of fascism, both nationally and internationally.

If any unusual activity is going on in the State Department as a result of the fall of Mussolini, it is being kept well hidden from the press. There is a Mr. Jones in charge of the Italian "desk" who reports to a new acting chief of the European division whose name I have mislaid. This new chief in turn is subordinate to James Clement Dunn, the department's political adviser for Western Europe and leader of the pro-Franco faction during the Spanish war and since. Over Dunn is Assistant Secretary Breckinridge Long, once our ambassador to Rome and an admirer of Mussolini. Attempts to talk with these officials were courteously discouraged.

In its feuds with newer agencies of the government the State Department insists that it should determine all questions of foreign policy. But when questions of foreign policy are put to it, correspondents are referred to the White House or the War Department or told to keep their minds on the war. Monday's press conference was typical. Secretary Hull was asked whether the government considers the House of Savoy a faction or a former faction of the Fascist authorities. This question — not asked by this correspondent — seemed to all of us a political question and one properly asked of the Secretary of State. Hull's answer was that he didn't know the attitude of the military and naval branches of the government on that question. Naturally, the Secretary continued, the war being still in progress in Italy, so far as the State Department is concerned, it simply had not come to that question. I report that reply as exactly as the rule against quotation marks permits. Is the State Department marking time until the war is over?

This same question seems to have bothered others. Harold Callender of the New York *Times* asked whether there was a danger that victory might come before we were prepared in a diplomatic and political sense. Hull's answer to this was, "Sufficient unto the day. . . ." He looked pleased with himself, as he did at his answer to the next question. Mr. Secretary, he was asked, what is our government doing, if anything, as a result of the developments in Rome yesterday? The answer was — permission to quote directly was later granted — "They are fighting like the devil." Keep your mind on that, Hull added, and we will win the war sooner.

Hull held on to the chair in front of him, blinked his eyes as though the light was too strong for them, occasionally lifted them to look at whatever correspondent asked a question, and spoke in a low-monotonous voice those present found it difficult to hear. (I checked all this with the transcript afterward.) He has a slight speech defect, almost a lisp. Unlike some old men, there is no youth in his eyes, and the fall of Mussolini does not seem to have affected his blood pressure. He said that there was no truth in reports that we had made contact with Badoglio,[1] and that he had heard of no contact with the Vatican in connection with

[1] Pietro Badoglio. Premier of Italy from the fall of Mussolini till 1944. He had previously been Governor of Libya, Viceroy of Ethiopia, and chief of the Italian general staff.

the change in the Italian government. When asked whether unconditional surrender applied also to other Axis allies — Hungary, Rumania, and Bulgaria — he referred the question to the War Department but ventured that the question would certainly be raised against any and all countries that have declared war at any time against the United States. When asked whether that applied to Finland, Hull said Finland was a marginal case. How the State Department loves little Finland!

Correspondents had to keep reminding themselves that the fall of Mussolini was an event. The President at his press conference Tuesday was casual, and when asked his reaction to the resignation of Il Duce, said he never had any reactions and that he was too old to have them. Since Mr. Roosevelt is one of those men who never really grow up — I mean this as a compliment — it seemed odd that the fall of fascism should leave him in so senescent a mood. He showed emotion only in denouncing the Sunday-night short-wave broadcast in which the OWI [Office of War Information] called Badoglio a "high-ranking Fascist" and quoted Samuel Grafton's characterization of Victor Emmanuel as "the moronic little king." I think it cause for disquiet that the warmest Administration reaction to the fall of Mussolini was an attack by the President on a distinguished anti-fascist columnist for the pro-New Deal New York *Post.*

The Administration is making some strange friends these days. Last Monday Cissie Patterson's editor, Frank Waldrop, took this correspondent to task for criticizing the President so severely last week. The Hearst-Patterson-McCormick press and Arthur Krock warmed up to the attack on the OWI and Grafton. Krock accused Grafton of following an "ideology that conforms much more closely to the Moscow than to the Washington-London line," although, as Victor Bernstein pointed out in *PM,* the *Times* the day before had editorially taken much the same line as Grafton toward the Badoglio government, calling it a "military dictatorship" trying by martial law "to protect the Fascist gangsters."

The whole affair has pleased the State Department greatly, for it has put the President in the position of fighting those who have been consistently critical of State Department policy. I am inclined to believe that we have been wrong to characterize it as State Department policy. "Off the record" information I am not privileged to reveal at this time leads me to conclude that the whole North African and French policies are the President's as much as the State Department's, if not more so. While there is a strong faction in the State Department which favors recognition of the French National Committee, as does the British government, the President is said to be strongly opposed. Incredible though it sounds, informed people whom I trust say that one reason for this is that the President still thinks another deal with Pétain may yet be possible and is prepared even to make a deal with Laval, if anything can be obtained from him.

French policy is made more, not less, important by Italian developments. For our military strategy would seem to call for the encirclement of Italy. The idea would be to strike across southern Italy and northward into the Balkans with one arm of the offensive, while the other moves up the Rhone Valley to Alsace. Since these are the obvious avenues of assault, I am revealing geography, not military secrets. The French underground should play an important part in that program, but from all indications the Administration seems unwilling to collaborate with popular forces. The ultra-conservative New York *Sun* in an editorial yesterday bluntly expressed what many officials here would be afraid to say publicly but are none the less acting on privately. The *Sun* said that what America and England were concerned with at the moment was "the prevention of anarchy in Italy," which I take to be a synonym for social revolution. The *Sun* found it "unpleasant to reflect" that the French National Committee "may have given undue weight to the unfortunate phrase that we are fighting to liberate the occupied countries."

Franklin D. Roosevelt is heading straight for a situation which may some day make the Four Freedoms seem as much a mockery to the common people of the world as the Fourteen Points. At home the State Department has obtained greater control of both economic warfare and the Lehman relief organization. Both can be used to give support to a Badoglio government, if it lasts long enough for that. The significance of the Grafton incident is that the President's attitude is giving the State Department the control it has long sought over the OWI's foreign broadcasts. Incidentally, Mayor LaGuardia should also be rebuked by the President, for he too warned the Italian people Sunday night not to be deceived by the substitution of Badoglio for Mussolini.

The situation abroad parallels the situation at home. The London *New Statesman and Nation* last week protested against the appointment of Lord Rennell of Rodd as chief civilian aide to General Sir Harold Alexander in charge of Amgot [Allied Military Government of Occupied Territories]. Lord Rennell was criticized as a financier, a member of the Oxford group, and a former friend of Volpi. He was general manager, so I am informed, of the Bank of International Settlements — that stratospheric refuge of high finance above the clamor of an anti-fascist struggle — and was a partner in Morgan, Grenfell, the London affiliate of J. P. Morgan and Company. Morgan loans and the Vatican blessing were two of the principal supports of the Fascist regime. Given Lord Rennel at the top and the use of Fascist officials at the bottom, Amgot would seem an ideal vehicle for restoring exactly the kind of Italy which bred fascism.

Amgot's sway, according to the present plans here, is to be extended over all of occupied Europe. The Nazi radio in France is already making use of this to dispirit the underground. I am beginning to feel that while we are ready to make deals with any of the crooks at the top except the full-fledged, fully labeled Nazis and Fascists, we are out to demand "unconditional surrender" of the peoples of Europe to what must begin to seem to them Anglo-American imperialism. The Europe that Amgot would restore is not a Europe in which the Four Freedoms could be achieved. The most dangerous development of all is that while Amgot was launched without consulting Moscow, Moscow has since launched a National Committee for a Free Germany without consulting London and Washington. If the present drift is allowed to continue, and without strong public pressure it will, Moscow will be supporting democratic regimes while we sponsor a revival of monarchy and reaction. That way, plain for all to see, lies World War III.

September 18, 1943

Washington Fog

〜ᐟ   ᐟ〜

THE NEWS FROM NEW YORK is that the Sanitation Department had to sweep up twenty-two tons of confetti, ticker tape, and waste paper after the report of Italy's unconditional surrender. No such burden was imposed on the authorities here, where official celebration was restrained. At the State Department Wednesday noon the press room was jammed, and we all felt happy and excited over the news. A bet was made that such an occasion could not fail to get a rise even from Secretary Hull, but your correspondent, who was one of the optimists, must report that he lost the wager. When the Secretary was asked whether he cared to comment on the surrender (after receipt of the official announcement by General Eisenhower), he said — this is as nearly verbatim as the rules allow — that he had nothing to give us, that he had no comment to make, and that he had nothing to say at that time. It would have been nice if the Secretary had at least smiled and said something like, "I haven't any formal comment but you all know how I feel. It's swell." But I suppose I'm being utopian again.

At the White House the only word Steve Early had from the President was that this was Eisenhower's show.

Yesterday Hull was slightly more informative. He said he hoped to be able to comment more fully, more definitely, at a little later stage. This would seem to indicate that there might be something more in the wind, though it is unsafe to rely on deduction from the Secretary's nebulous phrases. On Wednesday, for example, he was asked whether the Anglo-American-Soviet Mediterranean Commission would deal primarily with military matters. Hull's somewhat perplexing answer was that this was why he was not in a position to give out any information. That sounded as though the commission would be largely military and as though news of it would therefore have to be obtained from the War Department. But this morning Harold Callender, who has an inside track at the department, reported in the New York *Times* that through its representation on the commission the Soviet Union "will participate in economic and political decisions touching Italy and the entire Mediterranean basin."

The whole question of the Mediterranean Commission is mystifying. On Saturday, September 4, Churchill made a long "off the record" talk at a National Press Club luncheon. "Authoritative-source" stories followed in the next day's papers. The best of these was the four-column story by Paul W. Ward in the Baltimore *Sun,* and I recommend a careful reading of it to all who are interested in obtaining a clear view of British foreign policy at this time. Churchill is still the 1890 imperialist. At the luncheon it was revealed that there were under consideration plans, as yet tentative, for the creation of a Mediterranean Commission on which presumably Russia would have equal representation with Britain and the United States. Several days later this elicited some surprise "in the highest quarters" here. (I'm sorry to have to write this way but there are rules, and this will at least give the reader an idea of the fog in which reporters who cover foreign policy have to wander.) At the State Department Hull's first reaction seemed to be one of ignorance. It may be that the commission is a British idea and that the White House, with its close ties to the Vatican, is embarrassed at the prospect of Soviet participation in political decisions on Italy, even if Stalin is permitting the Russian Orthodox church to convoke a synod.

This talk of a three-power commission and General Eisenhower's announcement that the surrender terms had been approved by the Soviet as well as the American and British governments would seem to constitute the best news in some time on the diplomatic front. On what our government is planning for Italy's future I have, frankly, no real news. Neither has anyone else. I note that Salvemini and La Piana's excellent and indispensable new book, *What to Do with Italy,* agrees generally with the Kingsbury Smith crypto-official article, Our Government's Plan for a Defeated Italy, in the August issue of the *American Mercury,* though the former is written from the anti-clerical left, the latter from the piously pro-State Department right. Salvernini and La Piana say we are in Italy to prevent a republican social revolution; Kingsbury Smith, to prevent anarchy. It seems fairly clear that we do not intend to force democracy on the Italian people. With one exception, official pronouncements here and abroad to the Italian people are uniformly lacking in any appeal that might be construed as an invitation to establish free government. The one exception was Secretary of War Stimson's reference yesterday to the Risorgimento as "a glorious chapter in the history of human freedom." The Secretary said it was our purpose to recreate this freedom. But, then, Stimson is unregenerate in his democratic beliefs, as demonstrated once before by his public appeal for the lifting of the embargo against the Spanish Republic.

Whatever our plans for Italy, an attempt will be made to use Eisenhower's victory to consolidate Hull's position. Arthur Krock has already discovered that the unconditional surrender was a triumph of State Department policies, though aided of course by "General Eisenhower's military expedients, which logically progressed from them." This is certainly putting a wee little cart before a very big horse. A Krock scoop is the discovery that by refusing to grant full recognition to De Gaulle we "encouraged hope in Axis-subjugated nations that they will be left free to select their own civil governments." What he really means is that by our attitude toward De Gaulle we encouraged trimmers like Victor Emmanuel and Badoglio to believe that no attachment of ours to democratic and popular forces would stand in the way whenever they decided that it had become profitable to shift sides. Another reflection of this is the eagerness of the Hungarian, Rumanian, and Bulgarian ruling classes to jump on our bandwagon and get the protection of our troops against popular uprisings. This may hasten a Balkan invasion.

I never dreamed that Hull would some day force us to make a hero of Sumner Welles. An even stranger episode may be in the making. The indications are that Robert Murphy, now on his way home, will not return to North Africa. Department gossip suspects that Murphy has fallen out of favor with both Hull and Roosevelt because he was won over to full recognition of the French National Committee. Murphy seems to be regarded now as too favorable to the Gaullists. The President, it would seem, has never been closer in outlook to his Secretary of State. A new executive order is said to be in preparation which will greatly increase Hull's authority over Lend-Lease, Relief and Rehabilitation, the OEW [Office of Economic Warfare] and other agencies operating abroad. One proposal is to make Stettinius and Lehman Assistant Secretaries of State. Silence, meanwhile, continues to reign over the unmarked political grave of Sumner Welles. I am told that the Secretary will wait until Congress convenes before announcing the

Welles resignation and the name of his successor. It seems to be feared that an earlier announcement would give public opinion time to work up enough protest to make it difficult to obtain Senate confirmation of the new candidate for Under Secretary. If this is true, one would tend to conclude that Hull's choice is still someone of the type of Breckinridge Long or James Clement Dunn or Norman H. Davis.

October 9, 1943

Stettinius and State

THE INNER CIRCLE at the State Department suffered a defeat when the President appointed Edward R. Stettinius, Jr., Under Secretary of State and set up the new Foreign Economic Administration [FEA]. Secretary Hull would have preferred Breckinridge Long or Norman H. Davis as Under Secretary. Some of his closest departmental advisers had hoped to bring Lend-Lease, the Office of Economic Warfare [OEW], and Foreign Relief and Rehabilitation directly under State Department control. These agencies were assigned instead to the new FEA under Leo T. Crowley. According to the President's executive order, the new agency was also to take over the Office of Foreign Economic Coordination, which has been operating in the State Department under Assistant Secretary Dean Acheson. But this section of the executive order contained a parenthetic loophole — "(except such functions and personnel thereof as the Director of the Budget shall determine are not concerned with foreign economic operations)" — and the department at this writing seems to be hoping to salvage and retain this office and most of the men in it. It contains many new men and much fresh young blood.

One of the methods which Mr. Roosevelt uses to keep his audience from getting too restive is to shift the scenes and costumes from time to time. If a change had to be made, it wasn't a bad idea to place all foreign economic activities under a single agency, and it was a good idea to organize that new agency outside the State Department. One of the obstacles to good government is the tendency of departments to grow too large for any one man to handle, and a far better administrator than

Secretary Hull would have been a bottleneck if these activities had all been placed under his jurisdiction. Crowley has wisely announced that he will retain Lend-Lease, Relief and Rehabilitation, and Economic Warfare as divisions within the new FEA.

Crowley is not one of those characters who burn with a hard, gemlike flame. He has managed to keep several jobs and his health by letting well enough alone. As Alien Property Custodian, he has been nothing to write harshly to the Bank of International Settlements about. Where there has been no outside pressure, Crowley has let big business and the carteleers have their way. But he will also leave alone the progressives under him, provided only that there is peace and quiet. All things considered — I am beginning to feel like Boethius adjusting himself to the barbarians — those agencies could have a much worse boss than Crowley.

I would not speak harshly of the departed, but it is wise to remember that under Milo Perkins, for all his devoted work and courageous struggle, the Board of Economic Warfare [BEW] was beginning in many of its sections to be a little replica of the WPB [War Production Board]. By a gravitational process whose effects are visible everywhere in government, private interests were taking over control of the strategic posts directing them. Though Perkins is gone, the same private interests are still active. But Crowley has announced that Lauchlin Currie will remain as executive officer in charge of economic warfare, and I know of no abler or more genuine progressive in Washington. It is equally good news that Crowley has placed Murray Latimer in charge of foreign relief and rehabilitation. Latimer is an old and devoted New Dealer. I know little about Bernard Knollenberg, who was senior deputy administrator of Lend-Lease under Stettinius and is to remain acting administrator of this division under Crowley.

Almost everyone, including *The Nation*'s own dour correspondent, seemed pleased by the Stettinius appointment. Lindley likes him, Lippmann likes him, the *Daily Worker*'s Lapin likes him (though in moderation), and Helen Essary in Cissie Patterson's *Times-Herald* positively gurgled. "Mr. Hull, Mr. Stettinius, and Mr. Harriman," Mrs. Essary believes, "will make an elegant trio of good-looking, intelligent Americans when they bow to Mr. Stalin. . . . Long-legged ambassadors are always impressive — and smooth." Stettinius does seem to be what readers of less literate publications than *The Nation* would call a swell egg — an unfamiliar type in the State Department, where most of the officials seem to be trying hard to look like one of their own ancestral portraits. Since we are gathered together, however, to do more than size up a new recruit for a college fraternity, it might be well to subject the Stettinius appointment to dispassionate scrutiny.

Stettinius is a White House choice, and that means that the Under Secretaryship is once again to be held by a Roosevelt man rather than a Hull man. This is to the good, though the President and his Secretary are much closer than the former likes the liberals to think. Stettinius was acceptable to Hull. Stettinius did not object to giving the State Department greater control over the economic agencies. One plan was to place these agencies in the department and make the heads of each an Assistant Secretary. Stettinius, unlike Lehman, was reported to be in favor of this proposal. For Stettinius does not like to take too much responsibility. He was continually in hot water at the Defense Commission and the OPM [Office of Production Management] when he had to make decisions. He did not begin to make friends and influence people until he was placed in charge of Lend-Lease. Most decisions were made for Lend-Lease by other agencies. Materials were allocated to it by the WPB, food by the WFA [War Food Administration], munitions by a joint Anglo-American munitions board. Stettinius could make promises but not assure deliveries. That rested in other hands.

Stettinius is a likeable and unspoiled variety of the genus rich man's son. He was one of the big business men cultivated by Hopkins in order to give the New Deal some upper-class support. As head of United States Steel, Stettinius — like J. P. Morgan and Company, the firm's financial advisers — was relatively friendly to labor and enlightened on price problems. At the Defense Commission, where he was in charge of materials, he helped the basic raw-material monopolies, especially in steel and aluminum, to ward off expansion. At the OPM, where he was in charge of priorities, he failed to impose them strictly enough to end the waste of steel, aluminum, copper, rubber, and other vital materials by booming civilian industries. In neither case did his inaction spring from lack of patriotism. He naturally believed what he was told by his big-business colleagues and customers; he is that kind of man. At Lend-Lease, with many young New Dealers on his staff instead of Gano Dunns, dealing with matters which did not immediately affect his own business, Stettinius won the liking of men who had previously attacked him. Again like Morgan, he was friendly to Britain and the Soviets, and this is important in his new position.

He is a man of good-will, but he is not forceful, shrewd, or well-informed. The deft and subtle cliques in the State Department may find this big guileless boy scout easy pickings.

F.D.R.'s Victory

〜〜 〜〜

THE PRESIDENT, in one of his darkest hours, has won one of his greatest victories. Democratic national headquarters are in mourning; the election returns seem to foreshadow a Republican victory in 1944. The OPA [Office of Price Administration], main bastion of the home front, is in deepest gloom; large sections of labor, agriculture, and industry are wilfully insistent on price and wage increases likely to unloose a disastrous inflation. This is the moment at which the President, by consummate strategy, has at last succeeded in leading the United States out of isolationism and into a concert of powers for the preservation of peace. He has used a conservative Southern Democrat to bring about an entente between capitalist America and Communist Russia. And as this is being written tonight there is every indication that the Senate, where Wilson's hopes foundered, will by more than a two-thirds' vote approve the four-power pact at Moscow. This is a historic achievement, the first step toward preventing World War III; and except for a handful of mischief-makers here, there is a general feeling of satisfaction among men of the most diverse views over what Roosevelt and Secretary of State Hull have accomplished.

At the State Department, newspapermen who have been critical are being greeted with jubilation. The Moscow pact is felt to be a complete answer to the critics; the critics, for their part, are pleased with the results of the three-power conference — for which, they feel, they can claim some credit. The uproar over the Welles affair had made Secretary Hull exceedingly sensitive to the charge of being anti-Soviet and anxious to prove that he was as good a diplomat as his former subaltern. This was a propitious mood in which to send him off to Moscow. As one of the correspondents who have been most critical of Hull in the past, and will probably be so again in the future, I honor him for his achievement. In White House circles the Moscow pact is regarded as fully justifying the President's action in forcing the resignation of Welles at the price of keeping Hull. To have the Moscow agreement made by the idol of the anti-New Dealers, an irreproachable conservative, is considered to be worth many compromises.

Had the Moscow pact been presented to the Senate some time after the passage of the Connally resolution, the "but" brigade would have taken ample advantage of its vague wording and many loopholes. It is fortunate that the determined group of fourteen Senators led by Pepper and the sponsors of the B2H2 resolution had drawn out the debate and blocked a count on the Connally measure until the Moscow pact was announced. The release of the text in the midst of the debate caught the fence-straddlers and the quasi-isolationists off guard. They were forced to prove that they meant what they said when they claimed to be for international cooperation. All but the extreme isolationists at once claimed the Moscow pact as their own. Connally said "the sentiments therein expressed" were "in substantial conformity" with the terms of his resolution; the Pepper group welcomed the Moscow agreement as "the kind of clear declaration of principle" Pepper and his colleagues had sought to write into the Connally measure. The ignominious Taft thought that "on the whole the Moscow declaration is far more like the Mackinac resolution," and when Connally incorporated language from the Moscow announcement in his resolution, it was Vandenberg who suggested that by unanimous consent these additions be considered a part of the original resolution instead of an amendment. Senator Carter Glass deserves a large share of the credit for this move, which provides all but formal ratification and the force of a treaty to the Moscow agreement.

One of the principal fears expressed during the debate on the Connally resolution was that it might be construed as having approved in advance a treaty later to be negotiated by the Administration. The Washington *Star* quoted unnamed State Department officials as saying that the Moscow declaration had the force of a treaty, though it did not require ratification by the Senate. This evoked a statement from Connolly declaring that this anonymous report had been strongly denied by Under Secretary Stettinius. Whatever the value of the denial, and whatever the name applied to the Moscow declaration, it involves far more than a mere statement of generalities. It envisages continuous action through a joint political commission in London; it has already committed the powers to specific action in the case of Austria, and in the case of Italy to a general line of policy in regard to reconquered territory. The declaration involves a great deal more than most treaties, and it is obvious that in it the Administration has found another of its devices to circumvent the Senate on international policy. The passage of the Connally resolution in a form embodying language from the Moscow declaration places the President in a powerful position to carry on under its terms without further reference to the Senate. Mr. Roosevelt has outwitted his opponents again.

The Moscow agreement must be read in the light of the Soviet declaration that Russia's 1941 boundaries were not open to discussion. It is agreed here that nothing short of a successful war against them would lead the Soviets to give up what they consider the boundaries necessary to their security. A small group of Senatorial pseudo-isolationists, led by Reynolds and Wheeler, seemed anxious during the debate on the Connally resolution to lay the basis for just such an armed conflict. I called them pseudo-isolationists because the isolationist position they assumed during Hitler's period of expansion has been exchanged for the most open kind of interventionism against the Soviet Union. In these Senators the Atlantic Charter has found new and stronger devotees.

Reynolds, once the hero of the Bundists, seems to have become the chief reliance of the Poles, and he who glossed over Hitler's aggressions now tells the Senate, "If Soviet Russia intends to have and to hold the once-free Baltic republics and parts of Poland ... that intention must be resisted by force of arms or be permitted to prevail by default. ... Civilized nations have never been isolationist in their attitude toward international bandits and robbers." Reynolds has also become the champion of the colored peoples. He wants the Four Freedoms granted to "all colors of skin," but instead of starting his reforms in the army — as chairman of the Military Affairs Committee he is reported to be a powerful influence in promoting the segregation policy — he casts a demagogic eye on the British Empire. Wheeler, who excused the partition of Czechoslovakia at Munich, is worried about Soviet designs on Outer Mongolia.

This is the new isolationism. It speaks the language of idealism but parallels the Nazi line for the propagation of dissension among the Allies. The Senate rejected it by a vote of 70 to 15 in turning down the Danaher amendment, but all the Senatorial franks will spread the new brand of anti-Soviet poision assiduously. The same breed of men who once asked, "Why die for Danzig?" are now preparing to give their all for Bessarabia.

November 20, 1943

A Nation of Cry-Babies

P RICE AND WAGE STABILIZATION is complicated busi-
ness. You start with the simple concept of a ceiling, and you end by
analyzing the hind quarters of a steer to make sure that the price control
isn't circumvented by substituting an inferior cut of meat for a better.
You insert a control at one point in your war economy and find you have
twenty problems for each one you have solved. The present shenanigans
of the corn-hog ratio may serve to illustrate the complexities. If the price
of hogs gets too far ahead of the price of corn, it pays farmers better to
feed their corn to their hogs and sell it as pork than to put the corn on
the market *in persona propria*. The ratio at this time, though narrower
than a year ago, is still too wide. Chicago stockyards are glutted with
hogs, while the shortage of corn is hampering other branches of
agriculture (dairies, poultry, cattle) which also need corn for feed, and
many sections of war industry, which use it in making alcohol (converted
in turn into smokeless powder and synthetic rubber), plastics, paper, and
other materials.

Because so much corn grunts its way to Chicago as pork, scarce
tankers must be used to bring molasses from the Caribbean for alcohol,
and Great Lakes steamers needed for iron must be diverted to bring
wheat from Canada for Northeastern livestock. Politics doesn't make the
situation any simpler. The Department of Agriculture, largely responsible for this disarranged corn-hog ratio, has always been oriented
toward the Midwest and is as Republican-minded, even under Democratic Administrations, as the corn belt. While booming farm prices
haven't made the Midwest any less Republican — it turns slightly

Democratic only in adversity — the chief sufferers from the march of relatively low-priced corn into decidedly high-priced hogs have been Northeastern dairy and poultry farmers and Southwestern cattle raisers. The latter are Democrats by tradition, the former occasionally Democrats by persuasion. Neither tradition not persuasion is likely to hold them in line in the absence of plentiful feed supplies, and the 1944 election cannot be won without them.

On this, as on other sectors of the crumbling anti-inflation front, the Administration is trying to cushion the producer's feed-supply difficulties with a subsidy, instead, for example, of raising the price of milk. One virtue of this approach, as that excellent little farm paper *Spade* pointed out recently, is its economy: it would take a $2 price increase to put an equivalent $1 in the pocket of the farmer. It is cheaper to do it directly, by a subsidy, which has the added merit of holding down the cost of living. This virtue of the subsidy is its chief defect in the eyes of the distributor and the middleman. And if the truth be told, it does not appeal greatly to the farmer, whom the vagaries of nature have made a gambler. His hankering as a debtor for the roulette of inflation has haunted American politics for several generations, and like every other class and group in our country he is much quicker to see his immediate profit advantage as a producer than his ultimate fate in a general debacle. Far more serious than the corn-hog ratio is the hog-patriot ratio, which has never in our history been wider. In Congress the voices of moderation find it hard to be heard, and good men are stampeded — Voorhis and Pepper, for example, on citrus fruits — by the greedy squeals. All the great lobbies in action against price control and subsidies — oil, meat, citrus, milk — have been fattened by the war, but each feels a sense of grievance because his neighbor at the trough seems to be getting more swill.

With the exception of some low-paid workers — the canners and food processors in the so-called farm bloc are among the worst offenders — and a stratum of white-collar workers with fixed incomes, there is not a class or a group in this country which has not benefited by the war, which is not eating better — yes, eating better — and living better than it did before. Anyone who spends a few days covering the present price-control fight comes away with the impression that we are the world's greatest nation of cry-babies. It is a paradox of which we should feel ashamed that the weakest spot today in the United Nations is not among the poor battered Chinese, or the bombed and blasted British, or the Russians, heroic and virile amid their country's devastation, but on the home front of our own country, the one that has suffered least and benefited most and occupies the softest spot in the greatest war of human history. This is no reflection on our good men at the front, but only upon the snivelers at home, where everybody wants the cost of living held down, but everybody also wants his own income pushed up. This mathematical miracle would be too much for an Einstein, certainly for a Roosevelt.

I believe that were the President vigorously to roll back prices, he might yet save the country and himself, but his ability to do so without Congressional approval is constitutionally dubious and would be politically possible only in an atmosphere of crisis. At the bottom of the situation is the general feeling that the Russians will soon defeat Hitler, and then help us take care of the Japs. If this is correct, a general loosening of the line on wages and prices, the easiest course for the Administration and the one it will probably adopt, may do little harm. But if the Germans extricate enough of their men from the Russian front to put up a real fight in Western Europe, and the war lasts until the winter of 1944–45, the inflationary spiral will get out of control and the war may be lost on the home front. An inflation, at the very least, would lay the foundations for terrible economic maladjustments after the war and a strong fascist movement based on an impoverished middle class.

Never before has our democratic system seemed so clearly a wrangle of pressure groups rather than a voicing of the general will on the general welfare. Never before was it so necessary for the leaders of each group to forget the coming elections — political and trade union — and tell a few unpleasant economic truths to their own people. Our task is to do so on the labor front, where the cowardly surrender to Lewis has penalized the bulk of labor leadership, which better than any other group has helped hold the line. What needs to be said to labor, as steel prepares to follow coal, automobiles to follow steel, that three or four billions more in the pay envelopes of our workers will be worse than meaningless, since (1) there just aren't the goods to buy with it, and (2) it will only help push up other prices. Ultimately none will suffer more than labor if wages and prices begin chasing themselves around and up the inflationary Maypole. I know the main offender is the farm bloc and its processor allies. I know huge profits are being made in war industry. I know the Administration has been unable to keep its pledges regarding prices. I still say that a general rise in wages except for low-paid and fixed-pay workers is an illusion. It is unfortunate but it is true that the only course open to labor is to put up a fight to hold the cost-of-living line. Better to wage a slowly losing battle on that front than to kid ourselves into disaster.

December 11, 1943

The Indian Skeleton at Atlantic City

THE PRESSURE OF EVENTS is making it harder than ever for the Administration to maintain its docile silence on India. A series of recent events has rendered our tacit partnership in Churchill's imperialism all the more ignominious. The latest was the announcement from Cairo of freedom after the war for Korea. Earlier there was the Lebanon affair, where we meekly and quickly followed the British lead in rebuking the French for doing on a more moderate scale in the Levant what the British are doing in India and elsewhere. The Atlantic Charter[1] is being applied, with much fanfare, to a French mandate in the Near East and at least to one Japanese possession in the Far East, but is still in suspension in British Middle Asia.

The closing days of the United Nations Relief and Rehabilitation conference at Atlantic City provided another instance of the way in which India haunts the Anglo-American entente. India is asked to give 1 percent of its national income to relieve the hungry in liberated areas, but it was denied the right to speak of its own starving millions. Sir Girja Shankar Bajpai, "India's delegate" to the conference, with a propriety becoming in a servant of the British Raj, declined to raise the question. It was, the British delegation assured the press, outside the scope of the UNRRA [United Nations Relief and Rehabilitation Administration]. J. J. Singh of the India League of America threatened to disrupt these convenient diplomatic niceties by disclosing to the correspondents last Friday that the Chinese, Mexican, Chilean, New Zealand, South African,

[1]The Atlantic Charter (August 14, 1941) stated the peace aims of the U.S. and Britain and included a declaration of the right of self-determination of nations.

and Australian representatives were prepared to support India if the question of the famine were raised. Dr. T. F. Tsiang, head of the Chinese delegation, made a public statement supporting Singh. There was talk of a resolution whereby the UNRRA would ask the Combined Shipping Board to allocate some extra tonnage for food shipments to India, and it looked as if some unpleasant realities were no longer unavoidable. There was reason to believe that Governor Lehman, director general of the UNRRA, would have welcomed discussion of the Indian question.

There followed a hurried series of conferences between the Dominion delegations and Colonel John J. Llewellin, the chief British delegate, and a sudden announcement to the press by Colonel Llewellin that any resolution on India would be "out of order." No one had the temerity to ask how the British delegate, representing one nation out of forty-four, could take it upon himself to decide this question in advance. Colonel Llewellin and Assistant Secretary of State Dean Acheson dominated the proceedings, and it behooved the other delegates to behave. I doubt whether Acheson was happy over this brusque solution of the Indian problem, and at the closing session, with British approval, he was permitted to make a statement expressing sympathy with the people of India. Sir Girja rose to accept Acheson's little floral wreath with an appropriately brief statement, and the skeleton was back in the closet. But American officials here realize only too well that it will not stay put.

Every American official back from India brings the same message. There have been three official missions to India, and all brought back conclusions unpalatable to London. Colonel Louis Johnson, the President's first emissary, was accused by the British of having been "hypnotized" by Nehru. The Grady report was shelved because its proposals for expanding industrial production in India would have conflicted with British colonial policy. Indian henchmen of the Raj attacked it as "American imperialism." William Phillips, the second emissary, had one session with the President and another, at the President's request, with Churchill. The gossip is that the President was friendly but felt his hands were tied. As for Churchill, the talk around town is that Phillips got nowhere with him. "Phillips said Churchill simply refused to discuss the question; all he did was rant," was the version I picked up. If some of this gossip is unfair, the British and American governments have their own secrecy to thank for it. I was told that Phillips implied in talks with friends that he was not allowed to see Gandhi and Nehru because they were ready to discuss possible terms of settlement. I cannot vouch for this information and merely report what I heard from what I consider a fairly good source.

There is widespread dissatisfaction in the government with the Indian situation. Inside the State Department pro-British elements, fighting to give Britain a square deal after the war on such questions as shipping, are hampered by the use that anti-British and Irish Catholic sources inside and outside the department make of India. War production and export agencies, worried by the situation in the hungry machine-tool industry, wonder why we cannot ease the inflationary situation in India by exports of machinery for production of consumer goods. Agencies like the OWI [Office of War Information] and the Office of Strategic Services, which deal with questions of political warfare, feel that we are being compromised in the East by Britain's Indian policy. I have heard of the embarrassment felt by OWI officials in India on the receipt of posters showing how we were feeding the people of Sicily. India's treatment at Atlantic City and the discussion bound to take place at New Delhi when the Indian legislature is asked to ratify the 1 percent contribution will not make the OWI's task easier. The best propaganda now would be some additional food shipments, and I have found general agreement among officials dealing with shipping that it is nonsense to talk of a shipping shortage in connection with food for India. With some 50,000,000 tons available, much of it inadequately utilized, a few hundred thousand tons of shipping could easily be allocated to ease the famine.

The obstacle to acceptance of the recent Canadian offer of 100,000 tons of free wheat for India, and to purchases from the bumper crop glutting the Argentine, is not shipping but politics. The British position, as I get it here from British sources, is that the famine is due to hoarding, maldistribution, and inflation rather than to an actual shortage. Shipments made under pressure from public opinion would imply embarrassing admissions in British domestic politics, revive hopes of American interferences in India. I have no doubt in my own mind, after talking with American, British, and Indian authorities, that hoarding, maldistribution, inflation, and the hostility of Indian interests to effective food and price controls have played a much larger part in the present situation than Indians like to admit. Farm blocs are the same the world over. The real point, it seems to me, is that only a true national government of Indians could hope at a time like this to squeeze from the peasantry the necessary driblets of food by which urban India is normally fed. Conversely, the present government of India could hardly be expected to antagonize the large landowners, who are among its few supporters, by instituting really vigorous controls.

Many factors, some accidental, play their part in the present shortage, but the basic cause is imperialism. Britain has drained India of goods, paying for them in blocked sterling accounts in London against which paper is issued in India. India's new-found "wealth" in sterling is only a reflection of its impoverishment by the war effort. The one genuine solution for inflation would be greater production in India of consumer goods, but this would cut into Britain's post-war market. The other way to make the situation bearable would be to give India a responsible and representative government and make its people feel that this is their war. In normal times the heavy burden of debt and taxes forces the peasant to turn a portion of his scanty crop into cash. With the rise in prices this burden is reduced, and it is difficult to hold him down to a near-starvation diet. If Gandhi and Nehru were in office instead of in jail, they might appeal to his idealism. That task is beyond the power of the Viceroy and his kept Indians.

Grist for Goebbels

꙳Ꙩ

WERE THE PRINCIPAL EVENTS of the past week in Washington to be broadcast by the Axis radio, listeners in occupied Europe and Asia would be inclined to dismiss what they heard as typical Axis exaggerations, if not downright lies. They would hear that in America race prejudice was still so strong that sixteen Southern railroads preferred to suffer from a shortage of firemen rather than hire unemployed Negroes qualified by experience for such work. They would hear that in America respect for authority was so weak, recognition of the need for discipline in war time so rudimentary, that when a Presidential committee ordered those railroads to cease discriminating against Negroes, they publicly announced their refusal to obey and were applauded for it in Congress. Listeners under the Nazi heel, aware of the uses to which prejudice can be put, might be tempted to suspect American railroad "capitalists" of pitting race against race. But they would feel certain that they were listening to some more of Goebbels's handiwork if the Axis radio ventured to tell them that the action of the railroads was largely due to pressure from one of the most advanced sections of the American labor movement, the Railroad Brotherhoods. Past experience with Axis propaganda might lead listeners to scoff at the statement that these progressive unions had been forcing railroads to discharge Negro firemen and give their jobs to whites. The Axis radio would purport to quote a Malcolm Ross, chairman of the President's Fair Employment Practices Committee, as explaining that Negroes had done most of the work as firemen on Southern railroads for half a century "until automatic stokers and Diesel-powered engines changed the dirty, heavy work into desirable jobs." The implications of this would seem another of those ugly Nazi canards, aimed this time at the working class of the South. These same brotherhoods — let us imagine we are listening for a moment longer to that Axis radio — are prepared to tie up the whole American railroad system on the eve of the second-front invasion. The five operating brotherhoods have ordered a strike to begin on December 30, and this order is the work not of an irresponsible minority manipulating the unions but of democratic processes and majority vote. The term "majority vote" is inadequate. For the vote was almost unanimous: 97.7 per cent of the 350,000 operating workers cast their ballot for strike action.

Their grievance is that a government board granted a four-cents-an-hour raise. They had prepared to strike for eight cents. (Sophisticated French workers accustomed to the tactics used by the "capitalist" press to inflame soldiers against workers will think this familiar propaganda when they hear it over their radios.) The non-operating unions are also threatening a strike. They want an eight-cents-an-hour raise "straight across the board." They were awarded a raise ranging from ten cents an hour for the lowest-paid workers to four cents an hour for the highest. The difference between the award and the demand in terms of total aggregate wage increase for non-operating railway workers is estimated at less than 10 percent. (Imagine listening to this through the ears of a Chinese or a Yugoslav guerrilla.) Axis propaganda operates on the principle that the bigger the lie the harder it is for common folk to doubt it. But here we encounter the corollary: the more shameful the truth the harder it is for common folk to believe it.

I suppose that members of the brotherhoods will consider this unfair. Like everyone else, they have their grievances. The wages of the operating railroad workers have not risen as much as those of workers in manufacturing industries, but they were a good deal higher to start with. The question they must ask themselves is whether the difference between four cents an hour and eight cents an hour is worth a nation-wide strike call in the middle of a great war. I know that they feel pretty certain that there will be no strike. But what of the soldier abroad who hears of this strike call? What are his feelings likely to be? Will he be more friendly or less to the labor movement on his return, when American labor may face the greatest battle of its existence? Can brotherhoods which practice prejudice-as-usual and resort to strikes-as-usual expect to be considered on any better level than men who practice business-as-usual? The non-operating railroad workers have a stronger case than the operating, for they include some of the lowest-paid workers in the country. But the Vinson formula which they rejected would have given the lowest-paid third in their ranks more than an eight-cent raise. The question they must ask themselves is whether the minor differences between the Vinson award and the eight-cents-for-all that they want is worth the passage of the Truman resolution, a resolution which throws the doors open to a series of measures which will boost the cost of living.

The seventy-four-to-four vote in the Senate for the Truman resolution derived from many sources, few flattering to labor. One was the power of an organized minority like the brotherhoods. Another was the fear, expressed on the Senate floor, that the alternative would be a strike, and that the strike would lead to government operation of the roads, which are waxing fat on war profits. A third was the desire of the pro-inflationary forces in agriculture and industry further to compromise the hold-the-line fight, to make passage of subsidy legislation more difficult, to clear the way for similar legislation on milk, coal, oil, and a long list of other products. A Congress which talks as though it believes in laissez faire is entering with enthusiasm into the game of raising prices and wages by legislative fiat, an easy way to buy votes. The cost will be national disaster, with labor among the worst sufferers. A taste of what is coming may be obtained from the Disney bill to boost the price of crude oil, which passed the House 171 to 92, despite a brave fight by two oil-district Congressmen, Monroney of Oklahoma and Patman of Texas.

The pernicious parity concept, which tore a gap in the dike against inflation at the very beginning by boosting food prices, is extended by the Disney bill to petroleum. This threatens to launch a kind of leapfrog advance to inflation. The general commodity index, thanks largely to higher farm prices, has risen much more than prices of basic commodities like oil, which we have hitherto managed to hold down. "Parity" here means that we must provide an equivalent increase for crude oil. This in turn will push the general index still higher, laying the basis for further "parity" increases. Under this system the sky's the limit. There is no doubt that some marginal oil men have suffered from higher costs, and premium payments might well be used to stimulate the digging of new wells. But to grant a price boost of from thirty-five to seventy-four cents a barrel, as the Disney bill would, to all producers, further enriching some of the biggest profiteers in the war, is economically indefensible and politically scandalous.

PART VI

1944

January 8, 1944

What F.D.R. Forgot

~~~ ~~~

ONE OMISSION from the President's list of New Deal accomplishments seems to have escaped the attention of the press. This was the passage of the Wagner Act. The omission is symptomatic. With steel and railroad strikes threatening, the President may have thought it impolitic to boast of the part his Administration played in the organization of American labor and in guaranteeing the right of collective bargaining. I do not think the omission was accidental; if it was accidental, it was the kind of lapse of memory Freud explained for us. I am inclined to think it was deliberate, since the list of New Deal accomplishments and the Bunyanish parable about "Dr. New Deal" and "Dr. Win-the-War" were carefully prepared — though the President, like the artist that he is, gave them an air of improvisation.

Another accomplishment the President did not mention was the TVA, though he might easily have boasted of the great part it has played in war production. Perhaps the lambasting that Henry Wallace has taken for his reference to TVA's on the Danube helps to explain this omission. The President's list was prepared to evoke the shadow of the Hoover debacle. "Dr. New Deal," the President said, had established a sound banking system, saved homes and farms from foreclosure, and rescued agriculture from disaster. These accomplishments, which led his list, represent a good middle-class reform program; minimum wages and maximum hours were put down near the bottom. Mr. Roosevelt wanted a list that was difficult to assail politically. That he succeeded is indicated by the New York *Times*'s admission that "by and large it cannot be disputed that the New Deal introduced into American life a very considerable number of reforms which were long overdue." Once this is admitted, Mr. Roosevelt's opponents can only quarrel with him over details, and that, in the midst of a world war, hardly makes for an effective campaign.

The *Wall Street Journal,* surveying the prospects for 1944, reported succinctly if lugubriously, "Statistics Favor a G.O.P. Victory but Democrats Still Have Roosevelt." The President is off to a brilliant start. His New Deal press conference, taken in connection with the conference of the preceding Tuesday, was as deft a piece of political footwork as anything in his career. He knows that the attention of electorates, like that of children, flags easily and needs new phrases and faces. "Win the War" is new and is also the obvious slogan for 1944; F.D.R. has preempted it. The offhand way in which the change of slogans was announced was seized upon by the opposition as a confession of past error. The President, by defending an unassailable record and indicating — though very cautiously — that there may be more of the same after the war, has put himself in a position his opponents must envy. He can run in 1944 as a non-partisan Win-the-War President without losing his franchise as a New Dealer. It will take more than MacArthur's profile to beat that one.

The range of possibilities for a President is never a wide one; constitutional and political necessities impose narrow limits on the leadership he can exert. Mr. Roosevelt is now, as always, just a wee bit to left of center, a little ahead of majority opinion today as he was a little behind it in the greatest days of the New Deal. The New Deal has been a strange and changing thing since the beginning. Aside from this vague phrase, reminiscent of Teddy Roosevelt's Square Deal, Wilson's New Freedom, and poker, Mr. Roosevelt's chief difference from Mr. Hoover in the 1932 campaign was on public power, and the first steps he took in office were as vigorously deflationary as anything Mr. Hoover might have suggested.

In the curious combination of elements behind Mr. Roosevelt were a section of big business which wanted resolution of the anti-trust laws, farmers who wanted something like tariff protection for themselves, retail business men who understood the need for government spending. An older, more sophisticated, less vigorous capitalist class than ours might have used the NRA [National Recovery Administration] to move toward a form of corporate state, and would have understood the function of social demagogy in making it palatable. They took Mr. Roosevelt's rhetoric more seriously than it deserved, and by the violence of their attack tended in some degree to translate more of it into reality than was intended.

The demagogy of Section 7a in the old NRA was taken seriously by the workers, and their organization both pushed Mr. Roosevelt toward the left and made most of his reforms politically possible. This is what makes his omission of the Wagner Act from the list of his accomplishments indicative. Like the guaranty of bank deposits, the Wagner Act was one of those reforms Mr. Roosevelt sponsored most unwillingly. I hope Senator Wagner will some day write his memoirs and tell the whole story. Yet without the wave of unionization which forced passage of the Wagner Act and was in turn strengthened by it, Mr. Roosevelt's reelection in 1936 would hardly have been possible. The working class provided the firm base of the New Deal, gave it vitality and direction. The dissatisfaction of the middle class and of middle-class farmers provided the other essential element in the victorious coalition. When the fear of foreclosure passed, and fear of labor took its place after the Little Steel strike, the old coalition was broken, and with it passed the earlier vitality and idealism of the New Deal.

This is as good a time as any to take realistic stock of what the New Deal accomplished. In the field of social and economic reform Mr. Roosevelt enabled us to catch up with the England of Lloyd George and the Germany of Bismarck's Monarchical Socialism. Social insurance will not end the ups and downs of the business cycle, though it may moderate their impact. In the field of spending Mr. Roosevelt could never bring himself really to prime the pump vigorously enough for permanent revival. The 1938 "recession" indicated that his second term might have ended in another serious slump if the preparations for war had not provided a new method of spending palatable to the upper classes, which have profited so largely by it. This is not said to disparage Mr. Roosevelt or to deny the wisdom of his war preparations; his policies were determined by the stage of our national development, by public opinion, by international necessities. But it will help us to guide ourselves in the post-war period if we clearly recognize that in the last analysis it was only war that saved the second Roosevelt Administration and world capitalism from a new depression.

The New Deal approach isn't good enough to meet our post-war needs, and it is time that liberals began to think in fresh terms. No economy can go on forever paying men to rake leaves or build mausoleums, and I'm afraid the Rooseveltians would do little more than provide new WPA's in the post-war depression. Another depression is what we're headed for so long as the President leaves plans for reconversion to the big-business crowd. They are already thinking in terms of restoring a profitable scarcity and shutting down new capacity. Post-war New Deals, post-war stabilization measures must take steps from which Mr. Roosevelt has always held back, perhaps because he would have been forced back had he taken them. Only by vigorous government intervention to maintain a high level of output, only by the employment of the jobless in productive enterprise, only by boldly putting idle men at idle machines can reality be given to that new, glamorous, and socially explosive slogan of Full Employment. I am afraid that this is a goal only a new movement and a new leadership will be able to achieve, and then only after a period of reaction.

February 12, 1944

The Cartel Cancer

WHERE CARTELS EXIST, "competition is not eliminated, but regulated. Competition in quality, efficiency, and service takes the place of the crude method of price-cutting." This nonsense comes from the lips of Sir Felix J. C. Pole. Sir Felix is chairman of the Associated Electric Industries, Ltd., and his oleaginous description is being echoed, in a thousand variations, in the subterranean conversations going on here as to the shape of the post-war world. "There are indications," says Senator Harley M. Kilgore, chairman of the subcommittee on war mobilization of the Senate Military Affairs Committee, "that even though cartel and monopoly restrictions have been partly removed during the period of active fighting, cartel and monopoly thinking and planning have continued to thrive." This is putting it mildly.

The senior Senator from West Virginia and his colleagues on the subcommittee, in a series of historic hearings, have been looking into the role that cartel and monopoly restrictions play in preventing the full mobilization of our resources in war and peace. The subcommittee's special interest has been in our scientific and technological resources, that is, in brains shackled by monopoly. Today it released its first monograph, "Economic and Political Aspects of International Cartels." This deserves the widest attention.

Your government, ladies and gentlemen, has the most whimsical capacity for inconsistency. Within a few blocks of each other, administrative cheek by bureaucratic jowl, one may find a Wall Street nabob busily engaged in laying the foundations for a greater monopoly than ever in his favorite industry — as a means of furthering the war effort, of course — and a $4,500-a-year employee marshaling the evidence necessary to indict him for it. The battered citadel of the idealists is the Anti-Trust Division of the Department of Justice, a collection of poor, deluded, but tireless and exuberant warriors, slaphappy in defeat, ever hopeful that a really stiff sentence under the Sherman Act will rejuvenate a senescent "free" capitalism. Under pressure of the War and Navy departments, the WPB [War Production Board], and the White House, most anti-trust prosecutions have been suspended for the duration, and the Anti-Trust Division's safety valve — the boys are bursting with solid fact and honest indignation — has been to prosecute in the court of public opinion by presenting testimony to Congressional committees. The Kilgore committee is one of them, and this monograph was written for it by Corwin D. Edwards, chairman of the Anti-Trust Division's policy board.

The great value of Edward's able monograph is that it not only presents much new material that should long ago have been offered in the courts but classifies and analyzes the mass of facts on cartels which has been presented during the past two years before the Truman, Gillette, Bone, and Kilgore committees. Here one will find the definite and exhaustive answer to Sir Felix Pole's bland apologetics. "The central purpose of cartels," Edwards says, hitting it on the nose, "is to maintain prices at levels higher than would otherwise obtain." "A price war," as I. G. Farben expressed it in a 1934 letter to Winthrop Chemical, "is of benefit only to the consumer." Those inclined to believe that cartels substitute "competition in quality, efficiency, and service" for "the crude method of price-cutting" should read the evidence presented by Edwards on the light-bulb cartel. Its principal anxiety seems to have been to produce light bulbs that would wear out sooner and to keep consumers from finding out about the economies of fluorescent lighting. This is a typical, not an exceptional, case. Cartels either stifle technological development or hog its benefits. A striking instance is that of aluminum. At the beginning of 1939 the price of ingot aluminum was almost a cent higher than it had been in 1911. Subsidized competition and an anti-trust suit brought the price down 25 per cent during the war, but profits remained so high that in 1943 the government recovered $76,000,000 from Alcoa by renegotiation on less than $500,000,000 in contracts.

After two generations of American experience with trusts, it would seem unnecessary to repeat these obvious observations. But the town is full of mellifluous phonies assiduously selling the idea that after this war

let's have "good" cartels. One of these fellows is a Dutch executive of the
N. V. Philips combine, a worldwide network of concerns manufacturing
light bulbs and electrical equipment. His dulcet explanations of the need
to substitute "the interests of the community" for competition are hardly
distinguishable from those of the suaver Nazi theoreticians. The tip-off
on his proposals is his statement that "in democratic countries, where
freedom is the guiding principle, the primary parties to the [cartel]
agreements should be the producers." This is "self-regulation" of
business combinations on a larger scale than ever and hardly even in a
new guise.

The politically epicene source of this advice — advice which can be
duplicated from British and American sources — is indicated by Edwards's revelations on what has happened to the Philips combine since
the war began. This amazing story, never publicly told before, reveals
that the United Nations and Axis branches of this cartel have continued
to cooperate and communicate straight through the war. The American
trustees, on instructions from the Nazi-controlled main office in Holland,
helped a German cartel partner fight a patent suit in the Swedish courts
in 1942, turned over certain patents to the Spanish branch, and swapped
information with their Axis opposite members through a curiously
overstaffed Argentine branch. Yet so ingenious are the legal devices of
this cartel and so extensive is its political influence that its subsidiaries in
neutral countries have not been blacklisted and its properties in countries
belonging to the United Nations have not been taken over as enemy-
controlled. These are the kind of lice that helped sell out Europe to
Hitler and that will destroy free government elsewhere if given half a
chance.

It is a mistake to believe that the cartel system was a German plot to
curb American production of many vital war materials. Many of the
agreements restricting output and raising prices in this country were
invited by the American partner rather than initiated by the Germans.
Krupp's was selling tungsten carbide here at $50 a pound before General
Electric made the cartel deal that jacked it up to $453. The democracies
get the worst of these deals because their great monopoly capitalists are
hostile to the state and interested only in profit. To Alfred Sloan of
General Motors, answering a protest from a stockholder in April, 1939,
on its Nazi dealings, it seemed that "an international business — should
conduct its business in strictly business terms — without regard to
political beliefs." But business men feel differently in those countries
where they regard the state as their instrument rather than as an

unreliable servant susceptible to democratic twinges. "An international cartel," said the chairman of the board of Philips's German partner, "has no right of existence — if this cartel is acting against the common interests of Germany." This should be clear enough warning as to what will happen if we restore the cartel system and a capitalist Reich.

Unfortunately, this is exactly the direction in which we are headed. The cartel at home means the limitation of production to those levels the big producers consider profitable. Limitation of production means limitation of jobs, and without full employment there will be rich soil here for fascism after the war. No doubt these same big producers will cultivate it. The cartel abroad means the subordination once more of our legitimate national interests to the illegitimate objectives of a Germany bent on revenge. I hope next week to tackle the task of naming the men and influences in Washington which already make it seem an almost hopeless task to achieve full employment after the war and to prevent revival of the cartel system. The two are fatefully linked together.

The Cartels' Washington Friends

ᔕᢇ ᗆᔌ

LAST WEEK I said I would tackle the task of naming some of the men and influences in Washington "which already make it seem an almost hopeless task to achieve full employment after the war and to prevent revival of the cartel system." Here goes:

Jesse Jones. One of the best ways to maintain free enterprise after the war and to prevent further hardening of our economic arteries would be to use government-owned war plants as publicly operated yardsticks, TVA style, in basic industries. This is the only good weapon we have against cartelization; anti-trust prosecution is a Sisyphean task resulting at best in flea-bite penalties.

On paper, we are in an excellent position to carry out such a policy. We have built some 2,600 plants for war purposes; the investment in them is variously estimated at from $16 billion to $20 billion. These government-financed facilities include nearly all our synthetic-rubber and high-octane-gas plants, 92 per cent of our magnesium, 90 per cent of our aircraft plants, more than 50 per cent of our aluminum capacity, 50 per cent of our machine-tool capacity, and about 10 percent of our steel. The RFC [Reconstruction Finance Corporation] through the Defense Plant Corporation holds title to the bulk of these — 1, 753 in all. As Jesse Jones indicated in his speech before the New York Board of Trade last October, these include 534 aircraft plants, 164 iron-and-steel plants, 116 plants for the manufacture of machine tools, 98 plants for radio and similar equipment, 84 aluminum plants, 65 plants for ships and ship engines, 60 mining and smelter plants, 60 plants for synthetic rubber and its components, 35 plants for aviation gas, 6 pipe-lines for petroleum. This is far from a complete list.

A mere enumeration of products by no means indicates the full possibilities. The butadiene plants in the synthetic-rubber program provide the basis for infinite developments in plastics; the government's machine-tool capacity is a sleeping, and probably will soon be a chloroformed, giant, capable of spawning huge and multifarious industries. In a socialist America what wealth, comfort, and happiness for all could be drawn from these resources.

Here I plead only for a "mixed" system, for the operation of enough of this capacity on a "yardstick" basis to prevent renewed restriction of production and the fixing of uneconomic prices. Such a policy was advocated by the National Resources Planning Board; the NRPB has been abolished. The war plants are largely in the hands of Jesse Jones, and Jones is unlikely to permit their use for any such purpose — and would be back in Houston in a twinkling if he tried.

The trend of policy is to get rid of these plants as rapidly as possible, and there is little chance of an anti-monopolistic policy in disposing of them. Jones's policy in the RFC has been inimical to independent enterprise, helpful to monopoly. He will sell most war plants to their present operators; the majority of these are monopolistic and will emerge well fattened from the war. Standard Oil, Alcoa, and du Pont, are leading carteleers, and their allies will be in a stronger position than ever to dominate domestic and world markets. A huge portion of our war-plant facilities will go directly or indirectly to these three concerns.

Leo T. Crowley. Another small-town banker taken into the big time. As Alien Property Custodian, Crowley has his hands on a second great instrument for the preservation of free enterprise — in a real sense — and the prevention of a cartel system after the war. The alien patents and properties under his control were the heart of monopolies in chemicals, pharmaceuticals, dyestuffs, photographic materials, magnesium, and a long list of highly important industrial components and products. The policies he is pursuing will help keep these monopolies intact or make them stronger than ever.

Crowley boasts that he is making alien patents freely available to American business. But he makes two kinds of exceptions, and these are broad enough to permit maintenance and revival of the cartel system. He makes an exception when an American concern already has an exclusive license under an alien patent; such patents will not be available except under very special circumstances. But exclusive licenses of this kind are one of the basic cartel devices, and it is no secret that many American companies deliberately took out licenses under worthless German patents to give them a legal weapon against competitors at home and abroad. The second exception is in the case of patents used in the operations of a business taken over by the Alien Property Custodian. This means that a concern like General Aniline and Film, the principal German property in the United States and the foundation of Germany's imperial power in North and South American pharmaceuticals, chemicals, and other materials, continues in possession of these basic monopolistic devices.

Crowley is still drawing $75,000 a year as chairman and president of Standard Gas and Electric. He obtained that job from Victor Emanuel, president of Standard Power and Light, which controls Standard Gas. Emanuel himself came to power in Standard Gas and in Aviation Corporation, our most important holding company in aircraft and shipbuilding, with the financial backing of the Anglo-German banking house of J. Henry Schroder. The Schroder firms of London and New York are linked by family ties with the Schroder Brothers bank of Hamburg and by business ties with the Stein bank of Cologne. A leading partner in the latter is the Baron Kurt von Schroder who was the go-between in Hitler's negotiations with the Rhineland industrialists.

The Schroder bank in London was a member of the notoriously pro-Nazi Anglo-German Fellowship. In March, 1938, the London bank formed a company to finance the export of basic materials to the Reich. A year previously the Schroder bank in New York subscribed $300,000 to set up a corporation to facilitate barter of German products for American cotton.

Next to the Schroders, the most important banking interest in Standard Gas before the war was Chase National. No two banks in New York had more dealings with Nazi concerns and cartels than Chase National and the J. Henry Schroder Banking Corporation. I think it inexcusable that the Alien Property Custodian should be receiving $75,000 a year from Standard Gas, in view of the conflicting interests in which this double position might possibly involve him. Add the fact that Crowley is now head of the Foreign Economic Administration, and has actively furthered General Airline interests in Latin America, and you have a situation that hardly promises to weaken the great cartels after the war.

Nelson, Byrnes, Baruch. I only have a line left for these dominant figures in the reconversion of industry. Their policies, whatever their intentions, move in the direction of giving big business the inside track on reconversion. I hope to return to this subject again soon, but I think I have indicated how powerfully intrenched are the forces which make for great monopolies after the war and for the revival of cartels.

April 8, 1944

Reply to *the* Saturday Evening Post

I SEEM TO HAVE ALARMED the editors of the *Saturday Evening Post*. They shy at a remark made by your correspondent in an article on the "Cartel Cancer" in *The Nation* of February 12. The *Saturday Evening Post* for April 1 carries an editorial, "Soldiers' Doubts Reflect Our Wobbling War Aims," and in it the editors say:

> The confused American, who regards himself as a defender of "free enterprise," also finds a considerable propaganda not merely for destroying the military power of Germany but for using destruction of her military power as a pretext for destroying her industrial system as such. At any rate, I. F. Stone, writing on cartels for *The Nation,* hints dire consequences "if we restore the cartel system *and a capitalist Reich.* [The italics are the *Post's.*] In other words, we are supposed by a considerable group of Americans to be fighting to destroy in Germany the kind of economic setup we defend in America.

I have little quarrel with the *Saturday Evening Post's* editorial. It has much to say on the problem of war aims that is sober and sensible. I think most Americans will agree with its general conclusion. "The justice imposed by war," the *Post* says, "is rough at best, and this war will be no exception.... The purpose and spirit of an American army fighting on foreign soil will be most easily maintained if the issues are stated as simply as possible. Hitler and Tojo must be defeated because their success would mean our ruin." But I think most soldiers would agree that a further step would be helpful in maintaining morale. There are men fighting Germany today whose fathers fought Germany in the

First World War. I think these men would like some assurance that their sons will not have to fight Germany in a third war.

The *Saturday's Evening Post*'s attitude to the future of Germany rests on fallacious assumptions. These call for the most careful examination if we are not to drift into the reestablishment of pretty much the same kind of Germany we have had to fight twice in a generation.

Let us begin with the final sentence of the passage I quoted at the beginning of this letter. "In other words," the *Post* says, "we are supposed by a considerable group of Americans to be fighting to destroy in Germany the kind of economic setup we defend in America." This may at first glance appear conclusive and crushing, but it is really irrelevant. We may not be fighting to destroy capitalism in Germany, but we are certainly not fighting to maintain it. We are fighting to destroy the German threat to ourselves. And in making the peace we shall be concerned with only one thing — helping to bring to birth a Germany we shall not have to fight again.

I think the editors of the *Saturday Evening Post* would agree that we encouraged the reestablishment of capitalism in Germany after the last war. I think they would agree that if capitalism had been successful in Germany, the republic would not have fallen and Hitler would not have come to power. I think they would agree that if Hitler had not come to power, there would probably be no war in Europe today. Now the question is: After Hitler is defeated, are we to restore capitalism in Germany and run the risk of letting much the same sequence of events repeat itself? I think this is a reasonable question.

Now let us look at the first sentence of the passage I have quoted from the *Saturday Evening Post*. It links "free enterprise" in the mind of the reader with the German "industrial system." We are still fortunate enough to have large areas of free enterprise in American capitalism, but "free enterprise" was never even the ideal of German capitalism. There wasn't much free enterprise in Germany before Hitler, and there is a good deal less of it today. This is not because of National Socialism. The Führer no more meant to make the Reich national socialist, in the literal meaning of the term, than Huey Long intended to make every American a king. There is less free enterprise because, with democratic checks removed, the great trusts, combines, and cartels of the Reich have waxed stronger, gobbling up and strong-arming smaller businesses and independent enterprise. With a few unlucky exceptions like Thyssen, who lost out to shrewder rivals, the magnates who backed Hitler profited enormously by Nazism. Hitler's defeat will not deprive them of their dominant position in Germany's economy. The great capitalists of the Reich helped the Führer to power, benefited by his regime, and share in his guilt. Do the editors of the *Saturday Evening Post* propose to let them get away with their gains?

I am sure that the editors of the *Post* feel as hostile to those silent partners of Hitlerism as the rest of us do. But if we unthinkingly identify German monopoly capitalism with "free enterprise" and permit it to operate after Hitler has been defeated, we leave these men with their loot. They are counting on conventional thinking to help them do two things. One is through litigation and dummy corporations in neutral countries to salvage much of the property they stole in occupied Europe. The other is to retain their dominant position in the German economy. They look to our respect for property rights to help them in the first task and to our fear of communism to help them in the second. They have strong potential allies in America and Britain — first, among the corporations which own property in the Reich and, second, among German industry's opposite numbers in international cartel agreements. These cartel partners stand to benefit by the enhanced monopoly power of their old German associates, and may be expected to stand by them. One of the proposals already put forward here by a distinguished corporation lawyer is that American concerns be made "trustees" for the property of their cartel partners in the Reich. This would have an obvious advantage in protecting them from socialization.

This is not merely a moral problem. It is a problem in international security. These big German interests were unable to end unemployment in the Reich without dictatorship and war. There is no reason to believe that they can do better a second time. Peace will create difficulties for them; war would offer new profits and a new chance at world dominion. We know what they did to hamstring American production by cartel agreements before this war, and it would be folly to give them a chance to do it again. They are our enemies, as deeply and as permanently as the German military. Shall we leave them in power? Or shall we give the pent-up anger of the Reich's gagged working class a chance to sweep them away? And by nationalizing the great combines, and giving the small business man and farmer a chance at free enterprise in a mixed economic system, establish a Reich that can achieve prosperity without plundering its neighbors? I ask the editors of the *Saturday Evening Post* which course offers the better chance that our sons will not have to fight Germany again.

April 15, 1944

Washington Blues

A FEW NEW DEALERS have thought for some time that Mr. Roosevelt ought not to run for a fourth term. Their number has been increased by the defeat of Mr. Willkie in Wisconsin. The earlier argument against the fourth term was that Mr. Roosevelt, even if reelected, would probably have a Republican and certainly a more hostile Congress to contend with, and that he would be unable in these circumstances to solve the problems of demobilization.

It was argued that with Mr. Roosevelt in the White House, the ordinary voter would feel that the New Deal was in power, though virtually all key positions are already held by conservatives and the President is to a large extent their prisoner. Unemployment would be blamed on the New Deal, the reactionary trend intensified, and a liberal comeback long postponed. "The right is running the show," said one New Dealer back in uniform on a furlough from his post abroad. "Let them bear the responsibility."

This view assumes that there will be severe unemployment after the war, at least for some time — an assumption I share, since I see no evidence of any steps, private or public, that can insure anything like full employment. Others, who agree, are nevertheless all the more strongly for a fourth term, on the ground that Mr. Roosevelt's presence in the White House may provide some check in what may be a dangerously reactionary period. But those of the President's advisers who are thinking primarily in terms of international rather than domestic problems want Mr. Roosevelt reelected no matter what situation is likely to confront him at home. The more optimistic of these believe that Mr.

Willkie's withdrawal increases Mr. Roosevelt's chances. Previously they had regarded Mr. Willkie as the one Republican who might take progressive votes away from the President on domestic issues while winning the support of conservatives who would accept Mr. Roosevelt rather than risk any relapse into isolationism.

What worries the President's political advisers now is not so much what happened in Wisconsin as its effect in New York. Had Mr. Willkie made a strong showing, he and Governor Dewey might have killed each other off in the convention. Mr. Willkie's withdrawal now seems to have assured the Dewey nomination, and with that New York appears to be more than doubtful territory. The nomination of New York's governor plus the ugly sectarian quarrel in New York's American Labor Party makes many people here fear that Governor Dewey can carry New York against Mr. Roosevelt. If he can, a fourth term is unlikely. Talk in Congressional Democratic circles of a Byrd-Farley ticket reflects this feeling, and the open desertions from the not too crowded fourth-term band-wagon are evidence of how strong doubt has become. It is unlikely that Mr. Roosevelt will risk the great prestige he might possess and the influence he might exert as an undefeated elder statesman if he thinks his chance of winning is slight.

But few people here have the temerity to count Mr. Roosevelt out already. Many things may happen. The course of events in Europe, the opening of a second front, and the measure of its military success, will all have their effect. The American people may be much less war-weary when they are actually fighting on a major scale than they are when millions of men are being drafted for little visible purpose. Mr. Roosevelt is no quitter. He has shown his fighting heart and buoyant courage under circumstances that would break most men. At home he has provided the leadership in, and given his name to, one of the great periods of American history. He is, from every indication, determined to do what he can to bring a more stable international order into being. He must have personal commitments to and from Churchill, Stalin, and Chiang Kai-shek that would be endangered by his defeat. He must be far more strongly aware than most of us of the threat to a permanent peace settlement were the four-power coalition to break up. Part of his strength lies in that very wiliness for which we assorted idealists, liberals, and leftists are most apt to criticize him. The President may do things we shall find hard to justify in the next few months.

I admire and honor Mr. Willkie. It was a pleasure to hear and read the words of a man who said what he thought and proved that he was prepared to hear the consequence. But the consequences were serious. It was a pleasure that was also a luxury. Mr. Willkie demonstrated again that politics is no place for a man who chooses to speak plainly. It is only in times of extraordinary, imminent, and visible danger that he may hope to achieve leadership. I think the career of Mr. Churchill, a more conservative but no less outspoken personality, illustrates the same point; he was passed over for the mediocre and the equivocating until his country's great moment of peril, and in such a conjuncture Mr. Willkie may some day be called upon.

It is easy to oversimplify the results of the Wisconsin primaries. Wisconsin cannot be equated with the Midwest; many factors make it the worst possible place for a representative test of the general attitude toward foreign policy. The strong vote polled by former Governor Stassen of neighboring and equally Midwestern Minnesota, where both Stassen and Senator Ball are strongly pledged to international cooperation, indicates that Mr. Willkie's defeat was not simply an isolationist victory. But Mr. Willkie's failure, at this writing, to win even one pledged delegate indicates (1) on domestic issues, that even in Wisconsin, the home of progressive Republicanism, the liberal Republican and independent voters to whom Mr. Willkie thought he could appeal don't amount to very much; and (2) on foreign policy, that the active internationalist minority is far weaker than the active isolationist minority, while the inert mass in between doesn't feel deeply about the question — even so eloquent, attractive, and sincere a man as Mr. Willkie was unable sufficiently to move them. The result is not likely to lead Mr. Roosevelt to heed Mr. Willkie's advice and be more outspoken and clear in his foreign policy.

April 29, 1944

The Shadow Over the Capital

REPRESENTATIVE COX of Georgia is no longer chairman of the Special House Committee Investigating the Federal Communications Commission [FCC], and Eugene L. Garey is out as counsel, but these changes do not seem to have made much difference in the committee's approach and tactics. The questions asked Mrs. Hilda D. Shea, former chief of the Special Studies Section of the FCC's War Policies Division, deserve attention. Harry S. Barger, the committee's new counsel, seems to be carrying on in the Garey tradition. Garey is a partner of Liberty Leaguer Raoul E. Desvernine, and was counsel for I. G. Farben interests and allies in several suits designed to keep General Aniline and Film from American control. Garey appeared to think it one of his duties to find out which employees of the FCC were Jewish. Barger's questions were designed to elicit the fact that Mrs. Shea's maiden name was Jewish and that her father was a Russian immigrant. This information would, of course, be highly relevant in a Nazi court. Barger ought to go back where he should have come from.

Mrs. Shea was called upon to deny that she was a Communist or a Communist sympathizer, but she admitted — sit tight for a horrendous revelation! — that while employed as an attorney by the National Labor Relations Board [NLRB] she received a letter from Mrs. Beatrice M. Stern, an NLRB division chief, asking her to support Labor's Non-Partisan League. Barger pointed out that the league was sponsored by the C.I.O., which he no doubt regards as a subversive organization, but with striking forbearance made no reference to the fact that the league was equally notorious as a labor-front group designed to reelect

F— D— R— . Mrs. Shea was also asked whether she belonged to the National Lawyers' Guild, but she said she didn't. Barger disclosed that the guild had been described as a Communist-front organization. I can't imagine what Barger will be discovering next.

Barger is not a very funny joke. He and his committee are only one of the agencies fouling the air of Washington and making the city unlivable for progressive government employees. We have just seen the Dies and Kerr committees drive from public life so fine and honorable a man as Robert Morss Lovett. I note that Lovett, who is incorrigible, has just been reelected a vice-president of the League for Industrial Democracy, along with such other subversives as John Haynes Holmes, Alexander Meiklejohn, and Bishop Francis J. McConnell. Their careers may be found fully set forth in Mrs. Elizabeth Dilling's "The Red Network." While Mrs. Dilling is on trial for sedition, her faithful readers seem to be carrying on quite nicely at the Capitol.

It is not entirely irrelevant at this point to take note of the address delivered this week by J. Edgar Hoover, chief of the FBI, before the annual meeting of the Daughters of the American Revolution in New York. Hoover's principal animus, in the frankest speech this old hero of the Hearst-Patterson-McCormick press has permitted himself in several years, was aimed at "militant, self-seeking, loudly vocal groups of muddled emotionalists, parlor pinks, fellow-travelers, and avowed Communists." Hoover said the FBI keeps strictly out of politics. But at the beginning of a Presidential campaign one may wonder just what political movement was identified with Hoover's words by the good ladies of the D.A.R., who have long suspected the President and the New Deal of the worst.

I wonder what the ladies thought Hoover meant when he attacked "superficial sugar-coated panaceas that are neither democratic nor defensible" — these ladies who voted a resolution urging Congressmen to oppose passage of the Wagner-Murray-Dingell bill for compulsory federal health insurance. I am revealing no secrets when I report that the press corps here thought of pro-Roosevelt *PM* when Hoover criticized as "irresponsible" those editors who "not only proclaim their personal views but urge their readers to wire or write their demands urging this or that action." Had the wicked editors been named they would have grounds for libel action in Hoover's next sentence, "The fascist-minded tyrant is no different from the native-born communistic-minded corruptionist." If all this isn't sly dabbling in politics, the dictionary must have been revised since I last looked at it.

This revived appearance of a way of thinking some people hoped

J. Edgar Hoover had outgrown is a serious matter for the post-war period. The FBI will be in part responsible for the enforcement of New Deal legislation for the protection of labor's right to organize. It cannot function effectively if it is to be operated in political illiteracy and obscurantism, and the way in which it does comport itself may play a crucial role in the readjustment of our society to peace-time conditions. "The guarantees which the Constitution throws around civil liberties," the La Follette committee said in the first of its great reports on employers' associations and collective bargaining in California, "are neither pious declarations nor archaic echoes of the historic past; they are the ground plan for the healthy functioning of an industrial society. Their infraction will shatter our democratic society upon its internal conflicts; their fulfillment will enable it to achieve a strength and unity which no domestic or foreign enemy can challenge."

Before the war the FBI had become the top agency and in many ways the national coordinator for local and state police activities, and these were often aimed at the suppression of labor's rights. How the local and state authorities operated in California is dramatically set forth in the La Follette committee's latest report, Part VIII of the California series. This deals with the Associated Farmers and warns that "there is good reason to believe that the pattern of California in the years 1935–39 is the pattern for the United States today or tomorrow." It points out that from the days of Greece and Rome to "the struggles in Eastern Europe after World War No. 1, the relationship of men to the land they worked and to the fruits of their labor has been the nub of endless tyranny and conflict." It recalls "the participation of the landed Junkers in Hitler's rise to power, the place of the large landholders of rich Italian valleys in the vanguard of Mussolini's early maneuvers, the support of fascist rule in Spain and Hungary by similar groups."

These lessons, the La Follette committee says, "cannot be ignored." Agriculture is a major form of livelihood for the American people. California is the state which exhibits most clearly what may happen as large landholdings increase, as agriculture becomes more scientific, and as it develops into a big business rather than a way of life: "It is inevitable that the pattern set for employer-employee relationships in agriculture in California, if retrogressive, reactionary, or semi-fascist in tone, will be a great blow to the cause of economic democracy." Before the war, as the report shows, state and local police in California were often so closely interlocked with employer associations and their labor spies and provocateurs as to seem part of one great machine for the oppression of labor, agricultural and industrial. The Associated Farmers itself owed its financing largely to the California Packing Corporation and the Industrial Association of San Francisco; local and state police, hired thugs and vigilantes did the dirty work. Some of the principal police characters, such as "Red" Hynes of Los Angeles, who was paid $6,727.40 by the Associated Farmers from February, 1935, to May, 1937, exchanged information with the FBI.

If there is any hope of carrying over into the post-war period the better employee-employer relations developed during the war, much will depend on the FBI and the Department of Justice and their influence over local and state police. Much will also depend on the spirit prevailing in Washington, and especially in Congress. Among many business men, in California, here, and elsewhere, there are signs of a new spirit that is most encouraging. But I cannot report the same of official Washington.

Thomas E. Dewey

〜 〜

ALBANY FASCINATES ME, but I can't say the same for
Dewey. The capital of New York would inspire Dreiser and
depress De Tocqueville, but its Governor is a Republican Presidential
candidate, very standard model. I've waded through a foot-high pile of
Dewey messages, speeches, and statements kindly supplied by his affable
press secretary, James C. Hagerty. I listened to the Governor address the
American Newspaper Publishers' meeting in New York and watched
him being charming to the hopeful on the platform after it was over. I've
read almost everything written about him, except the Rupert Hughes
work, which seems to have confused him with George Washington and
Lucky Luciano with a cherry tree. I've talked to people who work closely
with him and to people who hate him, the latter being easy to find in
Albany and New York where Dewey has been seen in close-up. And all
I can report is that for the first time since becoming a Washington
correspondent and on one of the few occasions since I became a
newspaperman, I found myself with an assignment that bored me.

On international affairs, Dewey might be Warren G. Harding, an
internationalist but —. On domestic affairs, where straight Hooverism is
no longer possible even for a Republican, Dewey might be Alfred
Landon, unalterably opposed to the new Deal, four square against its
threat to the American way of life, but in agreement with its basic
principles, though he thinks they are poorly administered. As a public
figure, he is as familiar a type — the "clean government" reformer who
is death on all crooks except the really big and respectable ones of our
society. As a man, he is competent, courageous, hard-working, but

extraordinary only in his drive, his singleness of purpose, the intensity of his ambition. I don't think he is wicked, sinister, dishonest, or fascist, though I suppose he will have such epithets thrown at him when the campaign gets heated; I think he is a good American, very far removed from anti-democratic crackpots, racial bigots, and Bertie McCormicks. But the man is uninteresting because he presents no complexities, deviates in no way from type. I can see nothing but the commonplace in his mind. I sense no lift of idealism in his spirit; his motivations seem to me wholly self-seeking. And the personality is completely lacking in human warmth.

This may sound harsh and it may be unjust, but it is said only after much thought and consideration, and it checks with the reactions of people who are his friends as well as with those of his enemies. Dewey has been called "a boy scout," and he is one in the sense that he sees the problems of our society purely in the obvious and elementary terms of personal morality; I say obvious and elementary because he would not see the profounder immoralities in our customary ways of living and doing business. But he is not a boy scout in the sense that he would let a naive but praiseworthy and wholesome sense of duty stand in the way of personal aggrandizement. He chose the law as a profession because he thought it offered the prospect of greater and more secure financial rewards than singing; none of those who have written of him or who know him claim that he was attracted to the law as a useful way to spend one's life, or because he was inspired by the example of some great judge or advocate. There is nothing in him of the Galahad or the Quixote. His sensational splurge as prosecutor in New York was a quick stepping-stone to the Governorship, not the beginning of a job that he felt had to be completed in the interest of civic duty or clean government, and the Governorship is a stepping-stone to the Presidency. He is a kind of Get-Rich-Quick Wallingford in politics, a man who plays for the quick rise and the big profit. That the profit is in personal advancement rather than money is a detail, not an essential. Dewey's eye has always been on the headlines, not the stars. The men who worked with him as D.A. will tell you that the press was as constantly in their thoughts as the jury.

A certain humility makes a man lovable and marks him wise. Dewey reeks of self-assurance. You look at him on the platform and think of Browning's line, "A man's reach should exceed his grasp," but only because the two spring from such different worlds. It is only in the most superficial sense that Dewey would ever think of himself as unfit; he is said to be busy boning up on American history now in preparation for the Presidency. He would never think of himself as unworthy. Big men usually have a sense of fun. Roosevelt has it, Churchill has it, Lenin had it, so saintly a figure as Gandhi jokes and frolics. Dewey would never dream of making a joke at his own expense. His humor, or what passed for it, is heavy-footed, as when he referred to newsboys at the publishers' dinner in New York as "purveyors of your products." (I was there; I heard it.) He is not what we call a regular guy. There is nothing in him of Willkie's rich curiosity, human interest, or careless vitality. Dewey is small stuff and cold fish, handsomer and physically robust but really a good deal like Coolidge, frugal spiritually, a man who does not give himself freely.

I saw Dewey for the first time at the publishers' dinner, a trying event for most of those present because so many long-winded speakers preceded him, a trying occasion for him because Eric Johnston of the United States Chamber of Commerce tried to steal the show, and almost succeeded. Johnston's speech was the improvisation of a shrewd high-school boy, and I remember it chiefly for its gorgeously mixed metaphors, but it went over big with the publishers. Dewey seemed restive until his moment came. He went forward like a singer, chest out, enormously self-possessed. He sounded like a man who had studied with a first-rate elocutionist in a smallish town. One could have written a musical score for the speech. His gestures, the modulation of his voice, the measured emphasis and stress, were too perfect to be pleasant; the manner was conceited. When he praised Secretary of State Hull, it was with the gracious condescension that he might have used in patting a small boy on the head. The speech was expertly prepared and made Johnston's seem as amateurish as it was. Dewey gave an orotund solemnity to such hollow stuff as "When we have ceased to wage war, we shall have to wage peace," with the air of a man delivering an epigram.

In Albany I found those close to Dewey devoted to him. Four investigations are going here full blast, and the town is overrun with racket-busters who used to work for Dewey in New York. They like him, irrespective of political differences, for Dewey is competent, a good executive, and the young lawyer's ideal of a prosecutor. The young men in his immediate entourage are capable rather than brilliant, and already envisage themselves as the Harry Hopkinses and Louis Howes of the next Administration. It is a giddy thing to be on a Presidential band-wagon, and those few of them who have New Dealish backgrounds are rapidly throwing earlier ideas overboard as excess baggage. Even in this innermost circle one has the feeling that Dewey inspires fear and respect rather than affection. "He's very self-centered and never seems interested in you personally," said one racket-buster reflectively in answer to a question. But outside the circle of Deweyites, one encounters only dislike of the Governor.

In part, this dislike is to Dewey's credit. The town is comfortably corrupt. So is the Legislature. The Governor's attack on the local O'Connell machine brought reprisal in the shape of an O'Connell investigation of the Republican Legislature. Dewey was forced to take the investigation over to protect his party, but the man he chose as special prosecutor, Hiram C. Todd, is forceful and independent, and there will be difficulty in keeping the investigation within safe bounds. Dewey started out to investigate favoritism in assessments in Albany, the payment of current expenses out of bond issues, and election frauds. He hoped to duplicate in Albany the success he had achieved as a gang-buster in New York and break the one important Democratic machine upstate. But an investigation of the Legislature, which has been Republican-controlled for many years, was not part of his original plan. The fears this investigation has aroused in his own party have served to make Republican legislators subservient to him, and he has ruled the Legislature like a little dictator. But the inquiry itself will not be allowed to go too far because it would hurt the Republicans more than the Democrats in an election year and would inevitably involve big money interests with which Dewey is himself allied.

To understand the political problems that confront Dewey in Albany, one must understand this old Dutch town at the head of navigation on the Hudson. It exhibits the slatternly side of the Democratic process. For the first twenty years of the century it was solidly Republican. During the past twenty years it has been as solidly Democratic. During both periods it has been corrupt, and during both the respectable elements have shared widely in the benefits of machine government. They resent these investigations. The Democratic era began with an alliance between Dan O'Connell, son of a saloon keeper, and the old-family owner of the Alleghany-Ludlum steel works. Albany's political revolutions have not been the result of uprisings by an outraged citizenry but of internal feuds in aging political machines. A legislative investigation before the last war plus some fiery attacks by Teddy Roosevelt upon the Barnes political machine only increased the Republican vote at the next election, and there are many people here who think local resentment will enable the O'Connells to pile up a larger majority than ever before. Dewey's unpopularity in Albany might cost him New York State and the Presidency.

From all I can see, the O'Connell machine is still united and vigorous. Unless Dewey can unearth evidence of some major crime, it is unlikely that he can shake its popular strength. But the O'Connell machine has been in power so long that it has been many years since any rough tactics were required to keep either its henchmen or the populace in line. Public standards are higher than they were a generation ago, and in some respects conditions under the O'Connell regime are better than under Barnes. The "Gut," Albany's old tenderloin, no longer flaunts its red-light section. The principal "crimes" Dewey has been able to lay at the door of the O'Connell machine are not of a kind to bring ordinary Albany citizens tumbling from their beds in alarm. "Bookmaking" establishments operate pretty openly. There are plenty of slot machines around. Saloons are open all night selling Hedrick beer, the O'Connell family brew. Election frauds seem to be common, but the O'Connells have so tight a grip on grand and petit jury lists that not much could be done about them.

Albany's city government seems to have been holding down its tax rate by paying current expenditures out of capital borrowings. Assessments seem to be adjusted to aid the deserving and teach the independents a lesson; Dan O'Connell's first political job was as tax assessor, a post he used to good advantage in building his machine. These are dishonest practices no one could wish to condone — except the property owners and lawyers who benefit by them, and their beneficiaries are many. We Americans are for clean government in theory and political favors in practice. This makes the Dewey type popular — at a distance. One of Dewey's advisers in Albany is a nice young Republican lawyer who represents large property interests through his father-in-law's estate, helps run a leading real-estate firm, and does a substantial volume of business representing the Republican minority which has to take its assessment appeals to the courts instead of to the district leader. Dewey assigned him to investigate assessments, and the investigation will make it easier for a time to be a Republican in Albany, but an assessments scandal will neither break the O'Connell machine nor make dramatic headlines elsewhere.

In part Albany's dislike for Dewey is a result of his shortcomings as a person. Other Governors were gracious and became part of the life of the town. Mrs. Roosevelt and Mrs. Lehman lived, shopped, and entertained in Albany. Both were a familiar sight downtown. "Albanians," as they call themselves, have the civic patriotism of a Greek city-state. "We never see Mrs. Dewey," they complain. Albany feels that

Dewey is only a man on the make, hurrying through on his way somewhere else. It is contented in its corruption, thinks it civic misdeeds no worse than those of most cities, believes it is being smeared and sacrificed to provide a Dewey triumph, resents a certain ruthlessness and self-righteousness in the Governor's attitude toward it.

There are many complaints that Dewey is rude and standoffish in dealing with the townspeople. Lehman was chairman of Russian War Relief in Albany; as a matter of courtesy Dewey was invited to succeed him. The invitation went unanswered. The Inter-Racial Council runs a Booker T. Washington Center here. It held a musicale to raise funds. Tickets were sent the Governor. They were returned unacknowledged. The 4-H clubs held their annual meeting here. It is customary for Governors to address the meeting. Dewey refused because the Mayor of Albany had also been invited. He agreed to speak only when the Mayor withdrew. "He can't put his political ax aside for a moment," said one Albany newspaperman. Albany would agree with the irate Republican lady who once said, "You have to know Dewey to dislike him."

June 10, 1944

For the Jews — Life or Death?

At his press conference on June 2, after this article was written, the President indicated that he was considering the conversion of an army camp in this country into a "free port" for refugees. Unfortunately, as the New York Post has pointed out, "his statement was conditional, indefinite. The check is still on paper and we don't even know what the amount is." In these circumstances Mr. Stone's analysis of the urgency of the situation and his plea for public pressure to secure action from the Administration are no less valid than they were before Mr. Roosevelt spoke.

THIS LETTER, addressed specifically to fellow-newspapermen and to editors the country over, is an appeal for help. The establishment of temporary internment camps for refugees in the United States, vividly named "free ports" by Samuel Grafton of the New York *Post,* is in danger of bogging down. Every similar proposal here has bogged down until it was too late to save any lives. I have been over a mass of material, some of it confidential, dealing with the plight of the fast-disappearing Jews of Europe and with the fate of suggestions for aiding them, and it is a dreadful story.

Anything newspapermen can write about this in their own papers will help. It will help to save lives, the lives of people like ourselves. I wish I were eloquent, I wish I could put down on paper the picture that comes to me from the restrained and diplomatic language of the documents. As I write, the morning papers carry a dispatch from Lisbon, reporting that the "deadline" — the idiom was never more literal — has passed for the Jews of Hungary. It is approaching for the Jews of Bulgaria, where the Nazis yesterday set up a puppet regime.

I need not dwell upon the authenticated horrors of the Nazi internment camps and death chambers for Jews. That is not tragic but a kind of insane horror. It is our part in this which is tragic. The essence of tragedy is not the doing of evil by evil men but the doing of evil by good men, out of weakness, indecision, sloth, inability to act in accordance with what they know to be right. The tragic element in the fate of the Jews of Europe lies in the failure of their friends in the West to shake loose from customary ways and bureaucratic habit, to risk inexpediency and defy prejudice, to be whole-hearted, to care as deeply and fight as hard for the big words we use, for justice and for humanity, as the fanatic Nazi does for his master race or the fanatic Jap for his Emperor. A reporter in Washington cannot help seeing this weakness all about him. We are half-hearted about what little we could do to help the Jews of Europe as we are half-hearted about our economic warfare, about blacklisting those who help our enemies, about almost everything in the war except the actual fighting.

There is much we could have done to save the Jews of Europe before the war. There is much we could have done since the war began. There are still things we could do today which would give new lives to a few and hope to many. The hope that all is not black in the world for his children can be strong sustenance for a man starving in a camp or entering a gas chamber. But to feel that your friends and allies are wishy-washy folk who mean what they say but haven't got the gumption to live up to it must brew a poisonous despair. When Mr. Roosevelt established the War Refugee Board in January, he said it was "the policy of this government to take all measures within its power . . . consistent with the successful prosecution of the war . . . to rescue the victims of enemy oppression."

The facts are simple. Thanks to the International Red Cross and those good folk the Quakers, thanks to courageous non-Jewish friends in the occupied countries themselves and to intrepid Jews who run a kind of underground railway under Nazi noses, something can still be done to alleviate the suffering of the Jews in Europe and some Jews can still be got out. Even under the White Paper there are still 22,000 immigration visas available for entry into Palestine. The main problem is to get Jews over the Turkish border without a passport for transit to Palestine. "Free ports" in Turkey are needed, but the Turks, irritated by other pressures from England and the United States, are unwilling to do for Jewish refugees what we ourselves are still unwilling to do, that is, give them a temporary haven. Only an executive order by the President establishing "free ports" in this country can prove to the Turks that we are dealing with them in a good faith; under present circumstances they cannot but feel contemptuous of our pleas. And the longer we delay the fewer Jews there will be left to rescue, the slimmer the chances to get them out.

Between 4,000,000 and 5,000,000 European Jews have been killed since August, 1942, when the Nazi extermination campaign began.

There are people here who say the President cannot risk a move of this kind before election. I believe that an insult to the American public. I do not believe any but a few unworthy bigots would object to giving a few thousand refugees a temporary breathing spell in their flight from oppression. It is a question of Mr. Roosevelt's courage and good faith. All he is called upon to do, after all, is what Franco did months ago, yes, *Franco*. Franco established "free ports," internment camps, months ago for refugees who fled across his border, refugees, let us remember, from his own ally and patron, Hitler. Knowing the Führer's maniacal hatred for Jews, that kindness on Franco's part took considerably more courage than Mr. Roosevelt needs to face a few sneering editorials, perhaps, from the Chicago *Tribune*. I say "perhaps" because I do not know that even Colonel McCormick would in fact be hostile.

Official Washington's capacity for finding excuses for inaction is endless, and many people in the State and War departments who play a part in this matter can spend months sucking their legalistic thumbs over any problem. So many things that might have been done were attempted too late. A little more than a year ago Sweden offered to take 20,000 Jewish children from occupied Europe if Britain and the United States guaranteed their feeding and after the war their repatriation. The British were fairly rapid in this case, but it took three or four months to get these assurances from the American government, and by that time the situation had worsened to a point that seems to have blocked the whole project. In another case the Bulgarian government offered visas for 1,000 Jews if arrangements could be made within a certain time for their departure. A ship was obtained at once, but it took weeks for British officials to get clearance for the project from London, and by that time the time limit had been passed. The records, when they can be published, will show many similar incidents.

The news that the United States had established "free ports" would bring hope to people who have now no hope. It would encourage neutrals to let in more refugees because we could take out some of those they have already admitted. Most important, it would provide the argument of example and the evidence of sincerity in the negotiations for "free ports" in Turkey, last hope of the Balkan Jews. I ask fellow-newspapermen to show the President by their expression of opinion in their own papers that if he hesitates for fear of an unpleasant political reaction he badly misconstrues the real feelings of the American people.

June 17, 1944

How Washington Took the News

MOST OF THE WASHINGTON PRESS CORPS, like most of official Washington, slept peacefully through the early hours of D-Day. The first announcement that the second front had been opened came at 12:37 A.M., long after the usual deadlines of the morning-paper bureaus and long before that of the evenings. The German source of the news and the absence of any confirmation here or in London made bureau chiefs skeptical, and decided them against staff mobilizations. The few who came down town after the German broadcast noted the usual sights — an occasional light in the darkened Navy Department, the lonely sentries before the White House, the couples making love across the way in Lafayette Park. The moon was full, the weather mild.

The Secretary of War and the Chief of Staff had left their offices at 5 P.M. the day before and were safe abed. The big military secret was that Elmer Davis, on leaving the National Press Club at 9:30 that night, had gone back to his office at the OWI [Office of War Information]. The one exciting place in town was the foreign news bureau of the OWI in the Social Security Building near the Capitol, but in the huge adjoining press room as late as 3 A.M. there were only two reporters waiting for the big news — Libby Donahue of *PM* and Joe Laitin of the United Press, neither certain that anything would turn up. There was a guard at the door to keep them away from Elmer Davis's office, and a terrific clatter and clang issued from the foreign news room, with its huge battery of tickers, each with a bell that rings when particularly hot news comes over the wires. The bells rang often and the place was a mad scramble of OWI foreign staff members, but as Libby says, "those boys are crazy

even on a clear day," and one couldn't be sure. Five minute before
United Nations confirmation of the second front at 3:32 A.M. Miss
Donahue was confidentially informed from an authoritative source that
she might as well go home as there would be a long delay. She decided,
however, to stay.

By the time news of the invasion was confirmed, a Philadelphia
Inquirer reporter and an Acme photographer had also arrived, and all
were ushered into Elmer Davis's office to hear General Eisenhower's
broadcast over short wave. Davis looked tired and dazed but perked up
over General Eisenhower's delivery, which was good. "That man could
go places on radio when the war's over," Davis said admiringly.

The State Department moved its regular press conference from noon
to 11 A.M. on D-Day, perhaps out of a sense of the urgency of the
occasion. On the way there we saw a group of curious people, police, and
photographers waiting to get a glimpse of the visiting Polish Premier. He
had an appointment with Under Secretary Stettinius at 10:30, and the
latter, in full protocol, walked across the street to escort Mikolajczyk
over. What they said to each other, then or later, remains a secret, but the
Soviet Ambassador arrived at the department an hour afterward. In
between, the Under Secretary met the press. Hull was away resting at
Hershey, Pennsylvania, and as always it was a pleasure to see Stettinius's
youthful face and quick smile in his place. The Under Secretary read a
prepared statement, "The liberation of Europe has begun . . ." — one of
many like it on D-Day from departmental and embassy mimeographs.
Then he went on to announce recognition of the new Ecuadorean
government, the arrival of the Gripsholm at Jersey City, an agreement by
the Japanese government to pick up supplies at Vladivostok for interned
Allied nationals.

From embassies and department heads, press releases on the invasion
began to appear, but aside from these synthetic reactions there was little
excitement in the capital and — significant item — bond sales actually
fell off. J. Edgar Hoover called for alertness on the home front, and the
War Department asked Congress to establish sixty-nine new national
cemeteries. All over town, in government offices as well as in churches,
there were special prayer services, and many who do not ordinarily pray
joined in them with a sober sense of the struggle on distant beachheads
and its human cost. But on Capitol Hill, where some of us seemed to feel
prayer was most needed, it had little effect. The galleries were well filled,
mostly with visiting service men, but there were only eleven Senators
and a scattering of Representatives present when the day's session

opened. Minority Leader Martin told the house that "partisan politics . . . disappear as we think of the heroic deeds of our men and women" but this must be put down to poetic license. The Republican-Southern Democratic coalition soon got back to work in both houses with unabated enthusiasm. "I felt humble this morning when advised of the invasion," Majority Leader McCormack said. "A strange feeling came over me." The feeling was not widely shared.

Celler of New York tried to block a resolution to speed up the trial of Kimmel and Short[1] by pointing out that Pearl Harbor was in part due to an attitude of public "indifference and callousness . . . influenced by some of the isolationist remarks made in this very House . . . by the gentlemen who are the sponsors of this bill." Said Celler, "I have due respect for the gentlemen and I do not charge them with anything . . . they had a perfect right to their opinions." Retorted Dewey Short of Missouri boldly, "We still have them." The House passed his resolution for trial of Kimmel and Short within three months by a vote of 305 to 35, though trial may disrupt military-naval operations. The Senate went ahead on a bill which promises to hamstring the OPA [Office of Price Administration].

The big local event of the day was the President's regular press conference at 4 P.M., which drew a record crowd. Most of the President's official family, from Fala to Judge Rosenman, seemed to be with him in the executive offices, waiting in a kind of holiday mood to watch the old maestro handle the press. The President was happy and confident but tired, and he has aged. His hand shook a little when he lifted it to the same jaunty cigarette holder. He answers questions slowly, looking up at the ceiling, occasionally wriggling his face and scratching his chest between phrases. Our faces must have shown what most of us felt as we came in. For he began, after an extraordinary pause of several minutes in which no questions were asked and we all stood silent, by saying that the correspondents had the same look on their faces that people all over the country must have and that he thought this a very happy conference. I asked him toward the close to tell us what hopes he felt on this great day, and he said to win the war — 100 percent.

I thought the President's prayer that night a gauche affair, addressing God in familiar, conversational, and explanatory tone, as if it were a fireside chat beamed at heaven. But I am inclined to be charitable when I think of what D-Day means to Franklin D. Roosevelt, of the years since

[1] Rear Admiral Husband E. Kimmel and Major General Walter C. Short commanded, respectively, the U.S. naval and military forces at Pearl Harbor at the time of the Japanese attack.

the "quarantine" speech in which he tried to awaken the American people to their danger and to gird them against enemies they so long refused to recognize. How different it would have been could we have gone into France before it fell; how much easier our task. And how different it would have been if the Germans had turned west and south toward Africa and South America instead of east. How poorly prepared we were in 1941 to resist, and how poorly prepared we are even today to understand. D-Day's events in Congress, the slash last Saturday in UNRRA [United Nations Relief and Rehabilitation Administration] funds, the unseemly and ungrateful uproar over the lend-leasing of a cruiser to the Soviet Union indicate how backward public opinion continues to be, and how formidable is the task the President will face in making the peace. D-Day served to remind us that we are heavily in debt to the man in the White House as well as to the boys on the beachheads.

It's in the Bag for F.D.R.

CHICAGO IS MAGNIFICENT, a brutal force, an imperial city. Walt Whitman would have loved the splendor of its lake front, the skyline that challenges New York's, the luxury of Michigan Avenue and the flop houses of West Madison, the traveling salesmen and the tarts in the midtown hotels, the tireless human tides of the Loop. Little of that exuberant vitality was evident in the Republican National Convention, where droves of newspapermen foraged for scraps of news and delegates moved with bovine apathy into the Dewey camp. The Brickerites, with their boys' choir, lady cellist, and hymns, had something of the fervor of a Methodist revival, though with the sedateness proper in people from the right side of the tracks. The Stassenites were an isolated little band of Puritan internationalists, righteous, horrified, and impotent amid so much compromise with Colonel McCormick and sin. Willkie was only a voice offstage. The Dewey machine was modern, efficient, and triumphant, as slick as an advertising campaign by Batten, Barton, Durstine, and Osborn, proof to Chicago that politics is as susceptible to mass production as meat packing.

The convention itself required a strong stomach and a robust taste for humanity, not in the raw, where idealists may savor it, but in the pretentious and ribald package, human hamburger served up as Salisbury steak with a sprig of parsley. For this was country-club America gathering, respectable and prosperous America, the party of the small-town banker and lawyer as well as the party of Wall and State streets. Bald heads and well-lined paunches filled the rich lobbies of the Stevens. The pretty girl elevator operators got the libidinous eye of the men, the disapproving stare of big-bosomed battle-axes accustomed to preside over the better women's clubs. The convention was no place for anemic prigs or pallid political moralists; it is a little late in the day to demonstrate that the Republican Party does not sincerely intend to build socialism in one country. The best guidebook to the spectacle was not Aristotle or Bryce but Balzac and Sinclair Lewis; here was the petty bourgeoisie in all its greed, cunning, caution, and stupidity; here also was Main Street, standardized but energetic, the horizons narrow but the faces friendly. The delegate's conception of politics may be cretinish, but he's a nice guy to drink beer with at a bar.

The most devoted were the Brickerites, good papas and mamas from small Ohio towns, likable people who trim their lawns and teach their little boys to wash behind the ears. Dewey's girls — he flooded the town with them Sunday — were cover girls, of a well-pasteurized loveliness, from the better agencies, and at least one of them confessed that she was a Democrat. But Bricker's were soulful young things who really thought the big, handsome, gray-haired ham a hero. I was at a Bricker rally Saturday night and heard the Governor's people cheer as he said, "I have been all around this country during the last few months. I know the longings of its people. I know their heart-beats. I know what they want. They want a *real* American for President." Bricker wears his hair like William Butler Yeats, but he's pure Throttlebottom.

No such evangelism was visible in the Dewey camp. Typical scene was that in the Missouri caucus over the week-end, as reported to me second hand. "Now look, boys," was the appeal, "we got to be practical. Remember last time when Pennsylvania missed the boat. One of the best newspapermen in America tells me Dewey already has 840 delegates. He'll be nominated before they ever get to the M's on the roll call. Now let's send our pledges up to Jaeckle and Sprague." So the pledges rolled in, and it was clear that the last possibility of hopeless battle was over Wednesday morning when Joe Martin hammered away with his huge burlesque-show gavel and shouted, "I introduce the Governor of Ohio." Americans like a good loser, and Bricker had the delegates as well as the galleries with him as he withdrew in favor of Dewey. Dewey's nomination produced a five-minute ovation; the delegates cheered Bricker for seventeen. The resentment of the convention broke through when Senator Ball, his face refreshingly different from the pompous statesmen and Honest Johns crowding the platform, withdrew Stassen's candidacy. "Ours," he said angrily, "has been a clean fight."

The formal addresses, interminable in the Turkish-bath atmosphere of the triple-tiered Chicago stadium, were an anthology of cliches; the nominating speeches an orgy of mixed metaphor. Joe Martin said the convention was meeting "in a solemn moment of our history" while we were "locked in a deadly struggle" with "a cruel foe" and "pouring out our treasure," the last being particularly irksome to economy-minded Republicans. Local talent won by a nose in the mixed-metaphor sweepstakes, a Chicago judge calling Dewey a Galahad in shining armor out to get the Holy Grail to perform the Augean task of smashing gang rule forever.

The only good speech of the convention was one made by Colonel Romulo, MacArthur's aide on Bataan, a Filipino with his people's gift for rhetoric, ". . . tell them how we starved . . . tell them how we made bombs out of pop bottles. . . ." Everyone mentioned the war, but no one else made it seem real. Hoover, when he spoke, seemed tired and old. When he finished, the sweat poured from his face under the huge klieg lights and his hands shook so he could not put his glasses in his pocket. Elderly men in sweaty shirts with big cigars waved and cheered the last Republican President with affection felt for a vanished moment in their own youth.

The other speeches, in their standard hollowness and uproarious illiteracy, were not offensive; they invoked the standard semantic symbols of the party. The one speech in bad taste — a feeling I found shared by people whose political views are quite unlike my own — was Clare Luce's bedtime story in the Orphan Annie manner of how G. I. Jim was haunting the convention, "Yes, maybe he was brought here by General George Washington. All Americans know that the General's spirit has watched over every gathering where Presidents have been picked for 147 years. . . ." This was applying whimsy with a shovel. Her attack on the President, leading any stranger to assume that the Republican Party had been the lonely voice during the '30s against the Axis and isolationism, was cheap and contemptible.

The stage managers of the convention, who seemed to have a gift for anti-climax, made Dewey's triumphal entrance a trifle difficult Wednesday night by having the crowd sing "Mine eyes have seen the glory of the coming of the Lord," which was laying it on a bit thick. The nominee himself, sired by Horatio Alger out of Sullivan and Cromwell, looked young and vigorous, and he flushed red with pleasure on the platform. (My story wouldn't be complete without Mother Dewey's statement to the press, "I never thought of Tom's growing up to be President. I just wanted him to be a good boy and he was — most always.") Dewey was not turgid. He was brief, compact, and competent, but he didn't say anything, and I had the feeling that the crowd would have preferred the old-fashioned honey. The reception given him was short and sedate and quite unlike that customary at conventions. The lack of enthusiasm was not a good Republican sign for November.

Nowhere was the rubber-stamp character of the convention more apparent than in the extraordinary session Tuesday afternoon to adopt the platform. Starved for a story, some of us had hoped that the Willkie statement and the Edge protest would stir a fight on the floor against the foreign-policy plank. But not more than 10 per cent of the delegates put in an appearance at the platform session. The plank against more than two terms for President stirred the most applause. The response was mild even to the promise of "rigid economy," an old G.O.P. standby. There was a sprinkling of handclaps for a permanent FEPC [Fair Employment Practices Committee] and against lynching. But for the most part the delegates listened unresponsively as Taft read the entire platform. He moved its adoption. The motion was seconded. There was a scattering of "ayes" and no "noes." The Republicans had a platform.

I don't know what the foreign-policy plank means, but I think its best exposition may be found in the radio address Bricker made last Saturday night. "And finally," Bricker said, "the people of this nation want a foreign policy which will afford them reasonable assurance that their sons and daughters shall not again be asked to lay down their lives on the field of battle. They want America to be helpful in the world. They want America to have a place in a cooperative organization of sovereign nations, but" — and at this point Bricker faced the other way — "but they want no dictatorial world state, no military alliances, no international police force, and no international diplomacy that would lower our standard of living or deprive us of freedom of action." This is the 1920 catch-all formula over again, and those who want a fairly enduring peace can hardly be taken in by it. The Democratic plank will probably be little better than that. But the difference between Roosevelt and the Republican nominees is the difference between a man who wants some international order but is trimming his sails to placate the isolationists, and men who are opposed to an international order but are throwing out a few coy come-ons to those who want peace and security.

"I smell New Dealers," pudgy, raucous, but shrewd Gerald L. K. Smith cried in a speech to his followers last Sunday after they forced their way into the Stevens ballroom. The smell is strong in the domestic planks of the Republican platform. Like every Republican platform since

1936, it accepts the basic principles and legislation of the New Deal and in effect criticizes only their administration. Dewey and the men around him, though they stand naturally with the haves against the have-nots of our society, have no government philosophy of their own. They know it would be politically unsafe to call for repeal of New Deal legislation and are left only with the issue of efficient government. This is not a very exciting issue even when dressed up in unpopular words like "bureaucracy." In normal times natural dissatisfaction with the "ins" would make this a good-enough lever for Tweedledum to oust Tweedledee with. But this is not that kind of a year.

I think the general feeling here among the newspapermen and, in private, the politicians is that the Republican Party will not make its come-back until 1948, and Mark Sullivan has hinted as much. The time spent by the Republicans in answering the old saw about changing horses in midstream indicates that it has them worried. If the war is going well, Roosevelt's chances will be helped. If it should take a turn for the worse, the atmosphere will not be conducive to an all-out partisan campaign against him. On domestic issues the Republicans are New Dealers in spite of themselves, and have no clear line on which to fight. The biggest issue for the campaign will be that of American cooperation with a new world order, and that is an issue on which enough Republicans feel deeply to win several million crucial votes for Roosevelt. The Democrats will make a mistake if they place too much stress on Dewey's youth; they have too many old fogies hanging around Washington. But the question of Dewey's experience and maturity in dealing with leaders of other countries and in coping with the problems of peace is a real one and will also keep many votes in the Roosevelt column.

The Chicago convention was the convention of a do-nothing party run by say-nothing politicians hankering for the past but afraid to speak up for it — even Bricker attacked "reactionaries who would return to 'the good old days.'" With Willkie as its candidate, this party might have won enough progressives away from Roosevelt to win. With Dewey and Bricker, the party will only alienate enough conservative internationalist Republicans to lose. Mr. Roosevelt will win in November, and some chance of a decent world order will win with him.

July 22, 1944

Henry Wallace — a Great American

$\backsim$ $\sim$

I HAVE CHECKED and verified the Washington *Post* report that party leaders met with the President at dinner in the White House last Tuesday night and "ganged up" on Wallace. I can also report that with this dinner conference the anti-Wallace bloc shot its bolt and that it will be Wallace at Chicago. The politician-lobbyists, the municipal bosses, the right-wing Democrats, at least one timid white House adviser, and a whole covey of phony liberals have had their say, and it has not moved the President. Mr. Roosevelt made clear to all of them what he had previously told Ed Flynn of New York. He does not want a man over sixty as his running mate — which disposes of several aged hopefuls. He does not want a routine politician — which disposes of several more. He wants Henry A. Wallace of Iowa — which disposes of the rest of them. Wallace it will be.

The big interests of this country do not want Wallace, and they are well equipped with mouthpieces in the Democratic Party. Two of the more obvious were at the White House dinner. One is Oscar R. Ewing. Ewing is vice-chairman of the Democratic National Committee and also general counsel and principal Washington lobbyist for the Aluminum Company of America. Alcoa fears Wallace's anti-monopolistic views. Another is Edwin J. Pauley. Pauley is treasurer of the Democratic National Committee. He is an "independent" California oil operator who is curiously fraternal with the big oil companies, notably Standard of California, his principal competitor. The Standard Oil crowd hate Wallace for his anti-cartel views.

The "practical" politicians were there to reinforce these views with figures. They said Wallace would cost the ticket from 1,000,000 to 3,000,000 votes. Robert E. Hannegan, chairman of the Democratic National Committee, and most members of the committee have been part of the anti-Wallace block from the beginning. Their efforts broke on the rock of Mr. Roosevelt's "Dutch" stubbornness. The President, who has been prepared to compromise on many things, will not compromise on the choice of the man who might become his successor. From several sources in excellent positions to know his mind, I can report that the President feels that only with Wallace in office as Vice-President can he be sure that his great objectives at home and abroad will be pursued.

At least two high Administration figures went to see Wallace on his return from the Far East to ask him to withdraw. One was Judge Samuel M. Rosenman, who usually turns up on the rightist side of the fence in intra-Administration controversies. The other was Secretary of the Interior Ickes. Ickes has two links with the anti-Wallace forces. He is an old buddy of Pauley's, and he picked Ralph Davies of Standard of California as oil administrator partly on Pauley's recommendation. Ickes has been close to the oil trust and the oil trust hates Wallace. Both Ickes and Rosenman also have always been close to Tom Corcoran, who has been boosting Douglas as his first choice and Rayburn of Texas as his second choice against Wallace. As a leading figure in Sterling Drug, a company which was a long-time ally of I. G. Farben before the war and may be so again after it, Corcoran has a stake in revival of the cartel system Wallace has fought.

The weakness of the anti-Wallace block in 1940 was its failure to get together on a single candidate. This failure reflected the bloc's underestimate of Wallace's strength. The same weakness is apparent this time. Corcoran has tried in some degree to correct it by an alliance with the forces behind Rayburn, and at one time the Douglas crowd and the Rayburn crowd were prepared to swing over at Chicago to whichever of their respective candidates seemed the stronger. A grotesque incident in the annals of this alliance was Corcoran's effort to get Josephus Daniels to sign an article Corcoran had prepared extolling Rayburn. Daniels indignantly declined to serve as a stooge, and it looks now as though neither Douglas nor Rayburn will cut much of a figure at Chicago.

The chief hopes of the big-business crowd fighting Wallace have been centered on Barkley, and utility interests in New York are said to have used their affiliates out in the country (1) to drum up support for Barkley and (2) to titillate several state governors with the hint that if Wallace can be stopped maybe the lightning will strike them. Georgia Power and Light spokesmen, for example, "contacted" Governor Arnall of Georgia, but unsuccessfully. Similar overtures and soundings have been made by utility interests in Oklahoma, New Mexico, Chicago, and Jersey City. That they have failed is indicated by Hague's statement that he will support anybody the President wants for Vice-President and also by Senator Truman's statement that he does not want the nomination.

The anti-Wallace forces have been skillful in using the press, but unfortunately for them the President and not the press will decide the nomination. For several weeks the Douglas forces have tried to get leading labor leaders to indicate that they would support Douglas if they could not get Wallace. R. J. Thomas of the automobile workers was one of those approached, also unsuccessfully. Even the night before the joint Murray-Hillman press conference, some newspapermen fell for the report that the C.I.O. was considering a second choice in the event that Wallace could not be nominated. Ickes telephoned Hillman in an effort to get the Political Action chief to name an alternative. All that failed with Murray's statement, fully backed by Hillman, "We have no other choice and we're not doing any trading."

The argument that Wallace will lose the party votes is being combated here by two important groups. One is the C.I.O. and the other the Negroes. The C.I.O. has advanced the view that in several key Northern states, notably New York, the presence of Wallace on the ticket will increase enthusiasm and make it possible to get out a larger vote. I think the argument is a sound one, and I think that if Wallace loses the ticket any votes it will be largely in areas, such as the South, that Roosevelt will carry anyway.

The South's bargaining power has largely been destroyed by the strong position taken in the Republican platform on the FEPC [Fair Employment Practices Committee], lynching, discrimination in the armed forces, and the poll tax. Talk of a coalition between the Republicans and the right-wing Southern Democrats proved the idlest kind of speculation at the Republican National Convention, and no one there ever took the rumor of a Dewey-Byrd ticket seriously. Disgruntled Democrats in the South cannot affect the outcome in November, but the Negro vote might easily prove decisive. The convention of the National Association for the Advancement of Colored People in Chicago Sunday night is expected to indorse Wallace strongly, and his nomination might solve a leading Democratic problem. The party can weasel or keep silent on the Negro question in the platform, thus placating the Southerners, and still carry the bulk of the Negro vote by renominating Wallace. For Roosevelt and Wallace provide a better guaranty of better treatment for the Negro than any promises in the Republican platform.

For a day or so the anti-Wallace forces thought they had won something of a victory when the President announced that he would run without making Wallace's nomination a condition as he did in 1940. That belief was dissipated on reflection. The President could not say, "If the people command me ... I have as little right to withdraw as the soldier has to leave his post in the line," and then say that he would not run unless he had Wallace as his running mate. Those who know what the President has been thinking know that the key to his stand for Wallace is in the second paragraph from the end of his letter to Hannegan. The President wants as a possible successor a man who will carry on the objectives he set in that letter, the objectives of a permanent peace abroad and full employment and a higher standard of living at home. To Roosevelt, as to millions of Americans, that spells Wallace.

May I be permitted to cast my own vote on the eve of this historic decision? I have met and talked with the Vice-President, and in recent weeks I have questioned many people who have been associated with him in the Department of Agriculture and in the Board of Economic Warfare. I have been reading the newly published collection of his past speeches and articles in "Democracy Reborn." I think I have a good picture of his weaknesses and of his strength. He has not Mr. Roosevelt's robust human qualities or his extraordinary capacity for politics. He is not always wise in his judgment of people. He is shy and does not always "go over" with audiences. But he is extraordinary in his honesty, especially his honesty with himself, in his understanding of man and history, and in his vision.

Like Roosevelt, Wallace grew to wider understanding in Washington. But like Roosevelt, too, he compromised when the forces against him proved too strong, as in the famous purge of Jerome Frank, Lee Pressman, and Gardner Jackson in 1935 under pressure from the milk trust, the planters, and the packers. Like Roosevelt, he is not a revolutionist but a democratic leader trying within the limits of political possibility to correct the economic evils of our society and to help its underprivileged. He offers the kind of leadership that alone holds out hope of peaceful and gradual reform in our society, of the achievement of security and employment by combined private and governmental action. In a time of crisis, such as we may encounter after the war, he would acquit himself with greatness. Few people understand the problems of our society and of the world so well, and few have his broad humanity, his tolerance, his concern for people, few that genuine personal saintliness that is Wallace's. I think we may count our country fortunate in having in a single generation two leaders of the stature and vision of Franklin D. Roosevelt and Henry A. Wallace.

November 25, 1944

The 65-Cent Minimum

〜〜 〜〜

TWO BASIC DOMESTIC ISSUES have arisen here for progressives, and they call for the fullest possible measure of public understanding and pressure. Both are central to the problem of achieving full employment after the war, and on neither can we expect leadership from the White House. The first revolves around the appointment of the new Surplus Property Board; the second around the Pepper resolution for a 65-cent minimum wage, on which hearings opened Friday before a Senate labor and education subcommittee.

Something has been gained since I touched upon the first in last week's letter. Protests from Philip Murray of the C.I.O., James Patton of the National Farmers' Union, and several Senators, including Murray and Kilgore, have led the White House to withdraw one of its intended appointments to the Surplus Property Board and to hold up the other two. The appointment withdrawn is that of Colonel Joseph P. Woodlock, who has been executive assistant to Will Clayton as Surplus Property Administrator under an executive order issued last February. The two held up, after Senator Barkley told the President that a board controlled by the nominees of Jesse Jones and Will Clayton would not be confirmed in the Senate, are those of Sam H. Husbands and James Shepherd. Husbands is a faithful workhorse in the Jones-dominated RFC [Reconstruction Finance Corporation] and its subsidiaries — unimaginative, competent in a narrow way, totally unsuited to the task of using government-owned plants, lands, and commodities as a means to break monopoly and stimulate industrial expansion toward full employment. He was to be, and may still be, nominated for the chairmanship.

Shepherd, unknown here, is a partner in a corporation-law firm in Los Angeles. Such nominees are unfit for anything but maintenance of the semi-monopolistic status quo, which is exactly what the Jones-Clayton-Baruch-Byrnes crowd have in mind — and what the President appears prepared to acquiesce in, despite his talk of 60,000,000 jobs after the war. On this issue it would be most helpful if the White House heard some grumbling from the grass roots.

The second issue raises two questions, one ethical, the other economic. The first is whether at this late date we are to take a firm step toward that equality of sacrifice once promised us in the war. The second is whether we are to take the first small step toward providing the volume of mass purchasing power necessary to maintain full employment after the war. The 65-cents-an-hour resolution, for which we are all indebted to Senator Pepper of Florida, would do both. The Pepper measure has its origin in certain forlornly neglected provisions of the President's hold-the-line order of October 3, 1943. The National War Labor Board [NWLB] was ordered to stabilize wages except where increases were called for "to correct maladjustments or inequalities, to eliminate substandards of living, to correct gross inequalities, or to aid in the effective prosecution of the war." The WLB has moved but falteringly to correct inequalities or to eliminate "substandards of living," and the concurrent resolution introduced by Senator Pepper would declare it "the sense of the Congress that a straight-time hourly rate of 65 cents per hour is the minimum below which the National War Labor Board shall consider any wage substandard." At present employers may raise wages to 40 cents an hour without reference to the board, and regional boards may raise wages up to 50 cents an hour without reference to the national board. This is on the theory that wages below these levels are substandard. The Pepper resolution would increase the rate to 65 cents, but in the form of an authorization rather than a direction to the board.

A rate of 65 cents an hour adds up to $26 for a forty-hour week, or $1,352 a year for workers lucky enough to work fifty-two weeks a year. This is considerably below the so-called emergency budget for a family of four as figured out originally by the WPA [Works Progress Administration], with the warning that it was intended only "for an emergency standard which may be necessary under depressed conditions" and might prove "harmful to both health and morale" if too long continued. This budget, as adjusted to present prices, calls for an income of $1,730 a year, or an average hourly earning rate of 86-½ cents. Lest any reader think this too munificent, I give the budget as broken down into its constituent parts so he can compare it with his own household expenditures: food, $751; clothing, $214; housing, $201; household operation, $186; miscellaneous, $172; taxes, $44; war bonds, $62. This for four people, for one year. Its housing allowance — about $16 a month — will give you an idea of the living standard called for by this emergency budget, which is $378 a year more than would be made by a man working a forty-hour week the year round at 65 cents an hour.

Now despite war prosperity, and there is plenty of it in the middle and upper brackets, the testimony before the Pepper committee showed that 40 percent of America's workers are making less than 65 cents an hour. The number ranges from 3 per cent in mining to 86 percent in retail trade. In the manufacturing industries one worker in four is making less than 65 cents an hour. "The American economy," Philip Murray told the committee, "is still loaded down with low income groups. Thirty per cent of all consumer units in the United States were in 1943 still receiving less than $1,500 per year. There are still 7,093,000 consumer units which are earning less than $1,000 per year. The group between $1,000 and $1,500 numbered 5,120,000 consumer units. All of these families and single consumer units cannot even maintain the emergency level of living established by the Works Progress Administration for persons and families on relief."

Eleven million American workers are earning less than 65 cents an hour. It is clear that even under conditions of war prosperity, not one-third but two-fifths of the American working class is ill fed, ill clothed, ill housed. That their employers have done somewhat better in the war is indicated by testimony as to how much a 65-cent minimum would cost industry. "For industries involved," Emil Rieve of the Textile Workers' Union told the Pepper committee, "total profits in 1943, based on corporate tax returns, were 303 per cent above 1936–39. Increased wages under Senator Pepper's proposal represent only 7 per cent of 1943 profits in manufacturing industries, 1.1 per cent in mining industries, and 6.85 per cent in finance, insurance, and real-estate industries. This, it is plain, would still leave employers a substantial proportion of their increase in profits over 1936–39." It is also plain that the OPA [Office of Price Administration] has been a good deal more tender to business in fixing prices at a profitable level than the WLB has been thoughtful of labor in correcting "inequalities" and "eliminating substandard" wages.

This is not merely an ethical problem, it is also an economic one. Workers living on this level hardly provide the market we need for full employment after the war. The Shoe Workers' Union, pleading for the

65-cent minimum, pointed out that today 19.6 per cent of the women and 27.3 per cent of the men in this country can afford only one pair of shoes at a time and that 61.5 per cent of the population own two pairs or less. "If the American shoe industry wants a market," John Rackliffe said, "here it is." Frances Sayler of the United Electrical, Radio, and Machine Workers, after analyzing the sales figures in those industries, testified that if the annual income of the lower-paid workers were moved up into the $1,500–$3,000-a-year class, "it would mean a potential market for some 7,000,000 refrigerators where those products had never been bought before." That, she pointed out, is more than double the 1941 boom level production. Here, obviously, in raising low living standards, is the key to full employment of facilities and man-power.

Let no one imagine, however, that a mere increase of minimums to the 65-cent level is going to be anywhere near enough to create the post-war market we need. It is expected that with the defeat of Germany war production will slow down and overtime will be less necessary. The elimination of overtime in manufacturing would cut $2,153,000 from its wage bill — and that also means from its market for manufactures. As against this, the adoption of the 65-cent minimum in manufacturing would add but $935,000,000. In terms of purchasing power we shall have taken two steps backward to one step forward. Let us look at the figures in another way. Our gross national production is running at about $200 billion a year, of which $105 billion is war expenditure. That provides some idea of the gap which must be closed to get full employment after the war. The 65-cent minimum would contribute $5-½ billion in purchasing power toward the closing of that gap. It is little enough, but to get even this little will take a fight.

PART VII

1945

This Is What We Voted For

THE FIRST REACTIONS of the capital in the concrete and energetic communiqué from the Crimea Conference[1] indicates that this will rank as one of the President's greatest achievements. With Mr. Churchill and Marshal Stalin, he has taken us one firm step farther along the difficult road to a total victory and a stable peace. Much since November 7 has been disheartening to the day-by-day observer, but in the proceedings at Yalta the historic significance of Mr. Roosevelt's reelection is made plain — in foreign policy a continuation of close and friendly liaison among the leaders of the Big Three, the *sine qua non* of Axis defeat and post-war reconstruction. One can easily imagine Governor Dewey doing many of the same things and making many of the same appointments as Mr. Roosevelt since the election, but one cannot imagine a Republican President reaching the Crimea agreement on Poland, as one cannot imagine a Republican President appointing a man of Henry Wallace's outlook as Secretary of Commerce. Whatever his compromises on less important matters and however his evaluation of detail and his sense of timing may differ from those of some of his progressive supporters, Mr. Roosevelt's course clearly remains charted toward the two major objectives of an enduring peace abroad and full employment at home. This is what we voted for.

In the sphere of military action the Crimea communiqué is regarded here as foreshadowing a new offensive against the Reich, this time from

[1] At the February 1945 Crimea conference at Yalta, Roosevelt, Churchill, and Stalin planned the final defeat of Germany and the zones of occupation into which that country would be divided and agreed on free elections in Poland (a promise soon broken by Stalin); Russia agreed to enter the war on Japan; a San Francisco conference to plan the United Nations was approved.

the north, probably through Denmark. Should the Germans be forced to fight on a fourth front, their collapse would be hastened, and there is much hopeful speculation about the Russian agreement to sit in *with the Chinese* at the United Nations Security Conference to be held at San Francisco on April 25. The date is the deadline for denunciation of the non-aggression pact between the U.S.S.R. and Japan, and it is felt that the Soviets would not risk this announcement, with all it may imply in Tokyo, unless they were confident that final victory over the Reich will be close enough in the next few weeks to enable them to handle a surprise attack by Japan. This reflects confidence by the U.S.S.R. not only in its own strength but in the trustworthiness of its allies. A related indication of the ever closer relations among the Big Three is found in certain phrases in the communiqué which seem to doom any hopes that might have been nurtured by the "Free German" generals in Moscow.

When Stalin joins in expressing an "inflexible purpose to destroy German militarism ... to disarm and disband *all* German armed forces; break up *for all time* the German General Staff ... remove or destroy all German military equipment; eliminate or control all German industry that could be used for military production ... remove all Nazi *and militarist* influences from public office and from the cultural and economic life of the German people" (my italics), he must feel sure enough of his Western allies to shut the door on the use of the Marshal von Paulus crowd as an alternative instrument of Soviet policy. A declaration of intent to "disband *all* German armed forces" is a departure from earlier Stalin statements that seemed to promise the Reich the right to retain an army and opened an avenue of negotiation between Moscow and dissident German generals among its prisoners.* To use some of these generals as pawns against the West might at one time have seemed a grim political possibility in Moscow. Apparently the Crimea Conference has made Marshal Stalin feel that no such dangerous game will be necessary. This is regarded here as not the least of the President's achievements at Yalta.

Even so fruitful a conference as the one just closed cannot be expected to solve all mutual problems. It is noted here that while the leaders of the Big Three agreed on the establishment of a joint commission to discuss reparations, they have yet to establish a joint commission on war crimes. The communiqué does, indeed, speak of an inflexible resolve to bring all war criminals to just and swift punishment, but recent events have made it quite clear that this resolve is much less inflexible in Washington and

* "It is not our aim," Stalin said on November 6, 1942, "to destroy all military force in Germany."

London than it is in Moscow. It may be significant in this connection that the communiqué makes no reference to the industrial collaborators of the Nazis whom the Russians also wish to punish but some Anglo-American circles are anxious to protect. This may explain the failure to set up a joint body to handle the many complex problems involved in punishing Nazi higher-ups and the omission of any joint statement warning the neutrals not to grant asylum to Nazi leaders. In this sphere it would seem that leaders of the Big Three do not yet see eye to eye. Franco Spain is one of the neutrals which need renewed warning, and the Argentine is another. Here the differences among the powers are well known.

It is good to know that there will be closer cooperation and consultation among the Big Three in the future in regard to liberated countries, and it is hoped that they will also decide in the near future to begin informal but detailed discussion of the problems which will arise in the occupation of Germany. The announcement that the Reich will be split into three and almost certainly — when the French join in — four separate spheres of military control does not solve these problems; it only sets the stage for them. There will be a joint military commission in Berlin, but this also will not be enough to make certain that the occupying powers carry out their pledge to extirpate all traces of Nazism in the Reich. The Russians are better qualified for this task by political training, temperament, and the working-class basis of their regime. Unless there is mutual discussion, we may find Nazi elements taking refuge underground in the more equable and complacent climate of the English or American zone of occupation. This would be dangerous not only for the future of the Reich but for future relations among the occupying powers.

It is in the handling of these concrete problems that Allied unity and efficiency will be tested rather than in the formal details of voting rights and the structural charts for the projected world security organization. But it is on the latter and above all on the Polish settlement that discussion in Congress and by the opposition will center. The position to be taken by the Republican Party is not to be judged from the first approving statements evoked by the Crimea communiqué. Senators Austin of Vermont and White of Maine have applauded the results of the conference, but both are internationalist Republicans. Herbert Hoover, with unexpected and admirable magnanimity, has praised the President's work. But Vandenberg, the bell-wether of the party majority on foreign policy, indicated that he was undecided about the Polish settlement. It is on the Curzon line that the main battle will be fought. The danger is not from the extreme isolationists like Wheeler; they command the sympathies of only a negligible minority in the country and the Senate. The danger, as in the old League fight, lies in those who express themselves as fully in accord with the need for preventing German resurgence and establishing world peace but —. This time the leader of the "but" brigade is Vandenberg. Until the announced results of the Crimea Conference, he seemed to offer a bridge, however shaky, between the old isolationism and world cooperation. But the final settlement of the Polish question at Yalta brings fully into view the most treacherous aspects of the Vandenberg proposal. Now to propose the reopening of the Polish settlement after the war would be to disrupt the Allied unity and confidence on which not only the military strategy but the diplomatic decisions of the Crimea Conference were based. Not the slightest cost of the Vandenberg proposal would be Soviet cooperation in the war against Japan. To insist on perfectionism along the Pripet Marshes might mean payment in American lives on Pacific islands. That would be a high price to pay for Polish megalomania and American domestic politics.

The Pell Affair

〜 〜

I POINTED OUT in the last week's letter that the one disappointment in the Crimea communiqué was the failure of the Big Three to agree on joint action for the punishment of war criminals. There are obstacles to effective action in this field. One is the British Foreign Office, and the other is the American State Department. There are three reasons why progressive and labor pressure ought to be brought to bear against these obstacles. One is that the lives of several million prisoners of war and slave workers in the Reich may be endangered if the Nazis are led to believe that the British and American governments will be half-hearted in dealing with war criminals. The slaughter of slave workers, perhaps also of war prisoners, in the final hours before the Reich's fall would fit in with German plans to kill off as many of the non-German peoples of Europe as possible in preparation for a third attempt at world conquest. The second reason for acting quickly and effectively to punish Nazi war criminals is that we can thereby eliminate many of the party stalwarts who intend to go underground and prepare for the next war. The third reason is that the best way to lay the foundations for world security is to punish those responsible for the war and for the crimes committed in it.

The focus of progressive and labor pressure might well be the curious case of Herbert C. Pell, who was the American representative on the United Nations War Crimes Commission in London. Pell's return to London would be a victory for common sense and human decency. Pell was a Bull Moose Republican in 1912, later becoming a Democrat. He served a term in Congress after the last war, served as chairman of the

New York State Democratic Committee from 1921 to 1926, and was vice-chairman of the Democratic National Committee in 1936. In 1937 he was appointed Minister to Portugal and in 1941 to Hungary. He seems to be a man of considerable wealth and culture, and seven years in the foreign service have failed to harden his spiritual arteries. He was one of the few men in the service who was sympathetic to Jewish and other refugees, and it is quite clear he is not in agreement with the ultra-legalistic Nervous Nellies who seem to dominate interpretation of international law at the State Department and the British Foreign Office. Sir Cecil Hurst and Pell were the leading figures on the War Crimes Commission, and both were for effective action to punish war criminals. Sir Cecil resigned in disgust with the attitude of the Foreign Office. What happened to Pell is still something of a mystery.

There are, roughly speaking, three kinds of war crimes. In the first category are crimes against the civilians or captured soldiers of the United Nations; the men accused of these crimes are to be returned for trial to the country against whose nationals the crimes were committed. This category is the simplest from the standpoint of law and procedure, though British and American international lawyers may be counted on to mess it up with multitudinous technicalities. In the second category are the deeds of Axis higher-ups responsible for the policies of mass murder, looting, prostitution, and moral corruption applied in occupied countries as part of the German and Japanese war programs. For these criminals, whose crimes were not limited to any one country, special courts and special procedure will be required. The third category, the most difficult from a conventional legal point of view, is made up of crimes committed by the Nazis and German nationals on account of race, creed, or politics. The Foreign Office and State Department seem to be still in a dither on the second and third categories. Pell, like Sir Cecil and unlike many of the legalists, was for punishment of both these categories and returned here in December for further instructions.

As the American representative on the United Nations War Crimes Commission Pell was a Presidential and not a State Department appointee. He saw the President at the White House on the morning of January 9. He found Mr. Roosevelt in agreement with his views. Pell was encouraged and went to the State Department on the afternoon of that same day to pay his respects to Secretary of State Stettinius before returning to London. Stettinius told Pell he could not return to London because Congress had failed to make an appropriation to cover his salary and expenses. When Pell offered to pay his own way and serve without charge, he was told this would be illegal. The expenses of participation in the United Nations War Crimes Commission had been paid out of the President's emergency fund, but under the Russell amendment to the 1944 Appropriation Act Congressional authorization is required for such payments and activities. An authorization of $30,000 asked for the first half of this year had been refused by the House Appropriations Committee, approved by the Senate Appropriations Committee, and then eliminated in conference committee.

It seems strange that so small an item would create such difficulties. A minor State Department official testified before the House committee; Stettinius himself sent a letter to the Senate committee. Could it be that some State Department official privately egged the House committee on to kill this item? Such things happen in Washington. The conference committee eliminated the $30,000 item on December 16. Pell saw the President on January 9; neither knew at the time that the item had been eliminated. Why weren't the President and Pell informed earlier? The State Department interprets the Russell amendment as meaning that where Congress fails to provide an appropriation it automatically withdraws authorization for the activity which would be financed by that appropriation. But if this is the correct interpretation, why did Acting Secretary Grew announce on January 26 that the United States would be represented on the War Crimes Commission by Pell's former deputy, Lieutenant Colonel Joseph V. Hodgson, former Attorney General of Hawaii?

If Pell's elimination is merely due to Congressional action and not to State Department hostility, why did Grew decline to answer when asked whether Pell would return to London if Congress reconsidered and made the $30,000 available? Finally, I would like to note that Chairman Anderson of the House committee says he was under the impression that the State Department did not need the $30,000 but had enough to carry on until the fiscal year beginning July 1. Where did he get that impression? The chairman indicated that he would take a favorable attitude toward a request for a deficiency appropriation in the pending deficiency bill. But though other deficiency items from the State Department were sent to the committee ten days ago, the $30,000 item was not among them. The department blames the Bureau of the Budget. There is something fishy here.

"There will be no diminution," Grew said augustly in the Pell announcement on January 26, "in the interest or activity of this government in the general subject of the punishment of war criminals."

Would the editors of *The Nation* (page the shade of Godkin) permit me less augustly to say "horse feathers"? Pell had been back from London almost two months at the time that statement was made; yet the department hadn't been interested enough to arrange a conference at which Pell and Roosevelt would have a chance to discuss Pell's experience and problems in London with legal and other officers of the department. Nor was Pell given a chance to discuss them with Stettinius or Grew. Grew is the main source of our tender concern for Hirohito, and the State Department's international lawyers live in the shadow of the late James Brown Scott, who joined with the Japanese at the Versailles conference to help save the Kaiser and other heads of state from responsibility for war crimes. These departmental lawyers are more concerned with the hallowed antiquarianisms of academic international law than with punishing war criminals. International law today, like the common law and equity in the past, calls for robust and creative minds with enough faith in themselves to adapt past concepts to new needs. There is little evidence of their quality in the State Department. In London I am sure many Tories fear war-crime trials; were Hess or Ribbentrop to take the stand in his own defense, either might involve a good many members of the British aristocracy. There is also an undercurrent of Anglo-American upper-class hostility to the trial of war criminals; once begun, it would be almost impossible to protect financial and business opposite numbers in the Axis countries from punishment. There is a subtle international solidarity here that is not the least of the obstacles to just punishment of Axis murderers and the men who profited by Axis crimes.

Alcoa in Wonderland

THE ALUMINUM COMPANY OF AMERICA was formed in
1888. The Sherman Anti-Trust Act was passed in 1890. From 1893
until 1940 the company had a 100 per cent monopoly of all aluminum
produced in the United States. A court of last resort has at last held the
Aluminum Company of America a monopoly and a violator of the
Sherman Act. Thus does anti-trust adjudication move at snail's pace its
wonders to perform.

The case of the Aluminum Company evokes satire and despair. The
aluminum monopoly has been the subject of two court proceedings and
three investigations by the Federal Trade Commission. It has been
investigated five times by the Department of Justice. It has accepted two
consent decrees, one in 1912, another in 1942, rather than stand trial. It
has been sued by private litigants under the anti-trust laws on at least
four occasions — and grown steadily larger and more powerful.

The present proceedings began in 1933 and are still far from ended.
The record, 58,000 pages long, is already of Penguin Island pro-
portions — so huge that only two employees of the Department of
Justice have, between them, read the entire record, each concentrating on
one half and meeting midway in the legalistic morass. The current suit
was filed in 1933 and was met at once with a piquant argument that
required four years for its disposal. The Aluminum Company dug up
the long-ignored and violated consent decree of 1912 and sought to use
it as a shield. The company argued in substance that since the decree
forbade it to engage in the practices with which it was now charged by
the government, the new anti-trust suit was harassing, improper, and a

mere duplication of the earlier proceedings. The idea that a company could not only violate a consent decree with impunity but utilize the decree to exempt itself from further prosecution might have been the product of a law firm in which Lewis Carroll and James M. Barrie were the senior partners. The ingenious doctrine was learnedly rejected by the United States Supreme Court in 1937.

From the standpoint of the public interest, this litigation was not all waste motion. In the First World War Arthur V. Davis of the Aluminum Company was a member of the War Industries Board. During that war Alcoa raised the price of aluminum from 19 to 38 cents per pound. Over the objections of other members of the board, Davis maintained a differential between ingot, in which Alcoa had a complete monopoly, and fabricated aluminum, in which it had some competition, at a figure which put the squeeze on his competitors.

The current anti-trust action has at least served to keep Alcoa on the defensive. During the great depression, while the price of other non-ferrous metals fell from 39 to 71 per cent, the price of aluminum was augustly maintained at a point but 4 per cent below that of 1927. This was in accord with Davis's philosophy, as he once explained it to the French aluminum company, "that it was better to restrict production and sell at a higher price than it was to go ahead at full capacity and sell at a low price." But Alcoa dropped its price 2-½ cents in 1933 "because it feared some action" by the Department of Justice. The words are those of Judge Learned Hand in the new Alcoa decision. Successive reductions since the current Department of Justice investigation began have brought the price of aluminum down from its depression rate of 23.3 cents a pound to 15 cents a pound. This is in sharp contrast to the World War I price record and represents a sizable gain to the government. With aluminum production running upward of two billion pounds a year, a decline of 8.3 cents a pound in price is a saving of $166,000,000 a year. In this sphere at least, the heroically patient and tireless Don Quixotes of the Anti-Trust Division have not been engaged entirely in a futile task.

To their credit also must be marked up the education of a whole generation of progressive Senators and newspapermen. The Truman committee investigation was largely primed from the files of the Department of Justice and in its turn helped to make possible the vast war-time expansion of the aluminum industry against the wishes of Alcoa. Today we also have two independent producers of aluminum, Reynolds and Olin, with 202 million pounds of capacity between them and about 1,293 million pounds of capacity in government-owned plants.

Thanks also to the effects of this litigation and to the brave fight waged last year by former Assistant Attorney General Norman Littell against Will Clayton, we have a Surplus Property Act which directs the disposal of these and other surplus war plants in a way which will break the hold of monopoly on the industry. Attorney General Biddle and his Assistant Attorney General in charge of anti-trust enforcement, Wendell Berge, have considerable power under that act and are using it against the aluminum monopoly. We have gained some toe-holds in the ancient battle, and it would be unfair and defeatist not to recognize them, however pernicious we may suspect them to be.

The more encouraging aspect of the new Alcoa decision by Judge Hand and his two colleagues of the United States Circuit Court of Appeals is not its belated finding that Alcoa is a monopoly; nor its reversal, by way of a dictum of Cardozo's, of the old United States Steel case decision that "mere size" is not monopoly. "Mere size," the court now holds, if sufficient to dominate an industry, is itself a violation of the Sherman Act, a monopolistic situation subject to legal remedy. The present Supreme Court, had it not lacked a quorum to pass on the Aluminum case, would almost certainly have held likewise. But these are mere paper triumphs. Past experience has shown that the ingenuity of the corporate bar is sufficient to produce new devices for evasion far more rapidly than they can be disposed of in the staid tempo of judicial processes. The encouraging aspect of the decision is that it points to the anti-monopolistic provisions of the Surplus Property Act and puts Alcoa on notice that if government-owned aluminum plants are sold in such a way as to leave Alcoa in command of the industry, the company's dissolution may be ordered. Final action on the government's motion to dissolve the Aluminum Company was postponed until after the war and the disposal of government-owned plants. Thus the court calls attention to the only effective remedy for monopoly, the use of government-owned plants to restore competitive conditions. The remedy lies not in further anti-trust litigation but in the policy to be applied by Congress, the Surplus Property Board, and the Attorney General in the disposal of war plants.

For Judge Hand's decision underscores the futility of depending on the courts for effective action against monopoly. In the first place, the decision leaves the impression that public interest has been sacrificed to judicial good-fellowship. The lower-court decision by Federal District Judge Francis G. Caffey was extraordinarily obsequious to the Aluminum Company of America, and the Judge's conduct called either for rebuke or for a better defense than his brethren of the Circuit Court were able to furnish. I give a sample of his manner. At one point Judge Caffey declined to admit evidence unfavorable to Alcoa with the statement, "It is excluded. Proceed. I exclude it without looking at it. I don't care what is in it." The government was attempting to present evidence showing that Alcoa had bought up a Norwegian aluminum company to prevent General Motors and Ford from obtaining an independent source of supply for the light metal.

I give a sample of Judge Caffey's reasoning methods. One of the important questions in the case arose from the admitted fact that the same stockholders, the Mellon and Davis families, control both the Aluminum Company of America and Aluminum, Ltd., of Canada. This Canadian corporate alter ego engages in practices which would be illegal for an American company, notably in the field of cartels, while the American parent concern enjoys the fruits of these practices. Should an American corporation be allowed to evade the anti-trust laws through a Canadian affiliate? Judge Caffey said it should and buttressed his findings with an analogy of exceptional irrelevance and puerility. Suppose, Judge Caffey asked, ten men formed a steel company and then the "same stockholders at the same time also organized a corporation to engage in the production and sale of cornflakes. Could it be maintained that the fact that the stockholders in these two corporations were identical . . . would render them guilty of conspiracy?"

It is not surprising that the Department of Justice complained to the Circuit Court that Judge Caffey had "sweepingly granted the findings and conclusions of law requested by the appellees [Alcoa] upon virtually every issue." The department pointed out that in one case Judge Caffey denied the existence of unfair price differentials, although his own opinion elsewhere conceded that there were "twenty proved instances" of that very practice. A few of these rulings were too much even for the camaraderie of the Circuit Court, as in the case of Judge Caffey's conclusion that Alcoa only controlled an average of 32.87 per cent of the American aluminum-ingot market. The Circuit Court held that the percentage was above 90. Yet in most cases the Circuit Court declined to look into Judge Caffey's findings and treated them with a respect they rarely deserved. The Circuit Court said weakly of one whopper that it was "not so patently implausible an explanation that the Judge was bound to reject it."

This judicial equivalent of the old school tie entangles the Circuit Court in some odd situations. Judge Caffey found that Alcoa had followed a "long-established policy ... to live in harmony with the Sherman Act." The Circuit Court holds that Alcoa violated the act. The Circuit Court refers to "unlawful practices" and denies that Alcoa "was the passive beneficiary of a monopoly, following upon an involuntary elimination of competitors by automatically operative economic forces." But since the Circuit Court seemed to feel a gentlemanly compunction about upsetting Judge Caffey's findings, it ended, in all but one case, by accepting the district judge's inability to see the same "unlawful practices." The one case was a price-squeeze method Alcoa stopped using about twelve years ago. The net result is that while the Circuit Court recognizes that Alcoa was guilty of monopolistic practices, it doesn't seem disposed to do anything about it.

There is good ground for the Circuit Court's decision to postpone action on the government's motion for dissolution of Alcoa until after the war and the disposal of war plants. But there is no such excuse for the refusal to grant injunctive relief against specific monopolistic practices or to free Alcoa's patents for use on reasonable royalty by other business men. The greatest weakness of the decision is its unwillingness to divorce ownership of Alcoa from its Canadian Siamese twin; reluctance to take drastic action of this kind is typical of the history of the anti-trust laws. The Circuit Court did, indeed, hold the Canadian company guilty of violating the American anti-trust laws by joining in a world cartel which curtailed competition in the American market. The precedent is important on paper, but the ruling is enforceable only against foreign corporations with property in our jurisdiction. American corporations can evade it by arranging that their Canadian "Siamese twins" keep their funds and offices in Montreal. The real loophole is the use of Canadian subsidiaries as the vehicles for world cartel agreements, and this loophole is left open by Judge Hand and his colleagues.

April 14, 1945

No Shortage of Hogs

WHATEVER THE TRUTH about the meat situation, this country suffers from no shortage of hogs, especially in the food and textile industries. Relief for liberated Europe, as I indicated in last week's letter, is not held up by the UNRRA's [United Nations Relief and Rehabilitation Administration] minor political troubles but by the difficulty of mobilizing these industries to feed and clothe our allies. Food and textiles escaped effective mobilization for war and essential civilian needs. It is unlikely that after V-E day they can be mobilized effectively for relief to Europe. But whatever little we can do will help. Something can be accomplished if labor unions and other progressive organizations bring the essential facts to public notice, and press Congress, the War Production Board [WPB], the War Food Administration [WFA], and the Office of Price Administration [OPA] to act.

So far the WPB, the WFA, and the OPA have failed to provide even the home market during the war with adequate food and clothing at a fair price. All three are dominated by business men from the industries they are supposed to control. It would be untrue and unfair to enter a blanket indictment of all of them; many have shown considerable public spirit and willingness to rise above business considerations and personal interest. But the best of them have been much too weak in dealing with their old friends and associates. "They rape awful easy." Nor would it be true to say that there are not genuine grievances in these industries, and perhaps some few producers who cannot make both ends meet. But behind most of the squeals with which food and textile representatives have recently filled the halls of Congress is mere porcine resentment because somebody else is getting a little more swill.

I have before me as I write a release from the American Wool Council. The council objects to M-388, a belated and inadequate WPB order designed — ever so gently — to force the textile industry to produce a little more low-cost clothing. The council says M-388 is not an emergency measure at all but a "warmed-over" plan rejected in 1943. The council helpfully reveals for the first time that Richard N. Johnson, chief of the consumer-goods division of the WPB, prepared a plan in 1943 to ease the shortage of low-cost clothing. The plan was of course rejected. It would have cut into profits by channeling mill output into lower-cost fabrics and end-products into lower-price items. The Wool Council is exposing itself, not M-388. For if the textile crowd hadn't objected to the kind of supervision envisaged in the Johnson plan, the present emergency would not have arisen. The fact is that present textile problems were foreseen by Robert R. Guthrie of the WBP shortly after Pearl Harbor. Guthrie was then in charge of textiles, and he was fired by Donald M. Nelson for his courage. Some of the very dollar-a-year men to whom Guthrie boldly objected, though himself a business man, are still in the textile division, some fumbling, some sabotaging, the public interest.

The hearings before the reactionary Smith Committee on food and textiles have been unintentionally illuminating. One bit of testimony graphically indicates the attitude of mind with which we have to deal. One textile manufacturer who makes quality fabrics was asked whether it was not true that "physically the looms in the plant could be used for the manufacture of low-priced clothing." "A loom," he answered, "whether it is in our mill or in anyone else's mill, will still weave cloth, but the structure of a business must be taken into consideration." It is the "structure" of the business rather than of human beings that is the first consideration. In the depression of the early '30s these manufacturers found it possible to run out lower-price, lower-quality goods. They do not want to give up their lush war-time market for higher-price garments. Just how lush that market is may be seen from the fact that last year's textile-earnings before taxes ran close to $400,000,000, as compared to an annual average of $28,000,000 from 1936 to 1939.

In addition to their abnormal war profits, both food and textiles last year enjoyed special "windfall" profits. Under the Bankhead amendment to protect "parity" prices on cotton, and under some very queer accounting methods, the mills last year averaged a profit of about three cents a pound on the cotton they used; in other words, they were allowed parity prices on cotton but bought it for three cents a pound less. The next windfall from this source, after all adjustment, is estimated at $60,000,000 during 1944. The profits of the meat packers last year were seven times as great as their annual average profits from 1936 to 1939. Of their $162,000,000 in profits last year, a large portion is due to a "windfall" like that in cotton. They were given a rollback subsidy on the basis of a price of $15 a hundred for hogs, but the actual market price averaged about $12.50. During the current clamor, because of seasonal tightness in the livestock market, they have been granted additional increases: a subsidy of an extra $1 per hundred pounds on beef, elimination of the discount of 75 cents a hundred pounds formerly granted the army on carload-lot purchases of pork products. The new increases will guarantee profits of about $150,000,000 a year even if the price of livestock remains at current levels. While the big packers were getting these increases, the small, non-processing slaughterers were cut back by the OPA. These independents had been given an 80-cents-a-hundred differential on beef; this was cut to 30 cents.

The top executives of the OPA seem to be engaged in a terrific battle to hold down the cost of living, but these recent increases and current undercover compromises on the textile pricing program lead one to suspect that the hand is quicker than the eye. The new meat increases were made without submitting them to lower-level officials in operating divisions and without any real cost reports from the packers. I suspect that this is not unconnected with the resignation of one of the ablest and most devoted public servants the New Deal brought to Washington — Richard Gilbert, chief economic adviser to the OPA. Gilbert, who formerly taught Economics at Harvard and the Fletcher School, has been a key official in price regulation since the Defense Commission was established in May, 1940. He was the target of attack by William P. Jacobs, capital lobbyist for textile interests, and his resignation was requested by OPA Administrator Chester Bowles. Another able and hard-working New Dealer, Thomas A. Emerson, who was deputy administrator for enforcement, recently resigned in disgust and went to the Office of Economic Stabilization. These resignations are indicative.

"What actually is going on among textile manufacturers," James B. Carey of the C.I.O. told the Senate Banking and Currency Committee last year, "is exactly equivalent to a strike which, if engaged in by labor, would be loudly and properly condemned during war time. These manufacturers cut their output of the low-cost, less profitable items, demand higher price ceilings, finally get the higher ceilings, and still refuse to produce what is needed." It will take a lot of public pressure to hold them back from all-out production of higher-cost items after V-E Day. The situation in food is more serious and more sinister. As recently as last December War Food Administrator Marvin Jones told the White House there was no need for rationing. Jones did resist pressure to cut food-production goals for this year as sharply as the farm-and-food bloc wanted, but the consumer-conscious and well-informed C.I.O. *Automobile Worker* charges that much of the present food stringency "was planned by the War Food's production plans of two years ago." As I indicated last week, the big food interests want to end the war with bare shelves — and high prices.

Donald Montgomery, formerly of the Department of Agriculture, now the driving force of the C.I.O. Cost of Living Committee, last week sent a letter to Senator Elmer Thomas and Congressman Clinton Anderson, challenging Congress to investigate War Food Administration policy. Montgomery is prepared to prove that WFA policy "has been dictated more by a desire to protect the monetary value of food stocks . . . and the profits of food industries . . . than to protect the food needs of the people." The WFA has sought to distract popular resentment from itself by spreading the impression that food is short because of exports for relief. That was the effect of the action taken by Byrnes in naming the new food-export control committee under Leo T. Crowley. This was represented in Congress as a bold step to protect American supplies from being sent abroad. The truth is that pitifully little of our food has gone abroad except to our own armed forces, and that we can have plenty both for ourselves and for liberated Europe any time we muster the gumption to make the farm bloc and the food processors behave. Many will die in liberated Europe this winter of cold and hunger if we fail.

April 21, 1945

Farewell to F.D.R.

～～　～～

M R. ROOSEVELT'S BODY was brought back to Washington
today for the last time. The crowds began to gather early in
Lafayette Park opposite the White House, as they did all along the line
of the procession from Union Station. I got down to the park early and
stood with many others waiting. Some small boys climbed into a tree for
a better view. The gray tip of the Washington Monument showed above
the White House. The trees were in full green; tulips bloomed on the
lawn. Outside on the sidewalk there were soldiers in helmets every few
feet, and we could hear the harsh tones of command as the guard of
honor lined up on the White House lawn. Florists' trucks pulled up at
the door, and huge wreaths were taken inside. Cameras were set up on
the front porch, and camera men were perched on high ladders on the
sidewalks and among us in the park. Birds sang, but the crowd was
silent.

In the park I recognized a group of girls from the C.I.O. offices in
nearby Jackson Place, Walter Lippmann, and an Army and Navy Club
bellboy with a sensitive Negro face. There were soldiers and sailors,
Waves and Wacs. There were many Negroes, some of them quite
obviously housemaids. There were well-dressed women and men in shirt
sleeves. I noticed a small middle-aged priest, several grave and owlish
Chinese, many service men with their wives or sweethearts, a tired man
in overalls and blue-denim work cap. A tall gangling Negro boy in
jitterbug jacket and pork-pie hat towered above the crowd in front of
me. A man who seemed to be a hobo, unshaven and dirty, jarred the
silence with a loud laugh at something a child behind him had said.

There were close-mouthed New England faces, Jewish faces, Midwestern faces; workers and business men and housewives, all curiously alike in their patience and in the dumb stolidity that is often sorrow's aspect. A truck sped by on Pennsylvania Avenue. On the roof of the truck two navy men operated a movie camera, taking pictures of the crowd. Far above us, twenty-four Flying Fortresses roared across the skies in proud formation. One remembered the President's 50,000-plane speech, and choked. Motorcycle police heralded the procession's approach. The marching men, the solemn bands, the armored cars, the regiment of Negro soldiers, the uniformed women's detachments, the trucks filled with soldiers, and the black limousine carrying officials and the President's family went by slowly. They seemed part of an unreal pageant by comparison with the one glimpse of what we had come to see — the coffin covered with a flag. Many faces in the crowd puckered as it went past. In that one quick look thousands of us said our goodbye to a great and good man, and to an era.

I was at the *PM* office in New York Thursday when it happened. There was a commotion in the newsroom. A copyboy ran out of the wire-room with a piece of United Press copy in his hand. That first flash, "The President died this afternoon," seemed incredible; like something in a nightmare, far down under the horror was the comfortable feeling that you would wake to find it was all a dream. The Romans must have felt this way when word came that Caesar Augustus was dead. Later, when work was done, I went to a meeting of liberals in an apartment on Washington Square. It was a gloomy gathering, much too gloomy to honor so buoyant a spirit as Mr. Roosevelt's. Some felt that with his passing the Big Three would split up, that hope of a new world organization was dim. One of those present reported, apropos, that an automobile-company official in Detroit had told a delegation of visiting French newspapermen, "Next we fight the Soviet Union." Some thought the Nazis would be encouraged to hold out, that the war had been lengthened by the President's passing. Everyone seemed to feel that trouble, serious trouble, lay ahead.

I don't want to sound like Pollyanna, but I can remember so many crepe-hanging sessions of this kind since 1932. The Roosevelt era, for folk who scare easily, was a series of scares. Just before he took office, when the bonus marchers were driven out of Washington, revolution seemed to be around the corner. There was the banking crisis. The NRA [National Recovery Administration] was suspected of being the beginning of fascism; one of my friends in New York cautiously erased his name from the volumes of Marx and Lenin he owned; he felt the men with the bludgeons might be in his apartment any day. The Supreme Court knocked one piece of reform legislation after another on the head, and Mr. Roosevelt, when he set out to fight back, showed a deplorable disrespect for the constitutional amenities. There were the Chicago massacre and the Little Steel strike. There was Hitler. France fell when our armed forces were in good shape for a war with Nicaragua. The Japs sank most of the fleet at Pearl Harbor. It was a lush era for Cassandras.

Somehow we pulled through before, and somehow we'll pull through again. In part it was luck. In part it was Mr. Roosevelt's leadership. In part it was the quality of the country and its people. I don't know about the rest of the four freedoms, but one thing Mr. Roosevelt gave the United States in one crisis after another, and that was freedom from fear. Perhaps his most important contribution was the example, the superlative example, of his personal courage. Perhaps some of us will feel less gloomy if we remember it. Perhaps some of us will be more effective politically if we also learn from Mr. Roosevelt's robust realism, his ability to keep his eye on the main issue and not worry too much about the minor details.

I found the mood of the intellectuals and New Dealers in Washington this week-end quite different from that in New York. There has been much swapping of information and sidelights, and there is a good deal of confidence in the new President. No one, least of all Mr. Truman, an impressively modest man, expects him fully to fill Mr. Roosevelt's shoes. But the general feeling among those who know Mr. Truman is that he will surprise the skeptical. I can only record my own impression for whatever it is worth. I talked with Mr. Truman several years ago and liked him immediately and instinctively. The Presidency is a terrific job, and it remains to be seen how he will stand up under its pressure. But he is a good man, an honest man, a devoted man. Our country could be far more poorly served. Mr. Truman is a hard worker, decisive, a good executive. He works well with people. He is at once humble about his own knowledge and capacities, as a wise man should be, and quietly confident about his ability to learn and to rise to the occasion.

I hate to confess it, but I think Mr. Roosevelt was astute and farsighted in picking Mr. Truman rather than Mr. Wallace as his successor. At this particular moment in our history, Mr. Truman can do a better job. Mr. Wallace's accession might have split the country wide open, not because of Mr. Wallace but because of the feeling against him on the right. Mr. Truman has the good-will of both sides and is in a position to capitalize on the sobering influence of Mr. Roosevelt's passing. The heaviest task of the President lies in the field of foreign relations, and the biggest obstacle to its accomplishment is in the Senate. It is fortunate that Mr. Truman's greatest and most obvious political assets are his relations with the Senate. He is a friendly person, and was well liked on both sides of the aisle. Isolationists like Wheeler and La Follette are among his friends, and he may be able to exert an influence with them that the circumstances and the momentum of past events denied to Mr. Roosevelt. The chances of a two-thirds' vote in the Senate for the new peace organization are improved by the shift in the Presidency. I say this with no disrespect to our great departed leader.

I think Mr. Truman will carry on Mr. Roosevelt's work. He had been very effective in support of Mr. Roosevelt in the Senate. I can authoritatively report that the famous B2H2 resolution[1] originated in Mr. Truman's office. Three of the sponsors, Senator Ball, Burton, and Hatch, were members of the Truman committee. Mr. Truman's closest personal friends in the Senate were Kilgore of West Virginia and Wallgren of Washington, both sturdy progressives and good New Dealers. There will be changes in the Cabinet, perhaps some for the better. On domestic policy Mr. Truman's record is an excellent one, and labor has nothing to fear from him. The shock of Mr. Roosevelt's death has created an atmosphere in which the new President may be able to unite the nation more closely than ever and carry it forward to that stable peace Mr. Roosevelt so deeply desired.

---

[1] The historic bipartisan Senate resolution of 1943, sponsored by Senators Ball, Burton, Hill, and Hatch (hence B2H2) urging U.S. initiative in forming a United Nations.

Notes Before 'Frisco[1]

〜〜　〜〜

THE FIRST ESSENTIAL of world peace is full employment in the United States. This cannot be repeated too often. Our own country represents about half the world market, and if we are prosperous the rest of the world will be prosperous too. Only in such a context can the agreements reached at Bretton Woods[2] operate successfully. Only in such a context will other nations give up the weapons of economic self-defense and economic warfare — currency depreciation, quotas, barter agreements, licensing of exports and imports — which breed ill-feeling among nations. It has been said that if we wish to sell abroad we must be prepared to buy abroad. Only in a prosperous America can one hope for the political and economic climate which would permit any significant tariff reductions. The strong opposition in Congress to the Doughton bill for extension of the Reciprocal Trade Agreements Act indicates how far we are as a people from grasping the responsibilities and necessities of our creditor position. In a fully employed America the tariff problem would lose much of its urgency.

Several recent studies indicate that the volume of our import bears surprisingly little relation to the height of our tariff walls or to the price of foreign products. Calvin B. Hoover in his "Post-War Goals and Economic Reconstruction" reports that "the changes in volume of trade in commodities on which duties were raised during the Hoover

[1] Where the founding conference of the United Nations organization was held April 25–June 26, 1945.
[2] The United Nations Monetary and Financial Conference held July 1–22, 1944 at Bretton Woods, N.H. It created the International Monetary Fund and the International Bank for Reconstruction and Development.

Administration were not so strikingly different from the changes in the volume of imports of other commodities upon which duties were not raised." The factor that determines our volume of trade, Dr. Hoover finds, "is the volume of our own industrial production. If we have prosperity, then we have high imports and exports. If we have depression the opposite is true."

All this is far better understood abroad than at home. Washington embassies have shown unusual interest in the full-employment bill now before Congress. (It is worth noting that the new President when he was still a Senator signed promptly the Military Affairs Committee report indorsing the bill.) Some foreign governments, notably the Australian, are known to have begun diplomatic conversations on the full-employment problem with a view to some joint action or declaration at the world trade conference recently announced by Secretary Stettinius.

Full and stable employment in the United States necessarily means a lower rate of profit on capital. Some would like to evade this unpalatable fact and to dodge a terribly difficult problem by an intensified drive for foreign markets. Foreign markets, though important, cannot provide full employment. To place primary emphasis on foreign trade is also to intensify inevitable ill-feeling as American and British traders compete in Latin America and elsewhere. This would be imperialism in its classic form. For imperialism is the search abroad for that higher rate of profit which can no longer be obtained at home. I need hardly add that failure to achieve full employment would also provide the right emotional climate for imperialist adventures: disillusioned veterans, renewed isolationism, xenophobia, fascist movements. In such an atmosphere whatever is achieved at San Francisco would become worthless.

The second essential of a stable world peace is agreement among the Big Three on post-war treatment of Germany and Japan — not just agreement on generalities, but accord in the working out of detailed day-by-day decisions. The trust or mistrust bred in the process will determine the future relations of the great powers and decide the efficiency of the security organization to be set up at San Francisco. Here the political difficulties involved are enormous.

We must never forget that Hitlerism had a double root and can only be extirpated by double action. It was rooted not only in the German national pattern but also in the weaknesses of world capitalism. All the factors which enabled Hitler to reverse Lenin's famous slogan, which enabled the Nazis to turn civil war into imperialist war, are still present. The recurrent cyclical crises, the dead-end atmosphere of much upper-class thinking, the fear of change, the Communist bogy, the anti-Semitism characteristic of societies in decay are still with us. The two staples of Nazi propaganda — the "bulwark against Bolshevism" line for nice people, Jew-baiting for the others — will still be marketable after the war if there is considerable unemployment.

There is reason to believe that the "bulwark against Bolshevism" idea is already playing a part in British and American thinking in regard to Germany, as it also will in regard to Japan. Anti-Soviet fears and prejudices, though private, are prominent in the thinking of the State Department bureaucracy. James Clement Dunn and Julius Holmes are certainly among those to whom this applies. The tendency to favor a "soft peace" for Germany is also fed by cartel and commercial considerations, here as in Britain. The leak of the so-called "Morgenthau plan"[3] in distorted form was a deliberate job by the Senate Department crowd to which I refer, and it was contrived in a way most likely to kill the plan.

Mr. Hull himself, contrary to the general impression, was not for a soft peace, but for a year or more before his retirement he had little to do with the actual workings of the State Department. So long as Mr. Roosevelt was alive, the "hard peace" idea had the ascendancy, but since his death a change is already perceptible in inter-departmental discussions. The State Department opposition to drastic action against Germany has stiffened. It is possible that the department may take a stronger position on German war criminals and perhaps also against the Japanese Emperor as a means of covering up a softer policy toward both countries. No one yet knows what Mr. Truman's attitude toward the German and Japanese problems will be, but I suspect it will prove at least as stern as Mr. Roosevelt's.

It must be kept in mind that the Big Three did not have sense enough to stick together against the Nazi menace before the war. The U.S.S.R. and this country both waited to be attacked before entering the war. Joint occupation of the Reich may make it easier, not harder, for the Germans to play one side off against the other. Robert Murphy, who will be General Eisenhower's political adviser in the German occupation, is as dangerous as he is shrewd. Murphy is another of those whose thinking about Germany is colored by the desire for a "bulwark against Bolshevism." The grim fact is that the dominant forces in British and American society impel us to the reconstitution after the war of pretty much the same kind of Germany and Japan we are spending blood and

[3] For the conversion of Germany from an industrial to an agricultural economy.

billions to crush. Only large measures of socialism and a vigorous upper-class purge could remove the aggressive forces and the imperialist urges of Germany and Japan, establish mutual confidence among the Big Three, and make a third world war unlikely. These, too, are decisions which will determine the worth of what is done at San Francisco.

A less immediate and longer-range problem which will decide the stability of the peace is the treatment of the colored peoples. Here lies the possibility of conflicts more serious even than another falling out among the Europeans peoples. However "correct" the attitude of the Soviet Union, however conservative and conciliatory the policies of the Communist parties, the example of racial equality in the Soviet Union will be a constant reproach and irritant to colonialism, as Soviet full employment will be to capitalism. In this field, too, progressive forces in the West must press for reform if the unity of the Big Three is to be maintained.

Little has been said in the West of the spectacle provided by the farce of "India" at San Francisco and of "India" in the Assembly of the proposed new world organization. The delegation is made up entirely of British stooges, and it is Britain which will cast India's vote in the Assembly. We may be sure that the full implications of the sight will not be lost on the colonial peoples. "The trouble is," said a British representative to an American in a relaxed moment at the bar during the Bretton Woods conference, "we're too good to each other's niggers." He was referring, of course, to American interest in India and British interest in our treatment of Negroes; the remark is rich in overtones. In the handling of the colonial problem, we must either invoke prejudice and race hatred, fascist style, or move forward to the admission of the colonial and colored peoples into full equality and partnership. A few millions of European whites cannot forever dominate hundreds of millions of brown and yellow people. This is another of the fundamental questions which must be faced and answered if the San Francisco peace organization is to last.

May 5, 1945

The Same Old Codgers

~~~ ~~~

THIS IS A SPLENDIDLY VIGOROUS and beautiful city. Its lofty hills, great bay, clear skies, and fresh breezes make it an exhilarating place. The cable cars that crawl up and down its steep streets provide almost as exciting a ride as the chute-the-chutes of Coney Island, and the view from luxurious Nob Hill, where one feels closer to the stars at night, goes to one's head. For the press this has been a glamorous week spent scooting around between press conferences and plenary sessions. We saw and heard the bright, bird-like Dutch Foreign Minister, Van Kleffens; the school-masterish Deputy British Prime Minister, Clement Attlee; the monolithic but quick-witted Molotov; Nehru's fragile but intense sister, Mrs. Pandit; dapper Georges Bidault, the French Foreign Minister, who looks more like a care-free boulevardier than an under-ground leader; and, of course, Mr. Stettinius, our matinee-idol Secretary of State, whose press conferences are remarkable chiefly for his extraor-dinary facility in remembering the faces and names of reporters. It's the old apple sauce, but we lap it up just the same.

The press is housed in the huge Palace Hotel, on Market Street, down near the wharves, and the correspondents, for whom this is a kind of old-home week, obtain much of their mysteriously authoritative inside information by interviewing each other at the crowded bars and in the high glass-ceilinged dining-room. We are perpetually in transit, like skating bugs, from the Palace to Union Square, which is neat and fashionable and quite unlike its New York namesake; there, at the St. Francis, the Russians and the French are housed. Thence we go to Nob Hill, where the British and the Chinese are in the de luxe Mark

Hopkins, with its famous rooftop bar, and the American delegation in the equally plush if less famous Fairmont. Down-hill again we speed to the domed Opera House, where the conference sessions are held, and the big Veterans' Administration Building next door, which is the "press room" of the conference; there are batteries of typewriters and telegraph machines and a most delightful clatter.

Hollywood, as though fearful of being outshone, is well represented here. Your correspondent, as goggle-eyed as any movie fan, was introduced to Charles Boyer by a member of the French delegation and later that night in the lobby of the Palace to Edward G. Robinson. "Well," Robinson asked with that overtone of quiet menace for which he is famous, "is our side going to win?" It was definitely an "or else" question, and I hastened to assure him that all would be well.

The main event, the opening of the conference Wednesday afternoon, might have been an M-G-M opening. Crowds strained against the ropes for blocks around the Opera House to watch the arriving notables; the press flashed its cards with pride; the foreign delegates poured out of their black limousines, trying hard to look dignified and unmoved. Within, in an interior that seemed to have been done by Maxfield Parrish, floodlights lit up the gilded gesso, red plush, and stainless steel; against the blue background of the huge stage stood four brown pillars, symbols of the four freedoms, connected at the top by what appeared to be large segments of a boa constrictor. The press was with difficulty confined to the triple-tiered galleries by the feminine elite of San Francisco, among whom many heart-rending battles were fought for the honor of ushering at the occasion. But down below camera men swarmed among the delegates of the forty-six nations, kneeling in the aisles and all but hanging from the boxes to get their shots. Flashlight bulbs kept going off like summer lightning, and statesmen obediently composed their faces for the camera.

The affair itself was sobering. The speeches at the opening session were as banal as the juke-box music which was piped into the Opera House as the delegates arrived. The President's address was disappointing. The occasion called for either Lincolnian eloquence or plain, common-sense statement. Mr. Truman is fully capable in private of the latter, but he seems to have been prevailed upon to indulge instead in windy moralisms, turgid periods, and the kind of untruths which are regarded as inspirational. I pick one of the many examples from the speech. "None of us doubt," Mr. Truman said, "that with divine guidance, friendly cooperation, and hard work we shall find an adequate answer to the problem history has put before us." Mr. Truman would never talk that way in private to a visitor. Why does he in a speech? The statement is not true; some of the wisest of the delegates here certainly do doubt whether we shall find the "answer to the problem history has put before us." The rhetoric is false, the effect is hollow; it is hooey. In private Mr. Truman would say, "It's a tough job. I'm not sure we can do it. But we're going to try our best." Why not say that in public? That kind of plain talk inspires confidence. The tawdry and flatulent rhetoric which marked most of the speeches depressed me. The occasion was so momentous; the danger so grave; the need so great; the utterance so mediocre.

The San Francisco conference is as important as Versailles or the Congress of Vienna. But one's first impression of it is how mediocre is its leadership. The second is how little the cast of characters have changed since Geneva. To be quite frank about it, the conference, for all its glamour, is a meeting of pretty much those same old codgers to whose fumbling we owe World War II. They are still dishing out the same old platitudes and thinking in the same old terms. And so, I suspect, are many of the people they represent. The war, for all its terror and destruction, has not brought about that long-overdue revulsion against nationalism which can alone provide the basis for world order and security. The delegations assembled here indicate that the political parties and the dominant classes of the Western countries and of China are emerging from the conflict momentarily sobered, perhaps, but little changed. Except for the French and Yugoslav delegations, there is no sign here of the new men and forces which welled up from underground in continental Europe to fight fascism. The basic idea at San Francisco is that the big powers must stick together to maintain the peace; this was Metternich's idea in 1815; it is the kindergarten stage in education toward world security. The problem is how to keep the big powers together; it is the problem that these same men — the Halifaxes, the Edens, the Paul-Boncours, the Van Kleffenses — failed to solve at Geneva. Given the same men, the same parties, the same social systems, can one expect a different result?

These men lost the last peace, and unless they are replaced they will some day lose the next one. They can give us the first tentative framework of a world order; it is the job of progressive forces to take over from there as soon as possible. For whatever these men do on paper, they do not have the capacity to withstand and deal with real crises. The weak handling of the Polish issue, the clerical power politics focused upon it, the covert anti-Soviet urges associated with it, are indicative of the stresses and strains which peace will put on the relations of the big powers. It will take new leadership, deeper understanding, and firmer resolution if big-power unity is to be maintained when peace comes and trouble begins.

June 9, 1945

Truman and the State Department

THREE RECENT EVENTS indicate that President Truman does not see eye to eye with the State Department. The first was the sending of Mr. Davies to London and of Mr. Hopkins to Moscow. Both men are poison ivy to the State Department crowd, and their missions, as did similar ones under Mr. Roosevelt, constituted a serious reflection on it. They implied that in critical situations Mr. Truman, like Mr. Roosevelt before him, feels that he can rely neither on the ambassadors in those two key capitals nor on officials of the department. The situations referred to were created in part by the department's own stupid diplomacy, which has antagonized Moscow while giving a blank check to London. The State Department is fully capable of creating trouble but not of correcting it.

The second event was Mr. Stettinius's radio address[1] from San Francisco after a hurried trip to the White House for consultation. This address, as the New York *Herald Tribune* pointed out, constituted "a formal and almost point-by-point reversal of course on all those issues of policy concerning which Mr. Stettinius's pilotage has been most severely criticized."

The third was the release by the White House tonight of a letter from War Mobilization Director Vinson to Senator Wagner strongly indorsing the full-employment bill. The letter and the circumstances of its publication indicate that Mr. Truman as President intends to continue the fight he began as Senator, in the Murray-Truman report last December, for a full-employment economy after the war. This is in sharp contrast to the

[1] Edward R. Stettinius had succeeded Cordell Hull as Secretary of State in November 1944.

persistent opposition of the State Department and the American delegation at San Francisco to the inclusion either of the "right to work" or "full employment" in the new United Nations Charter.

Mr. Stettinius is reported to have come to Washington in great alarm and to have left chastened. Obviously one of the issues on which he was put on the carpet was Argentina. He assured his radio audience last Monday night that our vote for its admission "did not constitute a blanket indorsement of the policies of the Argentine government," but that on the contrary "with many of these policies both the government and the people of the United States have no sympathy." Arnaldo Cortesi's sensational report to the New York *Times* on Friday added to Mr. Stettinius's discomfiture. That afternoon, following an off-the-record conference with Latin American journalists, Mr. Truman took the unusual step of instructing a secretary to inform the press that when asked his views on the Argentine situation, he had replied, "I am not very happy about it."

Mr. Truman will find himself increasingly unhappy in this and other situations so long as he delays the essential task of naming a new Secretary of State and reorganizing the State Department. The dominant clique is as pro-Perón as it is pro-Franco. While Mr. Stettinius unhappily asserted that we would expect Argentina to fulfil the democratic pledges it made at Chapultepec, "seasoned Foreign Service officers" told the Washington *Post* "that this country has solemnly pledged not to interfere in the internal affairs of any Latin American country." The department's real attitude was revealed when Nelson Rockefeller told a group of Congressmen privately that Argentina was our best "bulwark against Bolshevism" in this hemisphere. The danger in this Goebbels-like line is indicated by two news items. One is an Allied labor-news dispatch from Montevideo which summarizes a book, "German Capital in Argentina," newly published in Montevideo by Luis Victor Sommi. Sommi charges that German trusts continue to control some two hundred corporations in Argentina. The other is the piece of apologetics on Argentina which leaked out of the American delegation in San Francisco to Russell Porter and was printed in yesterday's New York *Times.* Among other evidences of Argentina's helpfulness, Porter cited its "announced intention to liquidate any Axis firms not actually producing for the Allies' war effort." This is curious, and would seem to provide Axis firms with an interesting loophole through which to avoid seizure and continue profitably in business. Is it possible that we or the British are giving war contracts to Axis companies in Argentina? Could be.

The Argentine question is not the only one on which Mr. Stettinius's expression of regret and statement of pious generalities are less than convincing. His discussion of the trusteeship issue is inaccurate. His declaration that "freedom from want encompasses the right to work" may imply a change of heart on full employment or can be a formula for keeping it out of the charter on the ground that it is already implied by the Four Freedoms. Mr. Stettinius had hardly finished saying that "we must mediate" between the other great powers "when their interests conflict among themselves" before the State Department handed Great Britain another blank check in the Syria-Lebanon dispute. The unwillingness of either the United States or Great Britain to make any real concession to colonial aspirations on trusteeship makes our joint indignation over French demands for bases and other rights in Syria-Lebanon the rankest kind of hypocrisy. I would neither disparage just Arab grievances nor defend French colonial policy, but this whole affair has a strong smell of oil imperialism and of an Anglo-American attempt to muscle into a French sphere of influence.

Mr. Davies is said to have been instructed to tell the Foreign Office that Mr. Truman intends to carry on Mr. Roosevelt's policy, that is, presumably, the policy of playing a middle role between Moscow and London. Mr. Stettinius paid lip service to the same conception in his radio speech. But the actuality is that of an Anglo-American alliance with the leadership in London. This has a firm foundation in the system of combined boards, which have always been Anglo-American or Anglo-American-Canadian, and which continue to operate in raw materials, shipping, production, and other fields. There is Anglo-American military coordination through SHAEF [Supreme Headquarters of the Allied Expeditionary Forces], which some British sources would like to continue in the occupation of Germany and in the diplomatic sphere at San Francisco and elsewhere in the world; there is consistent Anglo-American teamwork, whether against De Gaulle, Moscow, or Tito. That is hardly the way to further the big-power "solidarity" of which Mr. Stettinius spoke.

A crucial test is coming in Germany, now that a coordinated control body is at long last being set up. Mr. Truman has signed excellent directives on reparations, the occupation of the Reich, and war crimes — directives which could be the basis for eliminating both the war-making potential and the trouble-making personnel of the German state. But the influence of the War Department and of the British has succeeded in preventing the publication of these directives. Their disclosure would inform the American and British public on our plans for the future of Germany and provide correspondents abroad with a means of checking the actual policies being applied by our military-control authorities. Private information here and stories seeping into the papers indicate that the military are moving in the direction of rebuilding German industry. This, as I reported some weeks ago, accords with the views of key State Department officials obsessed with the idea that a strong Germany is needed as a bulwark against you-know-what, and a similar idea seems to be favored in British Tory and financial circles. If there were a really joint policy on occupation, our military and diplomatic authorities would find it more difficult quietly to circumvent the Truman directives, and they may therefore do their best to continue separate administrations with separate policies.

Mr. Truman will have to decide whether he intends to run the State Department or to be run by it. The inside crowd is adept at doing things its own way while giving the appearance of carrying out orders. The longer it stays in office the more dearly it may cost us. As for Mr. Stettinius, he represents a special problem because he stands next in line for the Presidency. He is a genuinely nice person who intends no harm and harbors no sinister designs. Had Mr. Roosevelt lived, he would have been the willing instrument of the President's policies. But Mr. Stettinius's limitations of knowledge and capacity were appallingly obvious at San Francisco and created considerable amazement among other delegations. He doesn't have what it takes to be Secretary of State, and if anything happened to Mr. Truman it would be a calamity to have Mr. Stettinius become President. This opinion was shared privately by the overwhelming majority of newspapermen and delegates at San Francisco. Mr. Truman owes it to himself and the country to replace him as soon as possible, and to give us that long overdue State Department housecleaning.

June 23, 1945

Jim Crow Flies High

IN 1919, according to Malcolm Ross, chairman of the FEPC [Fair Employment Practices Committee], speaking before the House Appropriations Committee, "there were twenty-six race riots, most of them caused by this fight for jobs by unemployed people. We had no method of controlling those situations in 1919." We shall have no method of controlling such situations in 1945 after exactly fifteen days, unless public pressure forces action in the Senate on the FEPC appropriation for the next fiscal year or in the House on the bill for the permanent Fair Employment Practices Committee. A renewed appropriation for the FEPC and legislation to make it permanent are needed for three reasons: first, in order to continue measures for full mobilization of man-power until the Japanese war is over; second, to demonstrate to the colored peoples of the East, whose help we need in that war, that the United States is making progress away from race prejudice; third, to provide a post-war preventive measure to forestall racial outbreaks in the inevitable unemployment of the reconversion period. We do not want a repetition of the dreadful scenes which occurred under similar circumstances after the last war. W. E. B. Du Bois, in his book "Dusk of Dawn," has provided a vivid picture of the race riots of 1919. The dead included "thirty-eight killed in a Chicago riot of August; from twenty-five to fifty in Phillips County, Arkansas, and six killed in Washington." "For a day," Du Bois continues, "the city of Washington in July, 1919, was actually in the hands of a black mob fighting against the aggression of the whites with hand grenades."

It is not difficult to imagine outbreaks of this kind again in such cities as Washington and Detroit if nothing is done now to prevent them. The FEPC, despite all the hostility it has aroused, is a puny enough measure. A stepchild among Washington's swarming war agencies, it is probably the smallest agency of government in the capital, with a staff of but 127 persons all told, including stenographers and office boys. It is asking $599,000 for the next fiscal year, a drop in the bucket of the huge federal war budget. The FEPC has had a backlog of 2,500 cases for some time and has been just about able to close out enough old ones to balance the new cases coming in. If we were not so half-hearted and almost surreptitious in taking action against race prejudice, the FEPC would have an appropriation at least ten times what it is asking and has as yet been unable to obtain. The inadequacy of its funds becomes strikingly clear when one looks at its regional offices, where complaints are investigated and cases brought. A staff of seven, including three stenographers, handles all the New England states and New York. Three examiners and two stenographers are all the FEPC has for its Atlanta office, which takes care of five states — Georgia, Alabama, South Carolina, Tennessee, and Florida. There is a staff of three, including one stenographer, for the state of Michigan. From its San Antonio office two examiners and a stenographer must handle all the FEPC complaints of western Texas, New Mexico, Arizona, Idaho, Montana, Wyoming, Utah, and Colorado. It is a miracle that the FEPC has been able to accomplish as much as it has, and for that miracle great credit is due its chairman, Malcolm Ross. Bringing deep devotion and almost superhuman patience to his difficult task — the breaking down of race prejudice and discrimination in industry, primarily against the Negro — he has made a sizable contribution to the war effort.

About one worker in every twelve in war industry today is a Negro. Negroes are 12 per cent of the workers in shipbuilding, 10 per cent of those in combat vehicles and ammunition, 7 per cent of those in aircraft. The last to be hired, they are apt to be the first to be fired. In the Southern shipyards, in Detroit with its 260,000 Negroes, in Los Angeles with 150,000, in Portland, Oregon, where there has been a phenomenal increase in the Negro population, there may be serious trouble as cutbacks increase and industry shuts down or reconverts. Unfortunately, the FEPC as at present constituted by executive order is limited to war plants. It cannot offer protection to racial or religious minorities in business and factories reconverted to peace-time output, though that is where FEPC action is most needed. Today the FEPC is fighting for its life as a war agency, as well as asking for establishment as a permanent instrument of government.

The House Appropriations Committee, which spent three days grilling FEPC officials last year, was alarmingly swift in dealing with the committee this year. Hearings took little over a day, and the questioning was not much more than a formality. A majority of the committee had their minds made up to kill the FEPC appropriation. In the subcommittee the vote was four to four. Ludlow of Indiana and Dirksen of Illinois, the former a Democrat, the latter a Republican, led the fight for the FEPC, while Faber of New York, who watches the pennies for the G.O.P., led the Southern Democrats into battle against the agency. In the full committee Coffee of Washington and Koppleman of Connecticut fought hard to win approval for the requested appropriation, but lost eighteen to eleven. The committee reported ingenuously that since legislation to make the FEPC permanent was pending, "the only logical course" was to withhold action on the appropriation. This was an interesting squeeze play.

There is still a fighting chance for the appropriation in the Senate. A slim majority of the members of the Senate Appropriations Committee are friendly to the FEPC, though the chairman, Senator McKellar, is hostile. Last year McKellar had the annual appropriation bill printed without the FEPC items, and the committee had to overrule him and order a new bill printed. Should the appropriation lose in committee, which is possible, and be offered as an amendment from the floor, then McKellar as presiding officer would be in a position to rule it out of order. Some public pressure on the committee would be most useful. The men who need it on the Democratic side are Tydings of Maryland and McCarran of Nevada. The Republicans on the committee who are unfriendly to the FEPC are Bridges of New Hampshire, Wherry of Nebraska, White of Maine, Gurney of South Dakota, Reed of Kansas, and Willis of Indiana. Anyone who helps to build a fire under them on this issue will be doing a good deed.

Prodding is equally urgent on the bill to make the FEPC permanent. Progressives in Ohio might begin by taking some pot shots at Taft. The senior Senator from Ohio and leading corporation lawyer of Cincinnati was chairman of the committee which drafted the last Republican platform, and that platform said, "We pledge establishment by federal legislation of a permanent Fair Employment Practices Committee." But Taft himself was the only Republican member of the Senate Education and Labor Committee who voted against favorably reporting the Chavez bill for a permanent FEPC. The committee is a progressive one. The vote was twelve to six in favor of the bill, and it can be called up in the Senate at any time. In the Senate the Chavez bill was also sponsored by Senators Wagner, Murray, Downey, Aiken, Langer, and Capper.

Its counterpart in the House, the Norton bill, is a composite of bills for a permanent FEPC introduced by six Republicans and six Democrats. The Republicans are Baldwin, New York; Bender, Ohio; Clason, Massachusetts; Dirksen, Illinois; La Follette, Indiana; and Vorys, Ohio. The Democrats are Dawson, Illinois; Douglas, California; Doyle, California; Hook, Michigan; Norton, New Jersey; and Powell, New York. The House bill was reported favorably by the House Labor Committee, with only two dissenting votes, Hoffman of Michigan and Fisher of Texas. The former needs no introduction, as they say at banquets, to *Nation* readers. The latter is a sheep-raiser from southwestern Texas near the Mexican border. The House Bill was reported out three months ago and has been bottled up ever since in the Rules Committee.

The Rules Committee, theoretically, is the "traffic cop" of the House of Representatives. It is supposed to expedite action, not to block it. It is authorized to determine when it would be best to let a bill move to the floor and what limitations should be imposed on debate. It is not supposed to consider the merits of legislation. It does, of course, constantly exercise an unauthorized veto on legislation and is trying to do so in this case. Its chairman, Sabath, announced on the floor of the House last Wednesday that he was signing the petition for discharge of the Rules Committee so that a vote could be had on the bill. The fate of the discharge petition depends on the Republican Party, which supported the similar petition on the poll-tax bill last week but has until now played a devious role on the FEPC. The four Republican members of the House Rules Committee did indeed vote in favor of the Norton bill but only after helping the Southern Democrats to delay a vote for three months. And the Republicans did not vote for the bill until they were sure there were enough anti-FEPC Democrats present to block it.

July 7, 1945

Can Germany Fight Again?

THINKING ON GERMANY has suffered from the vices of a priori reasoning. There has been too much loose and often lazy-minded deduction from vague general principles, too little concrete knowledge. The great virtue of the hearings begun here before Senator Harley M. Kilgore of West Virginia and his colleagues of the "Kilgore committee" is that they are beginning to provide the facts.

The opening sessions have already furnished the first over-all view of the Reich's current assets and capacity for waging war again. These are considerable. Last September President Roosevelt instructed the Foreign Economic Administration [FEA] to initiate a series of "studies from the economic standpoint of what should be done to limit the power and capacity of Germany to make war in the future." Enough has been learned, Henry H. Fowler, director of the Enemy Branch of the FEA, now tells the Kilgore committee, "to safeguard an estimate that, if we were to leave Germany to its own devices and not to institute a program of economic and industrial disarmament, Germany could be far better prepared for war within five years than she was in 1939."

The effect of bombings has been overemphasized. "The most striking fact that should be understood in our current thinking," Fowler testified, "is that in late 1944 the German nation achieved the highest level of production in its entire history." Bombing was most effective where it was strategic, but strategic bombing sought out the bottlenecks of the German economy; it did not destroy German industry. "For the most part," Fowler said, "the great majority of the most important plants could today go into operation after very little repair." Fowler's industry-by-industry analysis should be required reading for all who wish to prevent a third German attempt at world conquest.

Dyestuffs is a basic war industry. The Reich has one plant "in perfect operating condition today ... that can turn out almost as much dye in one year as all the plants in the United States together." German steel capacity is at least 25,000,000 tons, and "practically all the great iron and steel furnaces of Germany are ready for operation or can be in operation with minor repairs." Germany, which consumed less than 4,000,000 tons of petroleum products in 1934, was producing 1,000,000 tons of natural and 5,500,000 tons of synthetic oil ten years later within the 1938 boundaries of the Reich. Oil plants were a high-priority target, "but it is believed," Fowler reported, "that a large part of Germany's 1944 capacity for producing petroleum products can be restored within a brief period." The Reich, with an aluminum-producing capacity of 40,000 tons annually in 1933, ended the war with a capacity of about 250,000 tons. German synthetic-rubber capacity today is still 80 per cent greater than the Reich's imports of rubber and semi-manufactured rubber goods in 1933.

The either-or oversimplification — shall we reduce the Reich to an agricultural country? — plays directly into German hands. The sober facts are that in many basic industries German capacity is in excess of legitimate German domestic and export needs, and considerable deindustrialization is necessary as a measure of security and to create a better-balanced European economy. German machine-tool and machine-tool-building capacity is out of all proportion to its peace-time requirements. This is also the case in steel. The Reich's 25,000,000-ton capacity would have been large enough, Fowler pointed out, to supply half of the United States' peace-time requirements, including those of "the tremendous transportation system, railroads, waterways, and highways necessary to keep together our economic and industrial structure, which is spread over an area sixteen times as large as that of Germany." The Reich cannot use that much steel "except for warfare."

The Kilgore hearings have also provided some insight into German plans to utilize nest eggs abroad to support a Nazi underground and to prepare the way for the revival of an aggressive Reich. Fowler submitted detailed memoranda on the flight of German capital abroad and the extent to which it has penetrated banking, industry, and trade in other countries, notably in Sweden, Spain, Argentina, and Switzerland. Here German plans are aided by the complaisance of the State Department toward Franco and Peron. The Kilgore committee had submitted a comprehensive series of detailed questions to the State Department and elicited a long statement in reply from Assistant Secretary of State Will Clayton. This disclosed, among other things, that the largest number of Axis "spearhead" firms are in Argentina, and that not a single one of these firms has been eliminated despite the Chapultepec pledges on which the Perón regime was ushered into the United Nations. The Franco pattern is repeating itself in the New World. The Fowler and Clayton statements are the strongest of arguments that there must be new and democratic regimes in Spain and Argentina if German plans for a third try are to be defeated.

The Kilgore committee will be neglecting its duty if it rests content with the prepared statements submitted to it. A real investigation is required. There was, for example, a frustrating air of unreality about Clayton's references to the black list and to our program for replacing Axis firms in Latin America. This replacement program was sabotaged in the Office of the Alien Property Custodian under Leo T. Crowley and withered away months ago. The facts were called to public attention by this correspondent in *The Nation* of last January 6 in a Washington letter called "Fumbling with I. G. Farben," and in *PM* last winter in the series of editorials "Report to the President." It is time the Senate found out how Nazi property and patents have been handled, what influences were brought to bear against the replacement program, and exactly what are the relations between Crowley and the Anglo-German banking firm of the Schroders. Crowley is still drawing the $75,000 a year paid him as head of Standard Gas and Electric, a job given him when the Schroders were the dominant stockholders in the Standard Gas holding-company system. The Schroders were leading bankers for Axis interests in London and New York before the war, and now have an important branch in Buenos Aires. One of their partners, Vlada-Mocarski, an ultra-reactionary White Russian, was appointed American consul in Zurich some months ago by the State Department, a key vantage post with respect to the flight of German capital abroad.

In the machinery of the military control commission in Germany, as in Washington, men closely linked with German cartels and friendly to German business and finance occupy key posts. The memberships of the Technical Industrial Disarmament Committees in the FEA at Washington were disclosed to the Kilgore committee, and they contain the names of many men from big concerns closely linked with I. G. Farben before the war. Testimony before the committee showed that the Germans are planning to utilize these old connections, and it is the duty of the Kilgore committee fully to explore them and to make the facts known. In this connection I want to call attention to an interesting statement on page 534 of the committee transcript, a passage in an FEA memo on German penetration of French finance during the occupation. This says that all enemy banks were put under German administration, including "American banks. The Chase Bank and Morgan et Cie., however, the only two American banks which continued operations, received special treatment." Why did these two leading American banks receive special treatment from the Germans? The question is of especial interest because Chase is the Rockefeller-Standard Oil bank.

I have no space to do more than praise the wise and statesman-like testimony by Baruch which opened the hearings. Or to do more than touch upon the complex political and social problems involved in ending the threat of renewed German aggression. One FEA memorandum on German rearmament after World War I vividly illustrates how the German General Staff was able to exploit Bolshevik fear of the West to rebuild the Reich's military power while German industry was able to utilize Western capitalist fear of "over-production" to increase the Reich's economic potential at the expense of its neighbors. The situation after this war is not greatly different. In the political sphere the unity of the big powers is again the first essential. In the economic and social sphere the task is even more difficult. It is the industrial reconstruction of Europe with a view to increasing (1) the potential of Germany's neighbors at the expense of the Reich, and (2) the productivity, the consuming power, the living standards of the Continent. This is impossible without socialist ownership and control of basic industry in Western Europe, and our chances of that depend on coming elections in France and Belgium and the willingness of Britain and America to permit considerable social reform in our sphere of influence.

July 14, 1945

Pearl Harbor Diplomats

IN THE FALL OF 1941 Joseph Clark Grew had been our ambassador in Japan for almost ten years. His second-in-command, the counselor of the American embassy in Tokyo, Eugene H. Dooman, was born in Japan, had entered the foreign service there in 1912, and had lived in Japan most of his life. Both were proud of their friendly relations with the highest circles of Japanese society. Dooman is one of the few Americans who read and speak Japanese with fluency. It was on these two officials that the American government was dependent for accurate information and appraisal of political developments in Japan.

Our main source of information on the views they transmitted to Washington is Grew's *Ten Years in Japan,* a carefully edited selection from his diaries and reports. Grew can boast of two warnings to the American government. "There is a lot of talk around town," he noted in his diary on January 27, 1941, "to the effect that the Japanese, in case of a break with the United States, are planning to go all out in a surprise attack on Pearl Harbor. Of course I informed our government." Grew does not seem to have taken this report seriously, for there is no further reference to it. But he did send home a grave warning in a report to the department on November 3, 1941. This report supplemented a previous report on September 29, 1941. It is odd that, unlike all the other diary entries and reports in Grew's books, these two documents are not provided in their original text. They are marked "(Substance)" and "(Paraphrase of original text prepared by Department of State)." The paraphrase says the Ambassador reported that "action by Japan which might render unavoidable an armed conflict with the United States may come with dangerous and dramatic suddenness."

These two isolated warnings must be read in context. The complete record may never become public, but even in *Ten Years in Japan,* which Dooman helped Grew to edit, the evidence is unmistakable: in the fateful autumn of 1941 Grew and Dooman completely misread events. They were guilty of wishful thinking not only about the Emperor and their aristocratic friends but also about Konoye[1] and Tojo,[2] and this wishful thinking continued even after Pearl Harbor. Their attitude of mind must bear its share of the responsibility for Japan's successful stab-in-the-back attack. And it needs to be recalled and analyzed because, unlike Kimmel and Short, Grew and Dooman were rewarded with new posts of influence and honor: Grew as head of the Division of Far Eastern Affairs of the State Department and then as Under Secretary, and Dooman as the department's leading adviser on Far Eastern affairs. Both men are likely to play major roles in shaping our post-war policy toward Japan. The talk in Washington is that while Grew may be removed as Under Secretary, he will be sent to the Far East as political adviser to MacArthur. His position, like his fundamental political outlook, would be comparable to that of Robert Murphy, political adviser to Eisenhower. Grew would almost certainly be accompanied by Dooman, whom Grew in *Ten Years in Japan* called "my *fidus Achates.*" The implied comparison is unfair to the friend and armor-bearer of Aeneas.

Grew's reports were prepared with the help of Dooman, a far abler man than his chief. In the preface to *Ten Years in Japan* Grew says he "counted greatly in the formulation through those years of the views herein set forth" on Dooman's "long experience in Japan, mature advice, and incisive diagnosis of political developments."

One is inclined to suspect from the views set forth in Grew's report to the Secretary of State on September 29, 1941, that this was made public in paraphrase rather than in text to protect Grew. It was a plea for further appeasement of Japan, and it was based on a ridiculous misconception of the character of the Konoye government, which had taken Japan a long way toward fascism and war. Soon after becoming Premier in July, 1940, Konoye abolished the Japanese General Federation of Labor. In September he signed a treaty of alliance with Germany and

---

[1] Fumimaro Konoye. Member of a noble Japanese family. Premier from July 1940 to October 1941.
[2] Hideki Tojo. Japanese general, leader of the military party. Premier October 1941 to July 1944. Approved the attack on Pearl Harbor.

Italy. In October he set up the Imperial Rule Assistance Association, Japan's closest approach to a totalitarian political party. At the end of 1940 he established a Supreme Economic Council. In January, 1941, he launched a ten-year program to expand food production in Manchuria. In April, preparing the way for a southward advance against British, Dutch, and American possessions, Konoye signed a neutrality pact with the Soviet Union and in June a trade agreement. After Hitler attacked the Soviet Union, Konoye moved troops into French Indo-China. In September, when Grew sent his report to the State Department, Konoye was trying to set up control associations for each basic industry, Fascist style.

What conclusions did Grew and Dooman draw from these developments? "The Ambassador," says the State Department paraphrase of the report of September 29, 1941, "recalls his reports to the department to the effect that Japanese foreign policies are inevitably changed by the impact of events abroad and that liberal elements might come to the top in due course as a result of the trend of events. He considers that such a time has arrived." The Ambassador thought there was "a good chance" of "Japan's falling into line" with the Atlantic Charter. He felt that the "impact of world developments" had "rendered Japan's political soil hospitable to the sowing of new seeds" which might "bring about the anticipated regeneration of Japanese thought and a complete readjustment of relations between Japan and the United States." The reader who desires to may study this fantastic analysis for himself on page 437 of *Ten Years in Japan.*

Grew pleaded with the American government in the negotiations then going on with Japan not to insist on "the sort of clear-cut, specific commitments which appear in any final formal convention or treaty." He asked instead that we place "a reasonable amount of confidence" in "the good faith of Prince Konoye." He pleaded that if we insisted on "clear-cut commitments" from Japan, the conversations would drag along indefinitely and Konoye would conclude "that the United States government is only playing for time." He warned that "the logical outcome of this will be the downfall of the Konoye Cabinet and the formation of a military dictatorship which will lack either the disposition or the temperament to avoid colliding head-on with the United States."

President Roosevelt was less trusting than Grew, and the conversations lagged. In October the Konoye Cabinet fell. On the 18th General Tojo became Prime Minister. It was announced that he would be his own War Minister and, significantly, that he was retaining his active rank in the

Japanese armed forces. The Tojo government was in fact a military dictatorship, and events were soon to make it clear that Tojo's accession to power was the signal that war with the United States had been decided upon. Tojo took power just fifty days before Pearl Harbor, and actual fleet and military preparations for the widespread attacks on December 7 must have begun soon after. But Grew and Dooman continued optimistic in their reports, and trustful in their Japanese informants. On the day of Tojo's appointment Grew recorded in his diary that Konoye's private secretary had "conveyed through him to me from Prince Konoye a very interesting explanation of the circumstances which had led to the fall of the Cabinet *and the successful efforts of the Prime Minister to insure the appointment of a successor who would continue the conversations with the United States*" (my italics). Grew himself noted, "Tojo was one of the original five members of the Konoye Cabinet last spring who supported the opening of conversations with the United States in the face of the opposition of Matsuoka. This is important."

On October 20 Grew's optimism has grown. He reported that he had learned from "a confidant of Prince Konoye" that Konoye resigned because he felt the negotiations with the United States "would make more rapid progress if our government were dealing with a Prime Minister whose power was based on ... the army, which is the controlling force in matters affecting policy." Grew concluded that it would be "premature to stigmatize the Tojo government as a military dictatorship" committed to policies which would "bring about armed conflict with the United States." On the contrary, Grew felt that Tojo, by "retaining his active rank in the army, will as a result be in a position to exercise a larger degree of control over army extremist groups."

Five days later Grew was jubilant. "A reliable Japanese informant" told him that before the fall of the Konoye government the Emperor demanded a guaranty from the army and navy that they would not involve Japan in war with the United States. "The Emperor's definite stand," Grew reported, "necessitated the selection of a Prime Minister who would be in a position effectively to control the army, hence the appointment of General Tojo." Grew wrote that his informant, "who is in contact with the highest circles," told him "that for the first time in ten years the situation at present and the existing political setup in Japan offer a possibility of reorientation of Japanese policy and action." There is not a line or phrase to indicate that Grew did not accept these statements as fact.

On October 29 Grew reported that the Germans were disappointed because they had hoped for "a definitely interventionist government" when Konoye resigned. Grew said the Germans were "uncertain" of what Japan would do if the United States went to war with the Reich. "The Germans," he wrote, "are at present working primarily for a Japanese attack on the Soviet." This was forty-one days before Pearl Harbor.

This extraordinary series of misjudgments was capped by the November 3 report, the second one which is presented only in State Department paraphrase. In this report, the paraphrase says, "the Ambassador refers to his various telegraphic reports during several months past analyzing the factors affecting policy in Japan and says he has nothing to add thereto nor any substantial revision to make thereof." This would imply that he still felt the moment had arrived when, as he said in the September 29 report quoted above, "liberal elements might come to the top in due course" if we did not insist on clear-cut commitments in our negotiations with the Japanese. It also implies that Grew did not think the formation of the Tojo government had brought about any fundamental change in the situation.

It is in this report, as part of a plea against economic sanctions and for "constructive conciliation" — a phrase Grew said was preferable to the term "appeasement" — that we come across the warning on which Grew and the State Department pride themselves. In the final paragraph of the paraphrase, we read, "The Ambassador sees no need for much anxiety respecting the bellicose tone and substance at present of the Japanese press." Obviously, then, he did not consider this anti-American propaganda as emotional preparation for war. But, as a final argument for "constructive conciliation," Grew adds that it would be "shortsighted" to think that "Japanese preparations are no more than saberrattling" and warns that action by Japan "which might render unavoidable an armed conflict with the United States may come with dangerous and dramatic suddenness." The phrasing is curious. Even a diplomat would hardly say that an attack on American territory "might render unavoidable an armed conflict." Strategically, the Dutch East Indies and Singapore could not be attacked without also attacking the Philippines. I believe that when and if the full facts are known we shall find that Grew still expected Japan to attack the Soviet Union.

One would be inclined to give Grew more credit for the November 3 warning if it were not followed by the same kind of wishful thinking and bad reporting which preceded it. But Grew is as blissfully idiotic about Kurusu[3] as he was about Tojo. On November 4, after the Kurusu mission was announced, Grew noted correctly that Kurusu "was last ambassador in Rome and then in Britain, and he it was who signed the Tripartite Pact," but he adds, "I have no reason to believe that he is any more friendly to the Nazis than to us." His basis for this conclusion is, "His wife is American, and his daughter, Jaye, was a great friend of Elsie's [Grew's daughter]. We had a long and very frank talk." Nor did Grew see anything other than "childishness" in the fact that even as Kurusu left for Washington the Japanese were continuing "to fill their press with hostile articles which tend to render an understanding impossible."

Grew went on happily whistling in the dark until the end. On November 20 he reports that the Japanese embassy in Berlin was embarrassed by the Kurusu mission "and resents it." Even Tojo's bellicose speech of November 29, in which he celebrated the anniversary of the Anti-Comintern Pact by threatening to "purge" American and British influence from East Asia, did not disturb Grew's cheerfulness. He thought the speech "utterly stupid ... of course, it was chiefly for domestic consumption." The Japanese, Grew concluded, "are really children and should be treated as children." The day before Pearl Harbor Grew was further cheered by "a Japanese informant of known reliability," who told him that "neither the Prime Minister nor any member of the Cabinet had seen the text of General Tojo's speech ... in advance." Since Tojo himself was Prime Minister, this is puzzling. But Grew was informed that the speech was "read by proxy, as is often done in Japan" and it was pointed out to him that "the substance and tone" of the speech "was different from all General Tojo's previous addresses." As they say in vaudeville, it must have been two other fellows.

Grew and Dooman were suckers to the end. Even Pearl Harbor did not end their weakness for gold-brick explanations. On December 9 Grew reports another happy discovery. Ohta, of the European section of the Japanese Foreign Office, called at the embassy that day. "Dooman asked Ohta," Grew recorded, "whether the Foreign Minister, in expressing reluctance to stay up very late to receive me, was trying to avoid having to meet me in person again after the beginning of the hostilities. Ohta burst out spontaneously and with considerable feeling. 'Not at all. The Foreign Minister knew nothing about the attack on

[3] Saburo Kurusu. Special envoy to Washington in 1941. He and the Japanese Ambassador, Admiral Kichisaburo Nomura, were negotiating when the attack on Pearl Harbor took place.

Hawaii until early the next morning.'" Dooman discussed this with Grew, and Grew concluded, "Without pressing the point too far, it seems clear that His Imperial Majesty's Minister for Foreign Affairs had no prior knowledge that an act of war was to be committed by the Japanese forces." Unversed as I am in Shinto legend, I doubt whether it contains any instances of more touching faith in the Emperor and his officials.

Grew's past record and diaries, James R. Young's *Behind the Rising Sun,* and talks with Americans who have served in Japan leave the impression that the Back Bay Bostonian, Grew, and Dooman, the son of poor Persian immigrants to Japan, are snobs and social climbers who were thrilled by the Imperial Court and aristocratic Japanese society. Their judgment was affected by their social contacts to the point of fatuity, and their eager gullibility was skillfully played upon by the Japanese for their own ends. They became pipe lines for misinformation intended to lull the United States into a false sense of security while Japan expanded in East Asia, and they cannot be trusted for realistic or rigorous advice as to the future of Japan. The Japanese, seeing the high positions Grew and Dooman will occupy in our government, must chuckle over an observation Grew confided to his diary in November, 1941, "The naivete of the Japanese," Grew observed, "is really amazing."

August 18, 1945

Washington Faces Peace

~~~ ~~~

B Y THE TIME THESE LINES appear in print the war will almost certainly be over. The prospect of sudden victory has created anxiety here as well as jubilation. For with the coming of peace, the classic crutch of war is kicked out from under American capitalism. The United States faces not only the same old problem but the same old problem in a more intense and exacerbated form. We emerge from the war the Midas of nations. While other countries rise from the ruins appalled by their poverty, we are baffled by our wealth. Our power to produce has increased by 50 per cent since 1940, and the task of raising living standards to match that output is of such magnitude that only government, and business men willing to cooperate with government, can accomplish it. A glimpse of what lies ahead is provided by *Post-War Markets* (Public Affairs Press, Washington), a business guide based on official information prepared by the Bureau of Foreign and Domestic Commerce. If post-war output should be no greater than it was in 1940 (when our economy was already stimulated by war orders) "there would be the 9,000,000 who were unemployed in 1940 plus the 2,500,000 added to the civilian labor force between 1940 and 1946 plus 8,000,000 who would be displaced by improvements in efficiency over the six years — a total of over 19,000,000 unemployed."

The figures are terrifying, but the only hope of arousing sufficient public pressure and Congressional concern is to step up such statistical bombardment. The lag between technological capacity and social organization is an old story, but the dimensions of that lag have nowhere and never before been so great as in the United States of 1945. The Mead committee, in its new report on reconversion problems, estimates that we must find 11,000,000 more jobs than in 1929, which is 6,000,000 more than our present civilian labor force. But employment in manufacturing industries last year was already 5,000,000 greater than in 1929 or 1939. "We must not only hold these productive gains," the Mead committee says, "but we must find productive work for 6,000,000 additional persons." Without strong countervailing pressure, the drift will be toward resumption of business on pre-war levels, with the government providing made-work for the jobless. The danger is made graphic by a War Production Board [WPB] survey cited by the Mead committee. In seventy-two industries, the "break-even operating rate" would be reached at a point where employment would be 25 per cent less than at present. Large sections of business could operate profitably enough for the owners on considerably less than capacity production. And no doubt many would prefer that to "government interference."

In a sardonic sense, the sudden surrender of Japan may well be regarded as its reprisal for atomic bombing. We were poorly enough prepared for a slow and comfortable period in which we could devote half our energies to war in the Pacific and half to the resumption of large-scale civilian output. We are completely unprepared for a Japanese collapse, and unless we act quickly and wisely may face an economic collapse ourselves. The President's letter last night to Chairman J. A. King of the War Production Board has already been overtaken by events. There is immediate need for a program which will smooth the transition from war to peace, and a longer-range, if hardly less urgent, need for a program which will insure that industry reconverts to a full-employment level. No government agency has been authorized to tackle the second job, though some headway is being made in Congress by the full-employment bill. But even the simpler and more immediate task of reconversion has yet to be mapped out adequately. Mr. King, an ex-TVA man with an N.A.M.[1] mind, believes that the problem can be met by hoopla; he would remove all restrictions as rapidly as possible and let industry scramble back to civilian output pretty much on a hit-or-miss basis. The OPA [Office of Price Administration], the War Labor Board, and the Office of Economic Stabilization feel that controls must be retained and used during the transitional period if it is to be negotiated successfully.

Mr. Truman, whose Senatorial experience made him conversant with the problems of industrial mobilization for war and peace, had to decide

[1] The National Association of Manufacturers, which had a reactionary reputation.

between these two points of view, and his letter is a victory for those who fear too quick a removal of restriction. But unfortunately it leaves Krug and the WPB crowd at the controls, and they are already interpreting the President's letter to suit themselves. The WPB is as much big-business as ever and cannot be trusted to handle reconversion on a basis fair to the smaller business man and the consumer. The big fellows would like to grab off materials quickly at the expense of the smaller. There is quick profit to be made in turning swiftly to production of higher-price items. The health of business enterprise requires a fair distribution of scarce materials during the transition, and the welfare of the consumer requires the allocation of channelling of materials into badly needed low-cost goods. The nation's economic safety depends on continued price controls during the transition and planning on an unprecedented scale for a higher level of output.

All this is repugnant to the WPB crowd, and Mr. Truman should know from past experience that it will handle these problems its own sweet way, irrespective of White-House directives. New agencies, new men, new ideas, new directions are necessary — and quickly — if we are not to suffer a relapse into chronic mass unemployment now that war's blood transfusions will no longer be available to an ailing capitalism.

August 25, 1945

Shake-up in the State Department

〜〜〜

IT WOULD BE PLEASANT to believe that the resignation of Joseph C. Grew as Under-Secretary of State indicated that President Truman and Secretary of State James F. Byrnes had begun to understand what a mistake they made in following Grew's advice on the Japanese Emperor. It is possible to state with assurance only that Grew's successor, Dean Acheson, sharply disagreed with our former Ambassador to Tokyo on the question of how far we could rely on Hirohito. In intra-departmental conferences, the new Under-Secretary was signally un-crushed by Grew's favorite retort, "Have you ever lived in Japan?" To be succeeded by Acheson must be a bitter pill for Grew, as for the whole inside clique in the State Department.

For Acheson has been in the minority on issues other than that of the Japanese Emperor. He has been pro-De Gaulle, anti-Franco, strongly opposed to the admission of Argentina to the United Nations, and friendly to the Soviet Union. He is not at all likely to be frightened by a Labor government in England, even if it carries out its socialist program. Of all the men now in the department, Acheson was by far the best choice for Under-Secretary, and it is no small advantage to pick a man who already knows a good deal about the inner machinery.

By all superficial marks, Acheson would appear to be a natural member of the snobbish clique which generally runs the department. He is a man of wealth and social standing, a Grotonian, a successful corporation lawyer. But his intellectual horizons and human sympathies transcend this background. He was once private secretary to Brandeis. He took time off from his corporate law practice to argue the constitutionality of minimum-wage legislation in the United States Supreme Court. He is not at all stuffy, and at fifty-two still has plenty of ginger in him.

There are differences of opinion in Washington as to how "strong" a man he is. He is strong enough to do a good job in the department if he is sufficiently supported by Secretary Byrnes and the White House. The job of Under-Secretary is as important as its holder and his chief choose to make it. He can be the actual administrative head of the department, or, as Sumner Welles was, he can be by-passed and rendered ineffective by the inside clique.

One of Acheson's assets lies in his relations with Congress. He deserves a generous share of the credit for the passage of the Bretton Woods legislation, and he played no inconsiderable part in the Senate's approval of the Charter. His ability to make friends and influence people in Congress is the kind of quality that impresses practical politicians like Truman and Byrnes. Within the department, Acheson's closest alliance has been with MacLeish and, among the new men brought in by Byrnes, with Benjamin V. Cohen. Cohen and Acheson laid the groundwork for the destroyers-for-bases deal with England, and have long been close friends.

Acheson disliked the "new team" put in charge of the department last year by President Roosevelt and submitted his resignation in January. He was persuaded to stay on to help put Bretton Woods through Congress and then to aid the Charter fight in the Senate. The strangest thing about Acheson's appointment is that it was obviously a surprise to him, and came three days after the New York *Times* reported that Byrnes had accepted his resignation as Assistant Secretary.

One of these days it is likely that the various agencies of government dealing with foreign economic and propaganda matters will either be merged into the State Department or brought closely under its control. This policy has much to recommend it from the standpoint of neat administrative arrangements, though not from a realistic point of view — so long as the department remains what it is. Under such circumstances it would be most useful to have as Under-Secretary a man with Acheson's knowledge and experience in handling foreign economic problems.

It would be well, however, not to expect too much. A real overhauling of the department has been long overdue but it is unlikely to be obtained from a Secretary of State as conservative as Byrnes. The resignations of Archibald MacLeish and Julius Holmes can hardly be fitted into any consistent pattern. The progressive MacLeish has worked hard under difficult circumstances to improve the Department's public relations and did an excellent educational job on the San Francisco Charter. The departure of Holmes is welcome news, for he is a combination of brass hat and cookie pusher, and as Assistant Secretary in charge of personnel was likely to multiply the snobs in the Department and the Foreign Service. I hope that Chase National Bank boy scout, Nelson Rockefeller, will follow him into retirement.

One of the discouraging factors in the situation is that Byrnes assigned the Budget Bureau to make a study of the State Department. The Budget Bureau is at best formalistic and academic, and at worst a nest of reactionary wire-pullers and intriguers. The task of finding out what is wrong with the Department should not have been intrusted to pundits who specialize in neat little blueprints.

The ideal way to prepare for a reorganization would be with a thorough series of hearings before the Senate Foreign Relations Committee. Congress and the country ought to hear from the men in other divisions of the government who have had to do business with the State Department, from the men who have left it in disgust, and if possible from some of the younger men within it. Only a full airing of policies and personalities could provide enough knowledge and arouse enough interest to establish the basis for a real housecleaning.

Brass Hats Undaunted

THE REPORT of the Naval Court of Inquiry on Pearl Harbor begins by explaining that the Pacific Fleet was organized in three main task forces. The operating schedule was so arranged that there was always one task force at sea, and usually two. "At no time during 1941," the Court of Inquiry assures us, "were all the vessels of the Fleet in Pearl Harbor." In accordance with this operating schedule, only Task Force One and part of Task Force Two were in Pearl Harbor at the time of the Japanese attack. Reading thus far, one feels that naval operations were wisely planned to avoid a situation in which the entire Pacific Fleet might have been destroyed in one enemy attack on the Hawaiian base. But then we read that "the preponderance of the battleship strength of the Fleet" was in Task Force One, and that all three of the battleships of Task Force Two were also in the harbor, and finally that "all battleships of the Pacific Fleet, except one undergoing overhaul at the Puget Sound Navy Yard, were in Pearl Harbor on 7 December." The Naval Court of Inquiry concludes, however, that this was "purely a coincidence." The disingenuous approach and the fatuous conclusion are alike characteristic of the report turned in by the three high admirals, Kalbfus, Murfin, and Andrews.

Despite this solemn rigmarole about the three task forces, the fact is that the Japanese attack had the effect, as the Army Board of Inquiry reports, "of immobilizing and substantially destroying the Pacific Fleet, which was a major threat to Japan's left flank in its southward move." To dismiss as "coincidence" the crucial blunder that concentrated all our battleships and most of the Pacific Fleet in Pearl Harbor that ghastly morning is to demonstrate the continued presence in the armed services of the brass-hat mentality responsible for that disaster. Admirals and generals are supposed to avoid "coincidences" of this kind when they know war is an imminent possibility, as they knew in the fall of 1941.

On a par with this Naval Court of Inquiry conclusion is its finding that "condition of readiness No. 3," in effect at the time of the attack, was "that best suited to the circumstances." This deserves to rank with the medical gag about the operation being highly successful though the patient died. It draws from Admiral King the tart comment that "condition of readiness No. 3" is that "normally maintained in port." In other words the high admirals of the Court of Inquiry still think the condition of readiness observed by a ship in Brooklyn in peacetime was "best suited" to the circumstances in Pearl Harbor on December 7, 1941. This finding will read better in Japanese.

As can be seen from these samples, the naval report on Pearl Harbor is hardly a masterpiece of forthright self-criticism. The report of the Army Board of Inquiry is by comparison a vigorous and outspoken document. The mealy-mouthed naval report is accompanied by separate statements from Admiral King, as commander-in-chief of the United States Fleet and Chief of Naval Operations, and from Secretary Forrestal. Both King and Forrestal indicate their displeasure with the Court of Inquiry and speak out with manly frankness on the navy's responsibility for Pearl Harbor. On the other hand, the army board's report is accompanied by a separate statement by Secretary Stimson which seeks to soften the criticism in that document and to rebut findings which place on the General Staff in Washington and on General Marshall, its chief, a substantial share of the blame for our unpreparedness at Pearl Harbor. The net effect of the reports and their accompanying statements is to leave the impression that the services as a whole are still far from prepared fully to admit the errors which made Pearl Harbor possible. That attitude does not promise well for the future.

Both the army and navy reports do a great deal of buck-passing. The prize specimen is the naval court's finding that "constitutional requirements that war be declared by Congress" made it difficult to prevent the attack on Pearl Harbor. This was neatly deflated in Secretary Forrestal's dour report, "The constitutional inhibition ... did not preclude long-distance reconnaissance." The army board's report blames the state of public opinion and isolationism, but itself contains isolationist overtones; noteworthy is the statement, in discussing contradictory tendencies at home, "we were arming our forces for war and at the same time giving

away much of such armament." Both reports have given fuel to the
isolationist press by blaming Secretary of State Hull for not continuing
to stall and appease the Japanese in the fall of 1941. That public opinion
bears a heavy share in the responsibility for Pearl Harbor is indisputable,
but irrelevant. For the question before the army and navy boards was
whether the armed services did all they could to prevent the disaster *with
the means at their disposal* and within the existing circumstances. The
answer to that question is sharply negative. It is only the criticism of
Hull, and by implication Roosevelt, which merits serious consideration.

Hull is blamed for presenting his ten-point proposal to the Japanese on
November 26, 1941, over the objections of General Marshall as Chief of
Staff and Admiral Stark as Chief of Naval Operations. Marshall and
Stark, supported by Stimson and Knox, said we were unprepared for
war and seemed to feel that Hull's proposals were so drastic as to make
war unavoidable. It is implied that Roosevelt ignored or overruled this
warning. But it is hard to see how Hull could have stalled the Japanese
any longer without in large part accepting their proposals of November
20, and those proposals would have made us a partner in Japanese
aggression. The Japs wanted us to supply them with all the oil they
needed, to unfreeze Japanese accounts in this country, to end all aid to
China, to "cooperate" with Japan in acquiring "these goods and
commodities which the two countries need in the Netherlands East
Indies." To accept such terms would have been to risk the complete
collapse of China and the dominance of the Dutch East Indies by Japan.
There was no assurance that paying this kind of blackmail would have
prevented further Japanese advances and an eventual attack upon us
anyway. It is to the credit of Hull and Roosevelt that they refused to
participate in a Far Eastern Munich and insisted, in the ten-point
proposal, on the evacuation of China as a condition for resuming friendly
relations with Japan.

The army and navy wanted more time, but we had already been
stalling and appeasing the Japanese for ten years. The price asked for
more time was so large that it would have benefited Japan more than the
United States. The refusal to pay that price undoubtedly precipitated the
long-prepared Japanese attack, and we were poorly prepared for war.
But the real point involved in the Pearl Harbor inquiry was whether that
disaster need necessarily have happened. And one test of the army-navy
plea for more time is what use the armed services made of the time they
did have. The services regarded the ten-point proposal as a virtual
ultimatum to Japan, and since they so regarded the proposal they were

under obligation to take steps immediately for war. But their record, as disclosed in the army and navy inquiries and in the earlier Roberts report, is one of unpardonable negligence and appalling stupidity. We would have had to fight a defensive war for months in any case, but we need not have lost our Pacific Fleet at Pearl Harbor and our air force at Manila in two quick, crushing surprise attacks. For the facts disclosed indicate that it was not a lack of knowledge but sheer stodgy unimaginative bureaucratic complacency at Washington, Pearl Harbor, and Manila which made the Japanese blitz possible.

In the first place, the joint army-navy defense plan for Hawaii signed on April 9, 1941, was, as the army board said, "prophetic in its accuracy." It was based on the assumption that the Japs would attack without warning, and the men who drew up that plan accurately forecast every basic detail of what happened at Pearl Harbor: the time of day, the type of task force used by the Japanese, the form the attack would take, even the fact that it might be preceded (as it actually was) by a single submarine foray in the harbor just before the big blow. The only trouble is that this army-navy defense agreement was neither implemented nor taken seriously by the military-naval command in Washington and in Hawaii. In the second place, President Roosevelt told the heads of the army and navy at a White House conference on November 25, the day before the ten-point proposal, to expect a surprise attack "perhaps as soon as next Monday," which was December 1. In the third place, from the time of that White House conference until December 7, "the record shows" (says the army report) "that from informers and other sources the War Department had complete and detailed information of Japanese intentions." Finally, at 9 o'clock on the morning of December 7, the War and Navy Departments were tipped off (four hours before the attack) that the Japanese would present an ultimatum or declaration of war at 1 P.M. Washington time. And a Commander Kramer in the navy was quick to point out that 1 P.M. Washington time would be dawn at Pearl Harbor, the very time at which our war plans predicted a surprise attack there.

General Marshall as Chief of Staff and Admiral Stark as Chief of Naval Operations failed to see to it that proper defense measures were taken at Pearl Harbor between November 25 and December 7. And they failed to react quickly enough to the advance knowledge that they had on the morning of Pearl Harbor. Stark didn't think the information was worth passing on and Marshall sent it to General Short by commercial cable when faster means of communication were available. The last warning left Washington 22 minutes before the attack and did not arrive until several hours after the attacking force had departed. Marshall could have telephoned Short, but his excuse was that he was expecting an attack on the Philippines rather than in Hawaii and telephoned MacArthur instead. This throws additional light on MacArthur's extraordinary incompetence as a commander at that juncture. For despite the pleas of subordinates to disperse his planes, MacArthur left them on the ground at Clark Field outside Manila, where almost his entire air force was destroyed by the Japanese ten hours after their attack on Pearl Harbor. MacArthur was more culpable than Kimmel and Short, and it is scandalous that there should never have been an investigation of his bungling in the Philippines.

Our military-naval command acted with indecent sedateness. Lacking daring itself, it did not expect daring from the Japanese. Even now, when we know how meticulously and minutely (and, let us confess, brilliantly) the Japanese planned their attacks, we still find the Army Board of Inquiry talking nonsense about "the Oriental mind" and attributing the Pearl Harbor blitz to "the violent and uncivilized reasoning of the Japanese." Our military-naval command did not keep abreast of new developments in warfare, notably the use of torpedoes from planes in shallow water. This was how the Japs did most of their damage at Pearl Harbor, and naval intelligence warned of this possibility months in advance. Our military-naval command underestimated the intelligence of the Japanese and they made the equally crucial mistake of underestimating the loyalty of our Japanese-American population. For it was the latter error which led General Short to institute the alert against sabotage instead of the alert against attack from without. Under this type of alert planes were parked wing to wing and unable to get off the ground in less than four hours. The attack on Pearl Harbor took only three, and most of the planes were destroyed.

Perhaps the crowning example of military stupidity is in the revelation that while our army's mobile anti-aircraft artillery was in state of instant readiness, it had no ammunition. The ammunition was in a crater a mile away. General Short and Ordnance had rejected pleas for artillery shells several days earlier on the ground that "they didn't want to issue any of the clean ammunition, let it get out and get dirty, and have to take it back in later on and renovate it." The slogan of the Pearl Harbor high command seems to have been, "Praise the Lord, but don't muss the ammunition."

The Truman Program

⤫

I HAVE BEEN OUT OF WASHINGTON for most of the summer, and there is much I have to learn. But I would like to venture a few observations in the wake of the President's message to Congress.

1. To understand the message and what is happening here one must keep in mind that Administration utterance, thought, and action reflect three diverse approaches to post-war problems. On what may best be termed the *theological* level the Administration bows the knee to "free enterprise"; the message invokes "free enterprise" fervently, as do the backers of the full-employment bill. A psychologist might say that the fervor of the worshipers increases in direct ratio to the volume of their secret doubts, for on the *practical* level the White House and its progressive allies are asking for a legislative program based on the belief that without extensive government intervention at many points in the economy full employment is unattainable. One would not need a full-employment bill if "free enterprise" were as magical as it is represented to be in the current liturgy. But there is more to the picture than these contrasting "theological" and practical attitudes. On the *emotional* level still another attitude is visible. The mood of the White House and of Democratic Party leadership generally seems to be as optimistic as that of the Republicans. The President remains, as he has always been, a New Dealer. It is the momentum of the New Deal, the logical consequences of its basic assumptions, the experience of the past, and the pressure of organized labor rather than any feeling of impending emergency which underlies the President's program. Basically, the

President, like most Americans at this moment, feels that "everything is going to be all right." There is a mystic faith in "pent-up" demand. There is an all too human failure of the imagination. We have been enjoying a fully employed economy for almost five years and find it hard to imagine any really drastic change. It is this mood which accounts for two facts, one about the Administration, the other about the President's program. The President has a New Deal program, but his Administration in its actual operating personnel, is less New Dealish even than Roosevelt's was after 1940; no one with a sense of urgency would bring so many mediocre politicians and conventional minds into posts of crucial importance. It is this which gives so many people here the feeling that the New Deal is over, though the President's program calls for its extension. The optimistic mood of the moment also explains why Truman recommends an immediate large-scale public-works program. The works on which immediate action is asked — public buildings and highways — are minor. The major projects — regional TVA's and housing — are presented in long range terms. Should coming unemployment be as severe as some of the ablest economists on lower Administration levels believe, we shall be caught unprepared, and the jobless will have to rake leaves again.

2. The President in his message has gone all out for a progressive program. He is for higher unemployment compensation and an increase in minimum wages under the Fair Labor Standards Act. He is for the full-employment bill and for a permanent Fair Employment Practices Committee. He is for slum clearance and for a federal research agency, as long advocated by his friend Senator Kilgore. He asks for repeal of the Johnson Act, for interim lending power to fill the gap left by the sudden cessation of Lend-Lease, and for an additional contribution of $1,350,000,000 for UNRRA [United Nations Relief and Rehabilitation Administration]. He wants a system of crop insurance, and he recommends only limited tax reductions. The little man from Missouri has courage.

But it will take more than courage to put this program over. Even the leader of a party newly come to power, with a full range of patronage at his disposal, could hardly hope to overcome all the special interests and prejudices sure to be antagonized by this program. Without an economic crisis and the public awakening it brings, little of this program can be enacted. If a large volume of unemployment develops quickly, Truman has a chance to put it over. If the crisis comes later, he must gamble politically on the advantage of having had a concrete program. He can blame the opposition for having defeated measures that might have prevented the crisis. The advantage of his politically bold message is that it clarifies the issues for 1946 and 1948, and behind this strategy is the sound observation that the Democratic Party nationally has never got anywhere except as a left-of-center party.

The Republicans will fight. The honeymoon is over. The reaction of the GOP Congressional leaders was curiously 1920-ish. They put their research experts to work estimating how much the Truman program *would cost.* They are thinking in terms of fiscal economy and "normalcy," and their statements bristle with the old horrid words that failed so signally against Roosevelt — "boot-strap legislation," "deficit financing," "regimentation." They are staking their hopes on a quick and fairly successful reconversion, with enough employment and business activity to keep the middle classes fairly content and thus to make possible a successful campaign on — as Chairman Halleck of the Republican Congressional Campaign Committee expressed it — "the old-fashioned issue of conservatism."

But this is not the whole of their strategy as it seems to be developing in Congress. The fight against higher unemployment compensation indicates that they will let conservative Southern Democrats take the leadership and the blame on the more unpopular issues. And Taft's amendments to the full-employment bill show that they will not risk frontal attacks on the basic measure but will seek instead to confuse the issue and accomplish their purpose by indirection. Last winter Taft sounded like a cross between Martin Dies ("with a Communist plot") and a sectarian Soviet ideologist (full employment can be made possible only by the socialist construction of society) when he discussed the full-employment bill. Now he claims to be all for its purposes but wants some "clarifying" amendments. The most important of these would take the right to work and clarify it out of existence. Unfortunately for Taft, the demand for full employment is too fundamental to be sidetracked by the kind of legalistic trickery one might use successfully in writing a mortgage or bond indenture.

3. The fundamental issue shaping up here is between those who want a fully employed economy and those who think they can get along profitably even if there is a large volume of unemployment. That a full-employment economy is the more profitable is demonstrated in the new War Production Board [WPB] report on the effect of the war on the industrial economy. Despite high wages and high taxes, low costs per unit of output under conditions of all-out production boosted profits,

after taxes, by 120 per cent over 1940 and to a point far over 1929. The basic questions raised by the WPB report is whether our expanded metal-working and chemical industries will shrink back to fit our pre-war economy or whether our economy will be expanded to fit these enlarged productive possibilities. The question is already being answered: capacity and output are being reduced in many of these industries. In part this is due to habitual patterns. "The modern industrial economy," the WPB report says in a sentence which deserves immortality, "has always been characterized by the low degree of utilization of its existing plant." The individual enterpriser operating on his own is safest when working within a comfortable margin of scarcity, including scarcity of jobs; thus prices are held up and wages down.

On paper, partial employment seems to have its advantages. The September 1 issue of *Business Week* estimates that if the excess-profits tax is repealed, business during the coming year can earn higher net profits than the war-time peak, even with 9,000,000 unemployed. "Why, then," the average business man may ask himself, "sail out on the uncharted seas of economic planning?" But what if the economy declines to stay neatly poised at a level profitable to the owners of industry, though miserable for many millions of jobless? What if a deflationary spiral sets in? Wouldn't the average business man be better off in an economy planned for full employment, however painful that might be to the sacred cow of "free enterprise"? It is on the answer to these questions that momentous changes will depend in the not too distant future of the U.S.A.

September 29, 1945

Behind the MacArthur Row

THREE THINGS make the White House statement on occupation
policy in Japan less impressive than it would otherwise be. The first
is the long delay in its publication. The document says, "The Japanese
people, and the world at large, shall be kept fully informed of the
objectives and policies of the occupation and of progress made in their
fulfilment." This is important, if the stated objectives are to be realized.
The publication of this basic directive in Japan would let democratic and
working-class leadership there know that it was our policy "to use the
existing form of government in Japan, not to support it"; that we favor
changes in the form of that government designed to modify "its feudal
and authoritarian tendences"; that we are not committed to "support the
Emperor or any other Japanese governmental authority in opposition to
evolutionary changes looking toward the attainment" of those objectives;
and that if force proves necessary against recalcitrant and reactionary
elements the Allied Supreme Commander is authorized to intervene
only where required to insure "the security of his forces and the
attainment of all other objectives of the occupation."

An equally important purpose is served by publication of the
document in this country: it provides the American people with a clear
picture of our post-war program for Japan, a solid basis for judging the
necessary duration and extent of occupation, "and a means of checking
for ourselves whether MacArthur and his subordinates are or are not
carrying out their instructions." Yet despite the pledge of full publicity,
the document remained secret until an unusual set of circumstances
made its release to the press necessary as a means of defending the State

Department, the War Department, and the Administration against a burst of criticism in Congress. The principles embodied in the document were agreed upon by the State, War, and Navy departments and transmitted to MacArthur on August 29; the actual text of the document, after approval by the President, was sent to MacArthur by messenger on September 6. But it was not made public by the White House until September 22, and even then, from all indications, only reluctantly and under pressure from the State and War departments. We still do not know whether the document will be made public in Japan, although it says that "the Japanese people shall be kept fully informed."

To formulate fine principles on paper and forget about them in practice is becoming a characteristic of American occupational policy. German experience provides the second reason for being uneasy about our post-war plans for Japan. The basic directives on German occupational policy are still a secret, but the main outlines of our program are known. The policy laid down for Japan turns out to be much like that laid down for Germany. In Japan as in Germany we seek — in principle, at least — the elimination of war industry, the breaking up of the big monopolies, a wider distribution of ownership and income, encouragement of democratic forces, the elimination of ultra-nationalist and military elements.

Hardly a day passes without new evidence that similar directives are being sabotaged by the military occupation authorities in the Reich. Big American industrial and financial interests interlock with those of Germany as of Japan. Their influence, plus brass-hat mulishness, is enough to nullify the most specific directives. For Germany these are severe and thorough, but that has not kept them from being ignored. Even so conspicuous a malefactor as I. G. Farben is successfully evading the fate decreed for it. I have seen the secret General Order No. 2 on I. G. Farben, issued last July 5 by Military Government authorities. It is very drastic, but it is not being obeyed. Instead of being liquidated in accordance with that order, I. G. is being rebuilt. I am reliably informed that the services of its old American subsidiary, General Aniline and Film, are being enlisted to provide technicians for the reconstruction of the German parent company. Only last Friday the United States reported from Frankfurt a press conference in which Colonel James Boyd, head of the United States Forces' Industry Branch, declared that I. G. Farben's war industries would be "switched" to peace-time output rather than destroyed. What is to prevent these facilities from being "switched" back again some day to war production? If this can happen in Germany, where the relationship of monopoly and militarism has been much more fully publicized, it can happen in Japan. If I. G. can thus save itself, so can Mitsui.

There is a third and more fundamental reason for not taking the White House program at face value. Its principles and purposes are sound, but the magnitude of the changes they require — and international security requires — in Japanese society calls for a military government of Japan. It takes little reflection to realize that we can hardly hope to break the power of Japan's ruling classes — the aristocracy, the plutocracy, the bureaucracy, and the military — if we confine ourselves to operating through a government which remains their instrument. To do so is to leave in power the very elements we are pledged to eradicate; to leave these elements in position to reassume full control once the occupation is over. The Associated Press reports from Tokyo today, "Japanese prominently associated with the incipient liberal movement say opposition of these strongly intrenched groups already has handicapped attempts toward settlement of the problems of national livelihood as well as social reformation."

From what little I can learn here in this highly secret field of national policy, one faction in Washington, now the dominant faction in the State Department, favored a military government and had plans drawn up for such a government. The decision against a military government of Japan seems to have been made at Potsdam. This is puzzling. The British may well have opposed any drastic policy toward Japan, but it is hard to believe that the Russians did. I cannot find out why plans for a military government were dropped, but my hunch is that they were abandoned because our other Pacific allies — including the Russians — would have had to be represented at the top policy level. I think many in army-navy circles would prefer a soft peace for Japan to Russian participation in the fundamental decisions of the occupation.

Soviet-American relations are the fundamental factor in determining the future of Japan as of Germany. It is worth noting in this connection that Assistant Secretary of War John J. McCloy, top War Department official on German occupation policy, is also the department's representative on the State-War-Navy committee which frames the basic directives for Japan. McCloy has long been regarded in our branches of the government dealing with the Reich as a man who operates on the assumption that we need a strong Germany as a bulwark against the U.S.S.R. and communism. There are some who believe we need a strong Japan and a meek Korea for the same reason, and it is significant that Landon coupled criticism of the Morgenthau plan for Gemrany with his defense of MacArthur. In Congress and in the press the old pro-Axis and anti-Soviet crowd is taking advantage of the demand for faster demobilization to plead for softer treatment of both Germany and Japan.

The Hearst-Patterson-McCormick press and its friends in Congress are engaged in an attempt to identify advocacy of a hard peace for the Axis countries with communism; this would make "reds" of Wainwright, Chennault, Halsey, Devereaux, and the other military figures who have warned us against a soft peace with the Japanese. The most ludicrous effort in this field was Arthur Krock's attempt today to make it appear that criticism of MacArthur came chiefly from "the pink publications." One of the "pink publications" which have been criticizing MacArthur and insisting on action against "Japan's own special kind of big business, the great industrial and financial concerns of Japan," is Krock's own paper, the New York *Times* (see its leading editorial, headed "Cleaning Up Japan," in the September 13 issue). The poor fellow seems to think he is writing for the Chicago *Tribune*.

The War Department is not above playing up to these reactionary elements. Last Tuesday, during the interminable debate going on in Congress over demobilization, Lemke of North Dakota told the House that one War Department official was reported to have said it was "all right to discharge the boys if you do not want as large an army as Russia." The War Department's quarrel with MacArthur is not the same as the State Department's. The War Department is angry because MacArthur's sudden statement that he would need only 200,000 soldiers to police Japan upset its plea that occupation needs necessitated a slower rate of demobilization. The War Department is inclined to think of a large army in terms of power politics vis-a-vis the Soviet Union rather than as a means of preventing renewed German and Japanese aggression. The State Department's quarrel with MacArthur has a different basis. There Grew, Dooman, and the Japanophiles are out; Acheson and younger "China hands" are now in charge of Far Eastern policy. They see MacArthur's occupation policies and his talk of a short occupation with comparatively few troops as endangering the hope of a durable peace in the Far East. They are fighting for a complete change in the present economic and social system of Japan, which makes for a will to war. It was for his courage in saying so that Acheson's confirmation as Under Secretary was held up in the Senate last Thursday. Who would have dreamed that within four years of Pearl Harbor a nominee for high office would be attacked in the Senate of the United States for advocating severe treatment of Japan?

Whatever success we achieve in preventing a renewal of Japanese aggression will depend on the patience and understanding of the American people. Unfortunately, army-navy clumsiness and inefficiency have created so much resentment against demobilization delays as to make it difficult reasonably to argue the need for considerable personnel and extended occupation in both Japan and Germany. The same papers and the same Congressmen who helped lull this country into a false feeling of security before Pearl Harbor are back at work on a repeat performance. MacArthur is playing to the old isolationist and crypto-fascist gallery. He is also playing to the human and understandable desire to "get the boys back" as quickly as possible. Congress is swamped with letters from home on the subject. The Axis thrived once before on democratic unwillingness to make some present sacrifice for the sake of future security, and can thrive on it again. Russell of Georgia, in an able and moving speech to the Senate Tuesday, introduced a resolution for the trial of Hirohito as a war criminal and sought to drive home the future consequences of a soft peace. But the Russells are being drowned out by the Rankins. And the Landons are ready to sacrifice national security to cheap politics. True, MacArthur today told Hugh Baillie of the United Press that Japan would never again be a world power or world menace. But in the fall of 1939 we were assured by as high a military authority that the Philippines were in no danger of attack from Japan. That was Douglas MacArthur, too.

October 6, 1945

The Plight of the Jews

ᓚᓅ ᓚᓓ

IT WAS WILLIAM O'DWYER'S FINAL REPORT as executive director of the War Refugee Board, issued on September 21, which first called attention to the Harrison mission, up to then a rather well-kept secret, only known to a few in close touch with Jewish affairs. O'Dwyer disclosed that in July Earl G. Harrison, United States representative on the Intergovernmental Committee on Refugees, had been sent by the government to investigate the needs and conditions of displaced persons in Western Europe, "particularly the Jews." The O'Dwyer report declared that while much had been done to improve conditions among these "displaced peoples," Harrison had found "glaring inhumanity ... prevailing in many areas." On inquiry it was learned that Harrison had made a report to the White House in the latter part of August and that publication had been promised but postponed. It was said in informed circles that the British had objected to release of the report, but it was pretty obvious that there were objections from within the Administration as well. At the State Department the report was in the hands of Loy W. Henderson, now top official for Near Eastern Affairs, and the first off-the-record response was that it would not be made public until Secretary of State James F. Byrnes returned from London. The newspaper *PM* ran an editorial calling attention to the withholding of the report and demanding its release. Late Saturday, some twenty-four hours before Governor Dewey was to address a Zionist mass-meeting in New York City, the White House, without waiting for the return of Byrnes, gave out the text of the report and of the letter Mr. Truman sent to General Eisenhower about it on August 31.

The report, as released, made it easy to understand why some people in the War and State departments and the British embassy preferred to keep its fierce light hidden under a bushel. Harrison is a leading Philadelphia lawyer, long prominent in the civic and charitable life of that city, a former United States Immigration Commissioner, now dean of the University of Pennsylvania Law School; his report is gratifying evidence that there is at least one man of heart and vigor on the mummified Intergovernmental Committee. He does not happen to be Jewish; he seems to be, in more than a nominal sense, a Christian. It would take more than a political reporter, it would take a Hebrew prophet, to discuss that report and its implications adequately. For let no one imagine comfortably that Harrison's story concerns only the tragedy of a few hundred thousand Jews and other stateless persons who too often found their liberators as callous and indifferent as their Nazi oppressors had been savage and sadistic; who found a passive replacing an active cruelty, the former in some ways harder to bear. That is only a small part of the tragedy. One who reads the Harrison report with discerning and imaginative mind will see reflected in it the fatal weaknesses of our society, the lurking shadow of a terrible retribution. Events since 1933 would seem amply to have demonstrated the consequences and the cost of anti-Semitism for all peoples and for civilization, the need for resolute action in stamping it out, the desirability of some great and graphic act of justice to the homeless of Jewry as an object lesson for the Nazi-infected peoples. The picture which emerges from the Harrison report is, by contrast, only likely to convince the enemies of world order in Central Europe, at home, and elsewhere that the democratic forces of the Anglo-American world are weak and irresolute, too half-hearted to live up to their grandiose moral pretensions, not genuinely anti-fascist, easily gulled, and perhaps next time, with more luck, to be defeated.

Can anyone be so foolish as to believe that we earn the respect of the Germans by treating their victims as Harrison reveals we have been treating them? Three months after V-E Day Harrison found many of the Jews and former slave laborers of the Nazis living in the same concentration camps, fed a diet "composed principally of bread and coffee," still clothed in hideous concentration-camp garb or, even more ignominiously, in S.S. uniforms left behind by their oppressors, facing fuelless months in quarters "clearly unfit for winter use," and often unable to present their grievances to Military Government authorities "because ironically they have been obliged to go through German employees, who have not facilitated matters." The liberated are treated far worse than the defeated. I do not refer to prisoners of war or war criminals — their food and housing are a paradise by contrast — but to ordinary Germans. Harrison found Germans "still the best-dressed population in all of Europe," with a diet "more varied and palatable," in rural areas at least, than that of their freed victims. Harrison asks — and the point was emphasized in the President's sharp letter to Eisenhower — whether this is the way to implement the Potsdam pledge "to convince the German people that they have suffered a total military defeat and that they cannot escape responsibility for what they have brought upon themselves."

There is another side to this picture which must give the Nazis even greater satisfaction. Harrison went abroad unsympathetic to Zionism. He found that the Nazis had succeeded in spreading anti-Semitism almost everywhere in the occupied countries. He found that of the 100,000 Jews surviving in the camps of Germany and Austria, very few of the German and Polish Jews wished to return to their old homes, nor did many of those from other East and Central European countries. They want to go home as others are going home, and this for most of them means going to Palestine. They had sought to live as Germans and Poles — and no one can deny what fervent patriots the German and Polish Jews have been in the past — but they were persecuted as Jews, and most of them now wish to live as Jews, to hold their heads up as Jews; they look to the colonization of the Holy Land as their one hope of restored self-respect, their deepest need. Harrison neither applauds nor deplores the feeling, but he recognizes that there is really nowhere else for them to go; covert anti-Semitism and xenophobia greet them even in America and England. Harrison asks that the gates of Palestine be opened to 100,000 at least and cites the past pledges of the British Labor Party as basis for an appeal to this effect by the American government. If the British people, oppressed by their own multitudinous troubles in the wake of a heroic struggle, are inclined to be tolerant of these broken pledges, let them ask themselves if the broken pledges on Palestine are not of the same pattern as the pledges the Attlees and Bevins[1] have made to British labor, and if they do not foreshadow similar disillusion for themselves. They may well ask themselves also whether this reluctance to do justice to the Jews in the matter of Palestine is not

[1] Clement Attlee and Ernest Bevin, respectively prime minister and foreign minister in the British Labour government of 1945–1951.

of the same pattern as the Chamberlain policies that were responsible for their own ruined homes and cities.

It is to Mr. Truman's honor that he has already acted on both aspects of the Harrison recommendations. He has ordered General Eisenhower to take immediate steps to improve conditions among the remaining Jewish and other stateless displaced persons in the Reich — and Eisenhower has made a personal trip through the Reich to see that this is done. The President has also asked the British formally to grant 100,000 entrance certificates for Palestine. But it will still take much public pressure to achieve these purposes.

The problem of enforcing both the President's recent order and previous directives on the treatment of refugees in the Reich is but part of the general problem of getting the military to obey Potsdam and Presidential directives designed to denazify the Reich. Let no one be deceived by the statements issuing from anonymous spokesmen at Patton headquarters. A New York *Times* dispatch from Frankfurt today reports not only that Patton is unwilling to requisition decent housing for refugees but that "large numbers of American troops are still living under canvas in Bavaria, while Germans, some of them Nazis, luxuriously entertain American officers in fine houses." The problem of Jewish immigration into Palestine is similarly part of the greater problem of substituting Allied cooperation for power politics. Pledges to the Jews on Palestine are being broken because of British imperialist desires to use the thin layer of the Arab ruling class as a pawn in a game of oil politics with America and power politics with the Soviet Union. The Arab league, from which much is being heard, is the creation and the tool of the British Foreign Office. A Palestine settlement beneficial to both Jews and Arabs is possible any time the British government wants it. If Truman can bring this about, he will do humanity as well as Jewry a historic service.

Jewry in a Blind Alley

⤙⤚

I CAME TO PALESTINE UNHAPPY, and during the first few days I became even unhappier trying to figure out solutions of the problems involved; but the longer I have been here the happier I have come to feel despite all that has happened and may happen in the next few days.

I stayed five days in Egypt visiting with many Egyptians and spending some time in a village near Cairo. I was able to see the sharp contrast in cleanliness and health between the Egyptian villager and urban poor and the Arab villager and urban poor in Palestine. I felt happy that the coming of the Jews had helped rather than hurt the Arabs.

I was deeply moved by my visits to the colonies here. From Gevulot, in the far south of the Negev desert wastes, to glorious Minara, 3,000 feet above the Upper Jordan on the far northern edge, I saw young Jews from every clime and country reclaiming the land and making something for themselves and their children under conditions which are truly heroic. This sense of consecration and common effort in the Jewish community most powerfully attract all who prize human courage, devotion, and idealism. I was not at all surprised to hear of two cases of non-Jewish demobilized British soldiers, formerly in service here, applying for admission to membership in the Jewish Kibbutzim, or communal settlements.

I felt happy to see that despite difficulties which from abroad appear insuperable there was a great and growing community here, and in visits both to Arab villages and neighboring Jewish colonies, I feel a huge reservoir of good-will between the Arab and Jew which can be tapped;

and I have not sensed in talks with Arabs either in Palestine or in Egypt, despite their differences, any feeling of race hatred or dislike of Jews as a people.

But at the cost of unpopularity perhaps in the Jewish community of America I wish to say as strongly as I know how that the new Bevin statement is only the latest indication of the blind alley into which Palestinian Jewry is being led by the failure to achieve any political understanding with the Arabs. And I wish to say just as strongly that political agreement will be impossible so long as a single Jewish state in Palestine is demanded.

We have been carrying on a campaign in America on the basis of half-truths, and on this basis no effective politics can be waged and no secure life built for Yishuv.[1] It is true that the Arabs have benefited by the Jews coming to Palestine, and it is true that there is plenty of room here for several millions more, but I cannot find a single Jew who can find a single Arab who favors a Jewish state in Palestine! It should not be hard to understand the natural dislike of any human being for being ruled by another people or his unwillingness to trust himself to such rule.

There is only one way in which a Jewish state here could be sold to the Arab world and that would be as part of a general settlement of Anglo-Egyptian and other Arab problems which would satisfy the aspiration of the Arabs for self-development and federation. That was what made Zionism acceptable in earlier days to the wise and far-seeing Feisal and other Arab leaders, but Britain's failure really to keep the promises given to the Arabs has made the Arabs naturally hostile to the promises given to the Jews. The Bevin statement is only another chapter in the record of broken promises to both.

The most significant point to be noted in the Bevin statement is that while consultation is assured the Arabs concerning any further Jewish immigration in accordance with the White Paper, not a single solitary word is said about a promise to consult with the Jews on the other major item in the White Paper — the undertaking to the Arabs that a start would be made in setting up self-governing institutions in Palestine within five years. I could not help noting also that in Egypt, if it were not for anti-Zionist political agitation, the British would be confronted immediately with a demand for a basic settlement of Anglo-Egyptian problems, including the Sudan, Suez, and British occupation.

It is true that the Jews are in a terrible position, on the one hand

[1] The Jewish community in Palestine.

asking to be beneficiaries of British imperialism and on the other serving as its lightning rod. Two political axioms seem to be completely forgotten by Jewish world leadership. One is that politics cannot be played unless one has alternatives; one cannot bargain unless one can obtain similar wares elsewhere. The other is that in politics one saves favors for those one must win over and does not waste them on elements already in one's pocket. So long as the Jews are dependent on Britain with no alternative policy for an agreement with the Arabs, the Jews are helpless. Incidentally the Arabs are also helpless until they reach some agreement with the Jews, because just enough will be given both sides, as by Bevin, to keep both dissatisfied and embroiled. Let us remember that as long as there is no solution of the Arab-Jewish problem, Britain has an excuse to keep ample troops near the Suez Canal. I realize this does an injustice to the subjective intent of many British leaders, but it is politically true none the less.

I understand, after being in this part of the world, why the Jews must fight against the conversion of the Yishuv into what the Royal Commission of 1937 called "one more cramped and dangerous ghetto." Consignment to minority status in an Arab state is a violation of pledges made to the Jews, fulfilment of which they have a moral right to demand. But I understand too why the Arabs in Palestine, who are also human beings and who also have historic rights here, are prepared to fight against any subjection to a Jewish state.

I know there are other Arab states, while there is only one possibility for a Jewish state; I know that proposals to divide Palestine into two national states, put forward several times by Jewish sources, have fallen on stony ground. Nevertheless, despite present public utterances by the leadership on both sides, I think that a division on these lines, with two national states created on a parity principle, is ethically right and politically feasible and would be acceptable to a great majority of Jews and Arabs if it were imposed from above by Anglo-American or United Nations decision. Certainly only on this basis can Arab-Jewish political understanding be reached.

I heard much talk in London against partition. I think it ducks the fundamental and inescapable question of the Middle East. For the Arabs, the removal of the Jews would be a calamity. I am convinced that the Jews have already contributed much and can in the future contribute even more toward the development of the Arab world. The Arabs are a great people with great potentialities. For the Jews, conversely, the basic problem here is to get along with the Arabs, to win them by helping them and by demonstrating a sincere desire to live together on an equal basis. This is a nobler and politically sounder goal than any narrow Jewish nationalism. If Britain and America wish peace with justice in this part of the world, with the Jew and Arab both here, I am convinced the solution lies in this, the only escape route from *divide et impera*.

December 8, 1945

Palestine Pilgrimage

∽ ∾

I FEEL a little like the hero of Jules Verne's "Around the World in Eighty Days," though he was a slowpoke by comparison. Last Tuesday I had tea in England and dinner in Ireland. I breakfasted the next day in Newfoundland and lunched in New York. I have just returned from a six weeks' trip abroad, a typical bit of American blitz journalism. My primary concern was Palestine, and the largest part of my time was spent there. But I had five days in London on my way and two days in Paris. I saw St. Peter's from the skies over Rome, and I climbed the Acropolis in awe during an overnight stop in Athens. I had five days in and around Cairo before I reached Palestine, and I saw every part of the Holy Land except the Dead Sea during my stay there. I spent two days and a night in the Lebanon, and stayed three days each in Cairo and London on my way back, with short descents from lonely night skies over Cyrenaica and Malta, and a breakfast near Marseilles.

It was my first trip abroad, and if a wandering newspaperman may be forgiven his enthusiasm, I came back drunk on the beauties of the world: that last look at Manhattan's heady towers on the way out; the infinite variety of sea and sky on the boat trip over; St. Paul's, mighty and melancholy amid the bomb ruins in a London dusk; Paris, as one had dreamed of it, miraculously unscathed by the war; a savage sunset over the wild Balkan headlands flying into Greece; the green delta stretching from horizon to horizon as one enters the Egyptian skies; the minarets and the stars over the Citadel in Cairo; dawn over the Negev from the watch tower at Gevulot, with Sinai far in the distance; Minara, my favorite colony, which shoulders the sky 3,000 feet above the Jordan across from the enormous Harmon, where Pan dwelt; and Jerusalem, clean, white, and lovely on its ancient hills. I was moved to tears twice on my trip, once when I walked for the first time into Notre Dame in Paris, and again when I came through the narrow winding streets of the Old City to the Wailing Wall in Jerusalem, and saw the few stones to which cling so many filial memories for a Jew.

I went over neither to uncover sensations nor to bolster preconceptions but to understand the British and the Arab as well as the Jewish point of view, to get the atmosphere of London and the flavor of Arab nationalism, and to see for myself what had been accomplished in Palestine. I dined with a Cabinet minister in London and had a two-hour off-the-record talk with Azzam Bey, head of the Arab League, in Cairo. My assignment, to achieve some grasp of the complexities and the tragedies involved in Britain's position, Arab aspirations, and urgent Jewish needs, was an assignment that called for an Isaiah, not a mere reporter. Perhaps I learned most from chance contact and talks with humbler folk — a devout English Catholic returning on the Queen Elizabeth from captivity in Japan, a cockney Jewish mother bombed out of her home in the East End of London, a Coptic doctor struggling against the disease and squalor of an Egyptian village, a young Sephardic Jew homeless in Athens whose Spanish passport had saved him in a German death camp, a brilliant Christian Arab leader in Beirut whose sympathetic understanding of Zionism surpassed that of any Zionist I encountered, a veteran English civil servant in Haifa, and above all the young men and women of the Jewish colonies I visited, the grandest young folk I have ever met.

I hated Egypt. I have never seen such poverty. There are wise and farseeing men in the Egyptian upper class, and I had the good fortune to speak with several. But there are also a whole horde of self-serving phonies, and some Egyptian officials seem to treat their own people with an arrogance and contempt beyond that of the worst foreign imperialist. The gap between rich and poor is unbelievably wide. Of all the villages in Egypt some fourteen now have health centers, and of these fourteen, five have doctors. It was to one of these show villages, near Gizeh, with the Pyramids visible not far away, that I was taken. The filth and squalor were beyond conception, and there, as in the Muski, the ancient quarter of Cairo, I saw a sight one cannot forget — flies feasting on the corrupted eyelids of little children. In the West one speaks of exploitation, but in the West the exploiting capitalist builds, constructs, produces; his activity adds as much as if not more than it subtracts. But in Egypt exploitation is of a different and almost one-sided character. The fellah lives on the Nile and the pasha lives on the fellah. In the West when we think of colonial nationalism, we think of Gandhi and Nehru. Egypt once had a Zaglul Pasha, responsive to his people's needs, but today one catches few if any overtones of idealism in the Wafdist movement he founded.

Egypt provides perspective on Palestine. There is the sharpest contrast between the markets of Egypt and the Arab markets in Palestine, as I saw them in the all-Arab town of Gaza or in the Arab sections of Jerusalem and Haifa. The Arab markets of Palestine are clean. The town and village Arab of Palestine is better dressed, healthier looking by far, than the Arab in Egypt, whose usual dress is a dirty, old-fashioned, single-piece garment which is almost an exact replica of the nightshirt grandpa in America used to wear. Passing from Egypt to Palestine one can see for oneself what is testified to in the Peel Royal Commission report on Palestine — that the coming of the Jews has not degraded the Arab but lifted his living standards.

I found myself immensely attracted by the life of the Yishuv, the Jewish community of Palestine. It is the one place in the world where Jews seem completely unafraid. I did not see the displaced persons' camps in Germany, but even in such free countries as England and France — and at home, in the United States — there are premonitory tremors in the Jewish communities, conscious or subconscious fears of the future. In Palestine a Jew can be a Jew. Period. Without apologies, and without any lengthy arguments as to whether Jews are a race, a religion, a myth, or an accident. He need explain to no one, and he feels profoundly at home; I am quite willing to attribute this to historic sentimentality, but it remains none the less a tremendous and inescapable fact. In the desert, on the barren mountains, in the once malarial marshes of the Emek, the Jew has done and is doing what seemed to reasonable men the impossible. Nowhere in the world have human beings surpassed what the Jewish colonists have accomplished in Palestine, and the consciousness of achievement, the sense of things growing, the exhilarating atmosphere of a great common effort infuses the daily life of the Yishuv. I came away feeling that no obstacles, no setbacks, nothing but perhaps a Third World War and atomic bombs in the Middle East, could stop this people.

It happens that I felt myself painfully impelled to disagree with majority opinion in the Yishuv. I am not in favor of a Jewish state in Palestine. But it would be foolish, and it would be completely to

misunderstand how history and human beings work, to disparage
Zionism. Only a passionate, narrow, and mystical national faith made it
possible for Jews to colonize areas the goats despised. Without the
Zionist movement, what has been achieved in Palestine would never
have come to pass. The closest parallel in American experience is
Puritanism, and Palestine is indeed much like the frontier in our own
country, both in colonial times and in the West. But the strength
associated with such a movement also has its corresponding defects, and
the defects of Zionism are reflected in its failure to take into account the
feelings and aspirations of the Palestinian Arab. The Arab has benefited
from the Jewish influx, but only indirectly. The Zionist has not hurt him,
but the Zionist has made him feel shut out. This exclusiveness is natural
and understandable, but it needs to be corrected if the Jews are to build
for themselves a secure life in the Middle East.

I understood after seeing Egypt and talking with Christian Arabs in
the Lebanon — many of them anti-Zionist only in public — why the
Yishuv will fight and has a right to fight against permanent minority
status under present conditions in an Arab state. But I also understand
why the Palestinian Arabs, to whom Palestine is also home, who has
fully as much right there as the Jew, does not wish to live as a minority
in a Jewish state. No one likes to be ruled by an alien people, and though
I, a Jew, found the friendliest sort of welcome visiting the Arabs, I found
no Palestinian Arab in favor of a Jewish state. Relations on the
day-to-day level between the two peoples are friendly and quite unlike
what one expects. There is no sense of race tension as one feels it in our
South or in encounters with anti-Semites in the Western world. The
Arab does not hate the Jew, but he fears being dominated by him, and
this fear must be allayed.

In a visit to Amir on the upper Jordan, where the Hadassah was
opening a new health center for Jews and Arabs, I encountered a feeling
among the Arabs that they somehow risked the displeasure of the British
governing authorities if they were friendly with the Jews. I found no
evidence to support this suspicion, but I believe that there is much the
British could do to improve relations between leaders of the two peoples.
I was told that at Haifa the chief engineer, the leading British civil
servant of the municipality, had done much in a quiet unobtrusive way
toward the success of the local government. Haifa's population — and its
City Council — is equally divided between Jews and Arabs. The
mayoralty was long held by a respected Arab, succeeded since his death
by his deputy, a Jew of Turkish origin. The chief engineer told me that

he could remember no occasion on which a split vote in the council had not found Jews and Arabs on both sides. Admittedly it is easier to run a municipality than a nation, but Haifa nevertheless illustrates the fact that the two races can get along in equal partnership.

The earlier day when Arab nationalist and Zionist could work together, as they did in the first honeymoon period after the war, came to an end for two reasons. One was Britain's failure to fulfil the promises made the Arabs on the basis of which their leaders accepted Zionism for Palestine. The other was the Jewish demand, first by implication and then explicitly, for a Jewish state in Palestine. The Jewish State slogan has made political cooperation between Jew and Arab impossible, and left the Jewish homeland completely dependent on British support. The British, feeling that the Jews had to support the Empire under any circumstances, have more and more made their concessions to the Arabs. These concessions have been at the expense of the Yishuv, of French interests, and of the minorities in the Middle East generally. It is because the Jews understand this and feel deeply the needs of their homeless brethren in Europe that they have launched the present civil-disobedience campaign. They scent an attempt to liquidate the Yishuv, and they scent another cruel Evian farce beneath Bevin's fine talk of finding a world solution for the Jewish problem. And I must confess that after being in London, and with all due respect for the good intentions of British Labor, I agree with Palestinian Jewry.

I came away with a great liking and respect for the English people but a great distrust of their officials. I understand the average Englishman's resentment over American interference, and I favor not only American sharing of responsibility but an international solution for the Middle East. British fears of an Arab uprising largely reflect a hobgoblin of their own making; the great powers can impose any solution they choose. I think the equitable solution would be a bi-national state for Palestine and international trusteeship until population parity has been reached between Jews and Arabs. I think the powers must recognize the Arab aspiration for some kind of league or federation and put bi-national Palestine into it, and I think they must then provide some form of international guaranty for the Christian Lebanon, the Jewish community in Palestine, and other minorities in the East, but a guaranty free from the taint of "capitulations" in Egypt, a system of protection much abused both by the imperialist powers and the minorities themselves. A settlement of this kind depends, of course, on whether London and Washington are sincerely concerned with stability in the Middle East or merely with appeasing the Arabs in preparation for a new war against the Soviet Union. I do not speak from surmise when I report that from Ernest Bevin down, the British Foreign Office and the Colonial Office seem to be suffering from an obsession on this score, and the Jews are its principle victims.

A bi-national settlement would provide enough immigration certificates over, say, the next five or ten years — about 650,000 — to take care of all Jews who must be given a refuge in Palestine. It would establish a Jewish community strong enough to hold its own in the Arab world. It would end Palestinian Arab fears of a Jewish state. It would genuinely fulfil Britain's obligations to both peoples, and it would lay the basis for a stable and developing order in the Middle East, in which British and world interests in communications and oil could be adequately safeguarded without infringing Arab independence. In that context, if the Jews give one-tenth the devotion to Arab relations that they have given to the land, they can build a secure homeland for themselves among their Semitic brethren. This way, I am deeply convinced, lies the only lasting and equitable solution for Palestine and the Middle East.

December 22, 1945

Another Inquiry Begins

〜 〜

THERE IS MUCH that is good to be said of President Truman's appointments to the Anglo-American Committee of Inquiry on Palestine. The American chairman, United States Circuit Court Judge Joseph C. Hutcheson of Houston, Texas, is best known for his decision in the Strecker case. Judge Hutcheson described the attempt to deny Strecker citizenship because of past membership in the Communist Party as "a kind of Pecksniffian righteousness, savoring strongly of hypocrisy and party bigotry." A majority of the Supreme Court agreed with him. Earlier, as a federal district judge, Hutcheson wrote a decision in the Osterloh case which widened the rights of aliens in deportation proceedings. Judge Hutcheson brings a free mind and a sympathetic spirit to the work of the committee.

Of the five men named with Judge Hutcheson, one has devoted a large part of his life to the refugee problem. James G. McDonald was made High Commissioner for German Refugees by the League of Nations in October, 1933. Two years later he resigned in protest against the League's half-hearted attitude. In one capacity or another he has been engaged ever since in trying to help the victims of Hitlerism. No one knows better the elaborate ritual of investigation, conference, and intergovernmental committee with which the Western powers have been accustomed to approach — and evade — the questions involved in this new inquiry.

The four other American members of the committee have had no direct contact with the problems of European Jewry or of Palestine, but there is no reason to believe any of them unfriendly. Former Under

Secretary of State William Phillips, once Ambassador to Rome under Mussolini, is a professional diplomat, a type which in the United States tends to be assimilated to the British point of view. But as Roosevelt's special representative to India during the war, Phillips demonstrated an independence that soon made him persona non grata with the Churchill government. Though his mission was to explore the possibilities of compromise with the Indian Nationalist movement, Phillips was denied access to Gandhi and Nehru. His report to the White House was critical of British imperial policy. That background may prove useful in the Middle East.

There is less to be reported about the remaining three committee members. O. Max Gardner, now practicing law in Washington, made a good record as Governor of North Carolina and is well regarded by Southern progressives. Frank W. Buxton is the respected veteran editor of the Boston *Herald*. He won a Pulitzer prize back in 1924 for an editorial called "Who Made Calvin Coolidge?" The editorial, reread today, inevitably has a kind of Currier and Ives flavor. It is unnecessary to produce credentials for Frank Aydelotte, director of the Institute for Advanced Study at Princeton. He is American secretary of the Rhodes Trust and a good friend of Britain — but one need not be an enemy of Britain to dislike the White Paper or distrust Ernest Bevin.

Of the six British members of the joint commission, the one known to us at *The Nation* — if only as his occasional, though admiring, readers — is R. H. S. Crossman, assistant editor of the London *New Statesman and Nation*. About the others the only facts available are the biographical details supplied by the British Ministry of Information. Lord Morrison of Tottenham is one of the New Labor peers, an old-timer in the party, once parliamentary secretary to Ramsay MacDonald. Sir Frederick William Leggett has been in the Ministry of Labor since 1917. Major Reginald Edward Manningham-Buller is a barrister and a Conservative M. P. Wilfred P. Crick is economic adviser to the Midland Bank, one of the so-called Big Four banks. Sir John Edward Singleton, chairman of the British contingent, has been a judge of the King's Bench since 1934. It is not an exciting list.

These are, I am sure, good men, and I intend no disrespect to them when I say that it is difficult to write of the new inquiry temperately. Such inquiries, to judge from past experience, represents a kind of "heads I win, tails you lose" gamble. If the commission finds that surviving European Jews are begging for a chance to stay in Germany and Poland, and only a handful of Zionists want to go to Palestine, we may be sure the findings will be fully and immediately "implemented." But if the commission finds that most of the survivors want to go to Palestine and should be permitted to go there, we may be equally sure that the recommendations will bog down. This process is well understood in Palestine.

I spent an evening, in Haifa, with one of the leaders of the current civil-disobedience campaign against the British authorities. I began by trying to convince him that it might be wise to do nothing until the committee had brought in its report. He ended by convincing me that the Jews of Palestine are justified in feeling that they cannot wait. Before the war, during the war, and now again since the war, they have seen a series of inquiries and conferences. There was one at Evian. There was another at Bermuda. Nothing came of them. As the number of inquiries grew, the number of Jews declined. Many Palestinian Jews feel — and I fully share that feeling — that a kind of "nonintervention" was practiced by the Western powers against European Jewry. "Six million Jews died in Europe while we waited for the democratic powers to act," said one Palestinian. "Thousands more of the remnants will die if we sit here with hands folded during the winter while they investigate again." The Palestinians, who did such quietly heroic work rescuing their brethren from Axis Europe, are going on with the job of rescuing them from "liberated" Europe — despite the White Paper.

In London I found the atmosphere as complacent as that in Palestine was desperate. The problem in London is just another of those headaches of empire. In Palestine half the Jews are folk who got away barely in time to escape Belsen and Oswiecim; the dead were their kinsfolk; the survivors are their kinsfolk, too, the last of whole families. I spoke with Jewish boys in British army uniform who had found friends and relatives in the camps. "More than food or clothing these people need hope — the hope of having a home at last." The British are a kind people, but they have troubles of their own. In Palestine the Jews are building a nation, and the plight of European Jewry is not merely sentimental or peripheral but as intense and central a matter as the massacre of Britons and the succor of the survivors would be for Englishmen. For Palestinians illegal immigration is a Jewish Dunkirk across the Mediterranean, an urgent and inescapable duty.

There are sympathetic folk in England who express the opinion that Bevin proposed the commission of inquiry as a means of giving him a way out with the Arabs. They point to the possibility of interim reports by committees as a wedge to open Palestine's doors to increased immigration. It is difficult to reconcile this theory with the news from Germany that Field Marshal Montgomery has ordered new refugees from anti-Semitic Poland turned back at the border of the British zone lest they "aggravate" the Palestine problem. It is hard to reconcile any optimistic theory with the British Labor government's foreign policy elsewhere, from Greece to Java, where Bekasi[1] seems to have provided a fair imitation of Lidice.[2] My own opinion is that Bevin wanted the inquiry in order to get America to share, not the responsibility for a genuinely equitable solution in the Middle East, but the odium of shutting off Palestine to further Jewish immigration. Bevin's concern is not a decent break for the surviving Jews of Europe but the building of an anti-Soviet bloc in the Middle East at the expense of Jewish aspirations for a refuge and a national home.

---

[1] At Bekasi, in the Netherlands East Indies, British troops were accused of burning and bombing the city in an effort to suppress nationalist forces and restore Dutch colonial rule.
[2] Czechoslovakian village destroyed by the Nazis and later rebuilt as a national memorial.

Index

〜 〜

About the Author

Born in 1907, I. F. Stone has been a working newspaperman since the age of fourteen when, during his sophomore year at a small-town high school, he launched a monthly, *The Progress,* which supported — among other causes — the League of Nations and Gandhi's first efforts at freedom for India.

While at school and college, he worked for daily newspapers in Camden, New Jersey, Philadelphia, and New York.

Since 1940 he has served in succession as a Washington correspondent and commentator for *The Nation,* the newspaper *PM,* the *New York Post,* and the *Daily Compass.* In 1953 he launched *I. F. Stone's Weekly,* a legendary venture in independent, one-man journalism, which he edited and published for nineteen years. He has written extensively for the *New York Review of Books* and long served as a contributing editor. He writes a Washington column at irregular intervals for *The Nation* and for many daily papers at home and abroad, including the *Philadelphia Inquirer,* on which he worked while he was in college.

In semiretirement Mr. Stone returned to the philosophy and classical history he had studied in college. He taught himself ancient Greek and wrote *The Trial of Socrates,* a controversial probe of the most famous free-speech case of all time, widely acclaimed on publication in 1988.

Mr. Stone and his wife, Esther, live in Washington. They have three married children.